12.99

CW01082316

Leading Innovation, Creativity and Enterprise

Leading Innovation, Creativity and Enterprise

Peter Cook

Bloomsbury Information
An imprint of Bloomsbury Publishing Plc

B L O O M S B U R Y
LONDON · OXFORD · NEW YORK · NEW DELHI · SYDNEY

Bloomsbury Information

An imprint of Bloomsbury Publishing Plc

50 Bedford Square	1385 Broadway
London	New York
WC1B 3DP	NY 10018
UK	USA

www.bloomsbury.com

BLOOMSBURY and the Diana logo are trademarks of Bloomsbury Publishing Plc

First published 2016

© Peter Cook, 2016

British Library Cataloguing-in-Publication Data

A catalogue record for this book is available from the British Library.

ISBN:	HB:	978-1-4729-2539-8
	ePDF:	978-1-4729-2541-1
	ePub:	978-1-4729-2540-4

Library of Congress Cataloging-in-Publication Data

A catalog record for this book is available from the Library of Congress.

Typeset by RefineCatch Limited, Bungay, Suffolk
Printed and bound in Great Britain

For Alison, James and Tom, the creative engines that power my world.

Contents

Acknowledgements

I am extremely grateful to these people, without whom this book would not have come to life:

Harry van der Velde and Simon Heath, who designed the visual concepts for this book. Harry is founder of Zicht www.zicht.com Simon is a corporate artist. Find him on Twitter@simonheath1

Sir Richard Branson, CEO of Virgin, for his interview www.virgin.com

Sir James Dyson, CEO of Dyson, for his interview www.dyson.co.uk

Malcolm Frier and Peter Kenehan at FujiFilm Speciality Ink Systems for their kind contribution of a case study into reinvention www.fujifilmsis.com

Christina Jansen, professional photographer to people as diverse as Muhammed Ali, Emma Thompson, Robert Plant, who took the photographs for this book www.cjansenphotography.com

Nadine Hack, CEO of Because for her insights into authentic leadership based on her experiences of working with Nelson Mandela, Barak Obama and world class enterprises www.because.net

Stephen Bourne, Professor Peter Childs, Shirley Craven, David D'Souza, Laurence Ghafar, Steve Gorton, Nicola Gunn, Dr Allègre Hadida, Chris Ham, Phil Hawthorn, Silvia Impellezzeri, Haydn Jones, Trevor Lee, Jack Preston and Rowena Sian Murphy for their wise and incisive counsel and insights on wide-ranging matters associated with writing this book.

Liam Tully, Head of Pfizer's Process Development Centre for the case study on practical creativity at work www.pfizer.com

Danny Harmer, Chief People Officer of Metro Bank for superb insights into the Metro culture www.metrobank.plc.uk

The staff at the Virgin Lounge in London and Karen's Diner, for allowing me to use their venues as mobile office locations.

Dan Barrett, Innovation Director of Innocent Drinks for his input on a creative climate at Innocent www.innocentdrinks.co.uk

Joel Casse, Global Head Leadership Development, Nokia and Nick Obolensky, author of *Complex Adaptive Leadership* for their insights into complex adaptive systems and change www.nokia.com www.complexadaptiveleadership.com

Dr. Andrew Sentance CBE, Senior Economic Adviser to PricewaterhouseCoopers and the product of a genetic fusion of John Maynard Keynes, Robert Plant and Peter Gabriel www.sentance.com

Professor Adrian Furnham, who offers a continuing source of inspiration, provocation and friendship www.adrianfurnham.com

Sheila E, world-class drummer and musical director for Prince, Stevie Wonder and Beyoncé for practical insights into the life of an eternally creative musician www.sheilae.com

Steve Plumridge, CEO of Cantium Scientific for his reflections on running a virtual business www.cantiumscientific.com

George Clinton, cited as one of the three founding innovators of funk and psychedelic music, alongside James Brown and Sly Stone www.georgeclinton.com

Patti Russo, Meatloaf's long-term singing partner and occasional chanteuse, for inspiration and insights into leadership that informed this book www.patti-rocks.com

Dr Julianne Halley, University of Cambridge, for her insights into biology and structure.

Alana Clogan and Elizabeth Hill at Bloomsbury for their foresight, patience and calm guidance to manage the process from inspiration to innovation.

John Varney, The Centre for Management Creativity for his insights into creative climate and LVT www.high-trenhouse.co.uk

Bill Nelson, a continuous source of creativity across my lifetime: musician, artist, writer, long-distance dreamer. Much of this book has been accompanied by Bill's music www.billnelson.com

Dr Stephen Leybourne at Boston State University for his collaborations on improvisation and innovation.

Bernie Tormé, guitar supremo, rock god, occasional musical sparring partner and a man who had provided deep insights into where creativity comes from beyond an academic textbook or guru www.barnroom.co.uk

John Mayall, Godfather of the Blues, the man who started the careers of Eric Clapton, Peter Green, Mick Fleetwood et al. and who effectively ran an innovation hothouse www.johnmayall.com

Roberto Ascione, CEO of Healthware International, for his insights into data and information management in the context of healthcare reform www.healthwareinternational.com

Marcus Anderson, sax player for Prince and Sheila E, for his wonderful insights into the mathematics of improvisation and the life of the creative artist www.marcusanderson.net

Dr Russ Derickson, engineer and maths genius for his probing insights into organisational structure and design.

Mark Brown, MD of Innovation Centre Europe, for his insights into The Dolphin Index www.dolphinindex.com

Justin Norvell, VP Product Development, for his insights into innovation at Fender www.fender.com

Mark Needham, MD of Widget, for insights into a creative climate at Psion www.widget.co.uk

Ethan Diamond, CEO of Bandcamp, for his case study www.bandcamp.com

Barbara Brooks Kimmel – Author of TRUST, Inc. Strategies for Building Your Company's Most Valuable Asset. Barbara is CEO of Next Decade Inc. who kindly supplied the FACTS® chart to support Nadine Hack's insights.

Cortney McDermott, CEO of Chime, for her support to the case study on authentic leadership www.cortneymcdermott.com

John Otway, two-hit wonder and rock'n'roll's greatest failure, for teaching me entrepreneurship in ways that textbooks do not come close to.

Anna Hill, CEO of SpaceSynapse, for her case study on democracy in space travel www.earthrider.eu

Dr Alan Drummond, Dr Patricia Seeman and Irene Becker for their insights into wicked problems.

Drs David Mayle, Jane Henry and John Martin at the Open University for their groundbreaking MBA programme Creativity, Innovation and Change, which continues to inspire and inform my thinking.

Sarah Winmill, University College London, Paul Deemer, NHS England, Gert Johannes Scholz and Michelle Zal, Chartered Institute of Personnel and Development for personal vignettes on creativity.

Introduction

We've travelled from the agrarian age through the industrial era to the information superhighway. At this tipping point in our evolution, we need Brain Based Enterprises (BBEs) rather than just Brawn Based Industries (BBIs). Enterprises based on brainpower need to understand higher order business questions of leadership, innovation and creativity to stay ahead. This book started with some questions that I would like to share with you:

1. Where does creativity and imagination come from?
2. How can we create circumstances where creativity occurs naturally?
3. What is combinatorial creativity? How can we use it to improve idea generation capability and capacity?
4. What kind of leadership is required to make innovation and creativity 'business as usual' in your enterprise?
5. What part do techniques play in engendering creativity within teams? What are the most effective and reliable tools for team-based creativity?
6. What is mathematical creativity and how can we use it for better ideas?
7. What ensures that creativity turns into innovation? What stops it?
8. How can you energise your enterprise for innovation and creativity?
9. How can you create an entrepreneurial culture inside an enterprise?
10. What are BBEs really doing beneath the veneer?
11. How does culture support or limit innovation and creativity?
12. How does organisation structure support or limit innovation and creativity? What can we do about it?
13. How may we become a genuine learning enterprise?

The concept of *Leading Innovation, Creativity and Enterprise* has matured for nearly 20 years, having written my first book on the topic in 1996. This represents tens of thousands of hours of diverse experience, working as a business practitioner across a wide range of sectors. I've accelerated my thinking via my work as an MBA academic and mental adventurer, working on the flagship 'Creativity, Innovation and Change' programme. During that time, the business environment we live and work in has become more volatile, uncertain, complex and ambiguous. This demands that individuals and enterprises become more ingenious to ride the turbulence that this produces, in order to be resilient and antifragile when challenged.

We divide our time between the individual and the world of business. Part 1: Innovation, Creativity and You focuses on personal factors that lead to innovation and creativity. Part 2: Innovation, Creativity and Enterprise focuses on organisational factors that lead to increased innovation, competitiveness and sustainability.

Part One: Innovation, creativity and you

Chapter 1: The roots of creativity

We begin with a deep dive to find the underlying natural sources of creativity. This area of study is relatively less travelled, but contains rich insights for anyone trying to think original thoughts or do new things.

- When people discuss creativity, what are the physiological and psychological states that are essential to create the conditions where 'mental escapology' is possible?
- Armed with such wisdom, can you call upon these states such that creativity is more frequent and better i.e. more directed to your desired outcome?
- Furthermore, is it possible to work directly from such states and therefore bypass the need to learn innovative thinking recipes and brainstorming techniques?
- What can we learn from the concept of combinatorial creativity to help us design à la carte states that improve our creative capability and capacity?

We gain our examples from business, art, mathematics, science and indeed any place where people have had a moment of creativity and paused for a moment of reflection and dissection of how it works, from Virgil to Virgin.

Chapter 2: Creativity and you

This chapter is about the infinitely complex variable that is you. Whilst there are many strategies for creating, they all depend on the mind, body and soul of the recipient. You are uniquely variable. This chapter is about understanding your creative preferences and those of others, so you can find out what works and adopt or adapt creativity strategies. Different things work in different circumstances for different people, so we need a repertoire and not a mantra.

We explore a number of psychological models in this chapter and link these with questions of ambiguity, problem finding, opportunity seeking, decision making and execution. In other words: the whole divergent and convergent thinking process. We also examine strategies for overcoming personal obstacles to creativity, which are sometimes the key to success in leading innovation, creativity and enterprise. We introduce mathematical creativity as a simple but effective strategy for ingenious thinking that anyone can use to supplement their own approaches.

Chapter 3: Creative leadership

Innovation depends, to a large degree, on the role of leadership in creating a climate and culture where ideas can arise, germinate and then become part of the fabric of society. In this chapter, we take an integrated view of leadership and management, since they cannot be separated as some pundits suggest. We also examine the triad of power, influence and authority and the question of elegance in leadership and management. In other words, what are the necessary and sufficient conditions for obtaining desired results in terms of influence and followership?

Whether you are a leader trying to encourage better ideas in your company, someone selling an embryonic idea as an entrepreneur or working inside an enterprise attempting to make new things happen across disciplines, you will need to use power, influence and authority in appropriate ways. We explore a range of approaches to help you improve relationships and influence people.

I dismiss the notion of the isolated lone leader in favour of the idea of distributed leadership. This is more like a jazz band where the 'baton' passes from person to person based on expertise and ability rather than using positional power and management by fear.

What knowledge, skills and values will help you adjust your own leadership posture and practice for maximum impact? We take a fresh look at some key values, strategies and tools to help you make wise decisions. We visit Johnson and Johnson, beCause and Pfizer as exemplars of leadership.

Chapter 4: Tools for creativity

We discussed personal states for creativity and combinatorial creativity in Chapter 1. These are the most direct routes to your creative core. When we work with others in teams and companies it helps to have some shared rituals and roadmaps for divergent and convergent thinking. Here we sample a suite of reliable tools for 'diverging with flair and converging with care', to convert fragile ideas into innovations. This is really the 'sheet music' for innovation and creativity, when working alone is not sufficient to achieve your goals and you need some shared rules of engagement.

Yet 'sheet music' will take you so far on the road to greatness. True masters of the art of thinking use imperfections and mistakes in order to reach beyond 'painting by numbers'. We contrast the sheet music approach to a 'free improvisation' approach to novel thinking.

We include some advice to help you design your own interventions and some thoughts on the gentle art of facilitating ingenious thinking in teams. These are based upon 20 years' experience of designing such interventions for companies as diverse as Johnson and Johnson, the United Nations, Unilever and Roche.

Chapter 5: The F word – Failure and success

When any serious entrepreneur or business leader is being honest about innovation, they will point to a succession of failures on the road to success. We visit a number of examples of failure in this chapter, ranging from insights from Sir Richard Branson, Pfizer, 3M, Space Synapse, Astra Zeneca, with lessons for those people trying to improve the ratio of failures:successes in their enterprises.

Amongst the many projects I've led and participated in, I worked on an audacious enterprise to conduct a record-breaking circumnavigation that turned into what can only be described as a glorious failure. I tell the unvarnished inside story of this enterprise with transferable lessons for leaders and entrepreneurs trying to do new things.

Failure can be more instructive than success in teaching us how to innovate if we are prepared to learn from it as individuals, teams and organisations. However, defensive routines can get in the way. We look at a range of strategies to help enterprises learn from their difficulties, be they simple improvements or more fundamental and transformational changes. These are based on the principles behind our mathematical creativity model, especially the minus and divide principles.

Part Two: Innovation, creativity and enterprise

Chapter 6: Innovation and enterprise

Once we multiply the need for innovation with larger numbers of people the issue of collective creativity and its conversion to innovation becomes more complex. Yet the real payoff comes when innovation and creativity is leveraged at the level of the whole enterprise. This does not mean the removal of individual flair by tying things up in standard approaches. However, there are undeniable tensions between individual creative activity and the desires of many enterprises to systematise work for reasons of efficiency. Brain Based Enterprises (BBEs) manage to successfully navigate these tensions, not by removing them, but by managing the inevitable paradoxes.

We start with a strategic view of innovation and then delve into the sub-elements, examining Metro Bank, Fender and Dyson as exemplars of innovation. As well as looking at what adds or multiplies innovation potential, leaders must remove innovation obstacles. We develop the concepts of mathematical creativity and the innovation pipeline to help you see the wood and the trees, subtract and divide ineffective strategies.

Chapter 7: Building an innovation culture

Culture trumps strategy every time in terms of whether an enterprise flourishes on a continuing basis or withers and eventually dies. Unfortunately culture is an intangible asset which is only possible to see via tangible manifestations, sometimes much later on in the business cycle. It cannot easily be quantified on a company balance sheet or other 'bean-counting devices' but we often know a great culture when we experience it as a customer or staff member, such as that at Psion, Virgin and Widget.

Here we examine the influence of culture on innovation and creativity, and identify the cultural conditions in which innovation and creativity is more probable. Cultures can and must be designed with care and flair for the good of employees, which ultimately impacts on customers and therefore shareholders and society. We develop the innovation pipeline model to identify opportunities for an improved ratio between ideas and innovations.

Chapter 8: Structuring for innovation

If culture sets the context for ingenious thinking, structures smooth the pathways to execute innovation. Structure includes both the formal and informal elements (e.g. organisation design, information and knowledge-based structures) and the less formal elements such as political structures and networks inside and outside the enterprise's boundaries. Whilst it is not necessarily true that good structures assist innovation and creativity, poor structures certainly impede them. Good structures should lead to higher ratios for the conversion of ideas to viable and sustainable innovations at lower cost, faster, with higher returns etc. Contrary to what many creativity gurus contend, structure is not the enemy of creativity, more its essential bedfellow. Like salt and pepper, sweet and sour, yin and yang etc. we need both to execute an idea. We extend the innovation pipeline model to accommodate the influence of structures on innovation and creativity to answer some of the following questions:

- How to harness the benefits of corporate size whilst preserving the nimbleness of a start up company ethos?
- How to make the most of matrix structures and the power of the crowd to harness innovative capacity from people you do not 'own'?
- How to develop collaborative structures that do not rely on formal authority and control to move faster along the innovation pipeline?

We examine Bandcamp and Cantium Scientific as examples of agile companies that have structured themselves differently in order to succeed.

Chapter 9: Developing innovation capacity and capability

Once a suitable culture and structure for innovation and creativity exist, the next questions to be addressed are the level, effectiveness and efficiency of creative activity and its conversion to innovation. In other words, the degree to which an enterprise leverages its skills and resources for innovative advantage:

- Is it best to 'make' or 'buy' creative capacity? How do you identify people who are creative but who also fit into a business context?
- What are the options to develop capacity and capability for a more healthy supply of better ideas?
- How do you develop and maintain the elusive concept of innovation climate such that people bring their brains, hearts and souls to work?
- How do you performance-manage creative people? How can you move beyond carrots and sticks to gain the prize of engagement?
- What part can finance and knowledge play in the development of a BBE? How can we shift from 90-degree data management to 360-degree knowledge leadership?

We visit Innocent Drinks, Virgin, Dyson and German software company Ingentis for examples.

Chapter 10: Becoming a true learning enterprise

When Peter Senge coined the concept of a learning company in the 1990s, it is probable that the idea was too far ahead of its time to gain widespread adoption. Change is now a continuous and more rapid process rather than a project with a clear start and end point in most businesses today. More than ever before the idea of being a nimble, adaptive or learning company has now come of age as a process innovation. In the future, there will be two sorts of company – the quick, creative, nimble, resilient, antifragile and the dead. Here we examine how to put your enterprise into the first camp, where flexibility, responsiveness and resilience are the hallmarks of your business strategy and where the strategy trickles down to every corporate corpuscle. In doing so, we cover a number of areas:

- How does change work in a VUCA environment?
- What does a true learning company look and feel like on a daily basis?

- How we can learn more rapidly through collaboration, creative swiping and using the power of the crowd to deliver sustainable innovations across the world?
- What are Nokia and FujiFilm doing to make learning a source of sustainable competitive advantage?

A 'pracademic' approach

In writing this book, I aimed to bring the three main pillars of my experience together. Considerable practical experience of leading innovative and creative enterprises, supported by many years in academia, teaching the subject at MBA level, plus experience from the artistic dimension, as a writer and performer of music. I have dubbed the blend of industrial pragmatism, art and academia 'pracademic'. A pracademic approach means:

1. Researching a number of innovative companies to provide a broad range of strategies and tactics for leveraging innovation and creativity in your enterprise. This should enable you to develop recipes that will work, not by slavishly 'copying and pasting' what others do, but by lavishly adapting and transforming the approaches into ones that fit your own circumstances. After all, this is the essence of sustainable competitive advantage and being a leader, not a follower.

2. I was also fortunate to spend my formative years working at The Wellcome Foundation, a philanthropic pharmaceutical company that understood the notion that, 'if you do good work, the profits will come'. Founded by two philanthropists in the ninetenth century, the company set out to rid the world of tropical diseases, ploughing its profits back into medical research. In common with Johnson and Johnson, Cadbury and Pilkington, Wellcome did many of the things that people now discuss under the heading of innovation, sustainability and ethical business. These companies were way ahead of their time and I have brought some of this forward here, lest it be lost through suffocation by the latest fads.

3. We are not confined to the world or businesses to look for innovation and creativity at work. As a musician, I am acutely aware of the parallels between successful improvisation, innovation and creativity in businesses, the arts and science. We gain our examples from

business, art, mathematics, science, as part of a magical mystery tour to find ideas that have practical relevance in even the most tightly controlled businesses.

4. An idea needs to be converted into an innovation to be truly creative. My wife, Alison, has tirelessly made suggestions, critiqued and improved the book with her sharp and witty pragmatism in ways that no other strategic adviser or business consultant could ever come close to.

I love to indulge in conversations with others about leadership, innovation and creativity at work and play. I can be contacted as follows:

Telephone: +44 (0) 7725 927585

Email: peter@humdyn.co.uk

Websites: www.humdyn.co.uk; www.academy-of-rock.co.uk
Book website http://humdyn.co.uk/books

Peter Cook
August 2015

Part One

Innovation, creativity and you

Chapter 1

The roots of creativity

Farming, information, creativity and innovation

Nearly 30 years ago, Fred Moody and Bill Gates recognised that the basis of competitive advantage had fundamentally shifted from the agrarian age to the industrial era to the information superhighway, when it was commented that Microsoft's only factory asset is the human imagination. The corresponding shift is from what could be crudely called Brawn Based Industries (BBIs) to Brain Based Enterprises (BBEs) even though human brain power was itself behind the creation of the first stone age tools.

In 2015, research by eminent neuroscientist Dr Daniel Levitin showed that our brains absorbed five times more information every day as compared with 1986. During our leisure time every day, each of us processes 34 gigabytes, or 100,000 words. Remember Bill Gates is also reputed to have said that 640 KB ought to be enough for anybody! At the point of writing this book Airbnb, the world's largest provider of accommodation owns no real estate, Uber, the world's largest taxi company owns no vehicles and Facebook, the world's largest social media company creates no content. We have moved from farming crops through industry to curating information through intelligence. A key asset in a BBE is the human imagination, where that imagination is distributed across networks, both human and cybernetic. In such a world, strategy changes from a long-range plan to a flexible posture, where the half-life of knowledge is in freefall and success depends on creativity as a key input and innovation a key output. Adapt, innovate or die has never been more true in an age of exponential information growth and discontinuity. Discontinuous change throws up fundamental challenges for leaders:

1. How shall we multiply individual brainpower and potential to develop a Brain Based Enterprise (BBE)? How do we establish a

connection between individual ingenuity and collective health, wealth and happiness at work?

2. How shall we combine precocious and diverse talents into innovative teams and whole BBEs? How can we do this through collaborating with people who we do not 'own' through traditional employer-employee relationships?

3. How shall we keep our BBE fresh, flexible, resilient and antifragile (an enterprise that improves its performance when shocked)? How shall we create the conditions for sustainable innovation and excellence in a world where people's knowledge, skills and experience are increasingly portable on a global scale?

We will begin our leadership journey with some definitions of creativity.

Art for art's sake

Creativity in the arts is sometimes considered as the generation of novelty for its own sake, without too much regard for its usefulness to society. Unfettered creativity matters because there are many situations where novelty is needed for its own value if we are to make progress as a society as a whole, be it within the arts, enterprise or industry. However, novelty without purpose in business leads to business for business's sake, for example a business concept without a customer or consumer. Most enterprises I have worked with are not impressed by the notion that the creative person may spend 20 years in an 'attic' before emerging with a good idea. Some companies want creativity to be available 'on tap', like a faucet, ultimately with the ability to turn the faucet on and off at will.

Appropriateness

Creativity is the thinking of novel and appropriate ideas
Dr William E Coyne, Senior Vice President, Research and Development, 3M

3M illustrate the importance of appropriateness. Thus, ideas (creativity) must be capable of being transformed into successful and sustainable results (innovation). This is what business author and speaker Tom Peters writes and talks about under the heading of strategy. Tom says that execution beats a good strategy every time and he is right. Appropriateness often relates to a market want or need. Timing is a key element of appropriateness. Leonardo Da Vinci may well have invented the helicopter in 1488, but we did not have the engineering skills to convert the invention to an innovation at that time. It is probable that Clive Sinclair's C5 environmental vehicle would have been more successful if introduced maybe 30 years later when environmental concerns had reached much greater levels than in the 1980s. Quite surprisingly automatic doors were conceived of in the first century BC by Heron of Alexandria, for use in temples and powered by steam. Being too early is just as important as being too late in many walks of life.

Windows of perception

Discovery consists of looking at the same thing as everyone else and thinking something different

Albert Szent Gyorgyi [IEEE, 1985]

Creative people see problems as opportunities by perceiving situations through different sets of lenses. The art and technique of reframing, whereby a different perspective is given to a problem by virtue of changing its frame of reference, captures the essence of the above definition. Szent Gyorgyi was the Nobel Prize Winner who 'discovered' Vitamin C, having initially focused his work on understanding why plants turned brown. Reframing and distorting the windows of perception are practical creative tools that I'm often called upon to use when we work on real life 'wicked' problems and opportunities.

Sometimes different perceptions arise out of requisite diversity. Diversity is not a 'nice to have' fluffy concept for the HR department to worry about. If you are serious about innovation, you need to be very serious about hiring and inspiring 'people who may be seen as outsiders'. We often see diversity played out in dyads. In the music, science and business worlds good examples of diverse dyads are Lennon and McCartney, Jobs and Wozniak, Roosevelt and Taft, Watson and Crick, Simon and Garfunkel, whose personality styles are different enough to induce what Peter Senge (1990) calls 'creative tension'. We also see this basic unit of diversity present within entrepreneurial start-ups. Creativity becomes more problematical when we get into large groups due to the complexities of communication that exists in such groups. The alternative to working together is to hire geniuses and polymaths. However, such people can be hard to find and do not always make great corporate colleagues or collaborators, sometimes preferring to work alone.

Process to progress

Some of my colleagues in engineering, science and technology based companies see innovation and creativity as a **process** consisting of a number of stages, which must be passed through to make progress. This is the view of creativity that says it can be turned on and off like a faucet. This is a laudable aim but not one that is totally realistic due to the iterative and sometimes random nature of the creative process. One of the timeless insights into process was produced by Wallas (1926). His construct has remained durable through time. He suggested five stages:

1. **First insight** – Problem/opportunity finding and redefinition.
2. **Preparation** – The groundwork is often done here.
3. **Incubation** – In many cases, this is where unconscious processes play their most important part.
4. **Illumination** – Often described as the 'aha' experience.
5. **Verification** – Where the idea is validated and accepted by others.

In life and especially business over the last few decades, impatience with the faucet promotes the 'disease of problem–solution thinking', or, worse still, 'solution thinking', in our attempts to find fast answers to problems that we face without any attempt to understand them and/or develop a range of options to address them. This is usually a huge mistake. For example, in our desire to rid the world of infectious disease through antibiotics we have unwittingly created a new problem of microbial resistance in the form of 'superbugs'. It is estimated that this will cause 300 million deaths at a cost of $100 trillion to the global economy by 2050, unless human ingenuity can find a way to deal with drug resistance. In this example, it was probably impossible to have foreseen the resistance problem, and a lot of lives were saved by using antibiotics, but we now need to redouble our intelligence to find new and better remedies for infectious diseases. So, except in the simplest of problems, there is always a need to understand the problem and identify alternative options before leaping to the 'solution'. Without this diagnostic phase, the 'solution' is likely to solve the wrong problem or even make it worse.

The development of the Periodic Table of the elements in chemistry is a great example of the importance of incubation (stage 3 in Wallas' terms) in the innovation process. It was Döbereiner that first noticed the idea of patterns of the elements. In 1828, he proposed the notion that the elements could be classified into triads, based on their properties. It took 30 more years for French geologist de Chancourtois to develop the idea. De Chancourtois organised the elements by their atomic weights and published his work in 1863. In 1865, John Newland came up with his theory of octaves for the elements, organising the elements into groups of eight. In 1866, he used music to explain his theories to the Chemical Society, who refused to publish his work, suggesting that it was frivolous due to his use of a musical metaphor to explain the idea. There were some flaws in Newland's theory as some elements did not quite 'fit' the law of octaves. It took a few more years until Mendeleev produced the essential breakthrough of what we now consider the basis of the modern periodic table. So confident was Mendeleev of his theory that he left spaces in the table for elements that had yet to be discovered. This is incubation on a massive scale over 50 years before reaching stage 5, or verification! This story also illustrates the importance of considering your audience when selling an idea and that getting it wrong is very much part of getting it right.

Roots and shoots of creativity

A wide range of accounts have been offered on where creativity comes from, ranging from divinity to luck through to what the ancient Greeks called *techné*. This implies that creativity can be planned and organised through the careful use of strategies and tools. Yet none of them on their own offer a complete account of the origins of creativity. Here are the main ideas to help you ponder your personal preferences. Importantly, they offer you opportunities where you might also look

The roots of creativity

Creativity can come from anywhere – find out what works for you

for more inspiration and imagination. This can be through the adoption of different strategies or what I call 'combinatorial creativity', where you combine approaches for unique advantages.

Acts of God

There are many accounts of individuals who seem to be inspired by a divine gift and there seems little doubt that certain people appear to be genuinely gifted. Tchaikovsky observed that he must give up everything else to develop and cultivate the germ that God had planted in him as an extreme example of this. The scientist Kekulé was said to have discovered the chemical structure of the benzene ring via a flash of inspiration, which involved connecting an image of a snake biting its own tail in a dream. Other accounts merely suggest that he was a good storyteller:

> I turned my chair to the fire and dozed. Again the atoms were gambolling before my eyes. This time the smaller groups kept modestly in the background. My mental eye, rendered more acute by repeated visions of this kind, could now distinguish larger

structures, of manifold conformation; long rows, sometimes more closely fitted together; all twining and twisting in snakelike motion. But look! What was that? One of the snakes had seized hold of its own tail, and the form whirled mockingly before my eyes. As if by a flash of lightning I awoke . . . Let us learn to dream gentlemen.

Kekulé, quoted in *The Act of Creation*,
Arthur Koestler, 1964

The practical difficulty with divinity as an approach to creativity at work is that there would appear to be little to be done if genius is supplied by the gods. Most businesses I've worked for are not content to hire a bunch of polymaths and wait for 20 years for them to be touched by divinity. Speaking with eminent psychologist Professor Adrian Furnham and others at University College London and Imperial College, it is apparent that even universities are now confounded by research targets and deadlines. Nevertheless, the divine perspective has appeal in some workplaces, in terms of employing gifted people and supporting them in the pursuit of their goals.

I should be so lucky

If I had thought about it, I wouldn't have done the experiment. The literature was full of examples that said you can't do this.

Spence Silver talking about the experiments that
led to the unique adhesives for 3M 'Post-it' Notes

There is much documented evidence that supports the 'lucky break' concept of creativity. Amongst the examples that are cited is the sweetening effect of saccharin, accidentally discovered by a chemist who happened to eat his lunch in the laboratory without washing his hands after some experiments. Of course this would not have happened in the modern age, due to our obsession with Health and Safety! As with divinity, pure luck is mostly an unattractive proposition to businesses that would rather have creativity as a resource that can be managed and developed. So, the attractive question for leaders becomes can we orchestrate luck? We will return to this when we examine organisation structures in Chapter 8.

Planning to be lucky

The more I practice, the luckier I get

Arnold Palmer, Golfer

Planned luck involves having a proactive mindset that consciously looks for more options and scans for opportunities. In other words, serendipitous creativity is much more probable if opportunities are seen and seized. It is the realm of entrepreneurs such as Sir Richard Branson and Steve Jobs. Planning to be lucky is a far more attractive proposition to businesses, since it implies that it is possible to arrange things such that productive creativity is more likely to occur and the frequency of those occurrences is greater.

The discovery of Sildenafil Citrate, the drug that became Viagra, is a great example of what I mean by planned luck. Sildenafil was originally intended as a treatment for angina but it was inactive. However, nurses noted that it produced penile erections. Had Pfizer not been required to keep copious notes about the side effects of clinical trials and analyse those results, it is likely that Viagra's activity would never have been discovered. It is thus an example of planning, analysis and serendipity. Creativity and analysis really are bedfellows where Viagra is concerned.

At enterprise level, creativity is not a deterministic quality which lends itself to 'cause and effect' analysis. Nonetheless, innovative enterprises such as W.L. Gore, FujiFilm and Pfizer design their businesses such that 'luck' is a highly probable and frequent occurrence.

Blood, sweat and tears

The endurance perspective contradicts the view that creativity is the sole domain of inspired 'poet in the attic'. The classic example is Thomas Edison, who recognised failure as an important step in success in his trial-and-error approach to innovation. After failing for the 1,000th time, he reputedly congratulated himself for finding yet another way not to invent a light bulb. James Dyson created 5,127 prototypes of his Dyson vacuum cleaner before it reached the market some 15 years later. Both cases used the so-called 'Edisonian' approach to systematic innovation, making just one change in each experiment so that it is possible to track your progress (or otherwise).

Creativity Strategies – Planned luck

What I would say is that it (inspiration) relates to the exploitation of the chance meeting on a non-suitable plane of two mutually distant realities

Max Ernst, quoted in *The Creative Process*,
Brewster Ghiselin, 1985

This insight suggests that Ernst subscribes to the notions of serendipity and bisociation to produce something novel. He effectively acknowledges the idea of planned luck on the part of the artist through the exploitation of chance. Strategy and creativity are not mutually exclusive bedfellows.

Techné

The ancient Greeks believed in the concept of *techné* or the accumulation of professional and institutional experience. There is a school of thought that says that creative people are born and not made. Whilst it seems that genius has a genetic component and that it may be distributed unevenly across personality types, these are tremendously limiting beliefs. They are also inconsistent with the evidence of the variety of people who have demonstrated creative capacity. Aspects of creativity can be studied and developed just like any other human capacity. There are a number of strategies and techniques that naturally creative people use, yet they may also be learned as 'method' to improve creativity in ordinarily 'less creative' people. This is rather like writing down sheet music or cookery recipes. During the research for this book, I asked people to offer me their 'recipes' for naïve creativity. Some of what they reported is included in this book as vignettes under the title 'Creativity Strategies'. We'll also examine some successful applications of technique when we examine Pfizer Ireland, who have made creativity part of business as usual. For now, we'll look at some of the more transferrable principles behind creativity methods.

Naturally occurring creativity strategies

We now turn our attention to the 'how' of creativity. Most proprietary creativity tools and techniques such as Synectics, Six Thinking Hats, Disney Creativity Strategy, TRIZ et al. are simply an assembly of the fundamental building blocks upon which many creativity techniques rest. I've found during 20 years of working with this subject that if you understand and practise using naturally occurring building blocks, you can assemble your own strategies, tools and techniques on demand. Indeed much of our success in facilitating innovation and creativity in companies has consisted of designing strategies and tools to best fit a particular business context or need, rather than using proprietary tools. Here are some building blocks.

Bisociation and focus

> Creativity is the ability to connect the seemingly unconnected
>
> William Plomer, South African
> Author, 1903–1973

As per Plomer's musing, there is a good deal of evidence that demonstrates the value in force-fitting apparently unrelated ideas together to produce novel ideas. Arthur Koestler coined the term 'bisociation' for such processes. Examples include:

- *Pilkington float glass* – Before the development of the float process by a research team led by Sir Alastair Pilkington, glass making was labour-intensive and time-consuming. This was mainly due to the need for grinding and polishing surfaces to achieve a brilliant finish. Pilkington's proprietary process involved floating the glass, after it was cast from a melting furnace, over a bath of molten tin about the size of a tennis court. The idea for rinsing glass came to Sir Alastair when he stood at his kitchen sink washing dishes. He was fascinated by the sight of a plate floating on water and wondered whether the principle could be applied to glass making. From this moment, he imagined a washing up bowl the size of a tennis court, full of molten tin, upon which one could float molten glass. I guess we've all had that thought! The really important thing that Pilkington went on to do was to actually do what he had imagined. This took seven years and a considerable sum of money. This is where perspiration succeeds over inspiration to produce innovation.

- *Cat's eyes* – The invention of 'cat's eyes' arose when Percy Shaw noticed that the tramlines had been removed in his town and that he had been using the polished strips of steel to navigate at night. He made the connection between the reflective properties of cat's eyes and the possibility of having reflective materials embedded into the road to improve driving vision at night.

Bisociation relies on the ability to think in at least two intellectual fields of expertise. As a consequence, specialists are likely to be at a disadvantage if they only have access to a single discipline. In such circumstances, the power of creative teams composed of people from unrelated disciplines becomes apparent. This explains the potential advantages to be gained from constituting brainstorming groups and 'think tanks' from a wide cross-section of disciplines, including using people who, at first sight, have little or no relevant contributions to make. In recent years, I've been lucky to participate in a number of these with colleagues from Imperial College London, working on ground-breaking inventions in aerospace and healthcare. A design principle of these events is to have a huge bandwidth of expertise to ensure that bisociation and fermentation occurs within and across disciplines.

The creativity checklist known as SCAMPER includes the word combine as one of its provocations to induce bisociation. Some creativity methodologies have as their subtext the introduction of random 'errors' as a means of distorting frames of thinking. Techniques such as morphological analysis, dialectical thinking and the eight I's method are good examples of methodologies that are built on bisociation. As well as deliberate errors introduced by such approaches, it is important to celebrate accidental errors as a way of finding an answer to a complex problem.

Some people gain greater value in focus and find it hard to gain access to novel ideas through force-fitting unrelated issues together.

Detachment and attachment
French Philosopher Simone Weil (1909–1943) talked of the idea of being detached or what we might think of as being 'off task' when she

suggested that reality can be attained only by someone who is detached. The history of creativity and innovation is littered with examples of people discovering things when they are detached or 'off-task', such as washing up, ironing, plastering, building, decorating etc. It is worth discovering what circumstances work for you. As well as the example of discovering gravity whilst sitting in the bath, Swiss Engineer George de Mestral saw the need for Velcro after returning from a walk to discover seedpods stuck to his socks. On examination, he realised that the pods had 'hooks,' which become entangled in the fibres of the wool. In other cases, it is essential to be fully immersed or attached to the topic at hand. Richard Feynman, Nobel Laureate physicist believed in getting his hands dirty and the value of experimentation, saying 'to develop working ideas efficiently, I try to fail as fast as I can'.

Leaders recognise that apparently low-value activity can be immensely important for generating ideas. As the saying goes, 'all work and no play'. They also understand that others need complete immersion in their ambition. Some new age approaches to creativity have attachment as an underlying design principle, such as meditation and hypnosis. Detachment features as an underlying design principle within creativity tools such as Projective methodologies, Six Thinking Hats, The Star Trek Method, Superheroes, Non-linear Conversations and so on.

One practical route into detachment comes from the discipline known as Neuro-Linguistic Programming (NLP) which considers there to be three perspectives from which you may view a problem or opportunity: the so-called 1st, 2nd and 3rd positions. The 1st position is the problem owner's view. The 2nd position is the view of a stakeholder, perhaps a customer or someone who sees the impact or benefit of any resolution. The 3rd position is that of the detached observer who has the beauty of detachment from the problem/opportunity and can bring an objective quality to the process.

Another manifestation of detachment is what I call the 'twilight zone'. Have you ever had a great idea whilst just falling asleep or half awake? Could you remember it later? It seems that a lot of people recognise that great ideas occur in the 'twilight zone'. We saw that Kekulé's insight that led to the discovery of benzene was a classic example of why dozing leads to great ideas.

Creativity Strategies

David Bowie – Force fitting and bisociation

David Bowie wrote many of his song lyrics by the random force fitting of words and phrases, which he cut up from larger pieces of writing. This was based on approaches pioneered by William Burroughs and The Beat Generation in the 1950s. Many proprietary creative and systemic thinking techniques rely on forced relationships between unrelated items. The use of Post-it notes, snowballing and LVT in Chapter 4 builds on this approach to song writing. A good example of this would be in his worldwide hit 'Ziggy Stardust and the Spiders from Mars', where Bowie builds a bizarre word picture of his alter ego from cut-up fragments. Brian Eno adopted some similar strategies with his creativity card deck 'Oblique Strategies', which inspired Bowie to produce a trilogy of albums in Berlin.

Solitude and gregariousness

I wandered lonely as a cloud . . .

William Wordsworth, 1807

In a study of thinking styles, more than 60% of the sample reported that they found solitude helped gain access to ideas. In some cases, this was simply a quiet place to reflect and think. In other cases, it was connected with engagement with some other activity (e.g. cooking, playing an instrument, sport, taking a shower, walking etc.). Some creativity writers emphasise the importance of interaction and teamwork in the generation of creative thought. I agree with their emphasis to the point that some people, especially extroverts, need to be gregarious to get inspired and think the unthinkable etc. However, solitude is also a place where personal reflection can take place and it is of great importance for people who need 'personal thinking space'. You will access more from your introvert thinkers this way. Just think of the implications of this for the way in which work, buildings and meetings are designed.

Some creativity methodologies emphasise working alone (e.g. brainwriting), which allows each individual to contribute as an individual versus brainstorming which advantages the extrovert team player. Research confirms that more radical ideas are produced through the private brainwriting process, although this can be dramatically affected by the quality of the facilitator. Computer-based innovative thinking methods also allow for solitude, although some have other disadvantages which must be taken into account. In Chapter 4, we will examine 'solo creativity approaches' as well as those more suitable for those who gain more from teams.

Naivety and expertise

If stupidity got us into this mess, then why can't it get us out?

Will Rogers, Actor, 1879–1935

In some cases, experience in a field over an extended period is essential to break free of a paradigm. For others the more experience we have the less likely we are to produce novel ideas. Taking naivety first, Harry Beck conceived the idea for the modern London Underground map in 1931. It was a radical innovation in two ways:

• He enlarged the inner London area to improve readability.
• He ignored geographical conventions, using only horizontal, vertical and 45-degree lines to simplify people's ability to navigate.

The result was a much more dynamic and readable map. Although it has been revised many times, the fundamental innovations in Beck's original design have remained as the 'dominant design' for the modern-day map. The design is widely copied for metro maps around the world. Harry Beck was an electrical engineering draughtsman and his diagram owed more to electrical circuit diagrams rather than the conventions of cartography. This is a good example of creativity springing from a naïve perspective. Had Beck been an expert mapmaker, it is unlikely that we would have the tube map in its present form. This example crucially relied on naivety, or the 'clever idiot' for success.

Moving on to expertise, in drug discovery it is thought that really good science only begins to emerge from scientists after they have spent up to ten years working in a particular field. This is the so-called 10,000 hours phenomenon, coined by Malcolm Gladwell. There is a massive implication for innovation here in a world where many individuals become restless for career improvement every three years or so and it is considered unfashionable to stick at a discipline for extended periods of time.

Creativity Strategies

Gert Johannes Scholz – A walk in the park

My most productive creative writing occurs when there is interplay between convergent and divergent thinking, and between deliberative and free-associative thinking. I use a simple method to draw on these modes of thinking and cognition.

On a given morning I set aside three to four hours for working, beginning with focusing on the theme and information at hand, synthesizing and formulating ideas on paper by way of deliberate attention. This process draws on convergent thinking as I distil the essence of various schema's and paradigms. Whilst immersed in sources of information and formulating ideas consciously onto paper, my mind is taking in and processing more than which I am consciously absorbing.

After about an hour of work I go for a fifteen-minute stroll. I switch my mind off to take in the environment. These are the moments when the brain pulls together disparate shreds of thought and binds them into a new single conscious idea; those 'aha!' moments, when two formerly disconnected fragments of thought suddenly merge into a new meaning. On a typical writing morning I will do about three hours of actual writing – every hour broken by a short fifteen-minute 'walk in the park'.

Constraints and freedom

> I subscribe to the myth that an artist's creativity comes from torment. Once that's fixed, what do you draw on?
>
> David Byrne, Press Interview, *The Guardian* 27 April 2001

In the film '*It Might Get Loud*', guitarist Jack White suggests that technology makes us lazy and laziness is bad for creativity. He is right. My first guitar cost £10, the strings stood about a centimetre (slight exaggeration but not much) from the neck. This made my fingers work much harder to play the instrument than normal. As a result, people tell me that I can bend strings an incredible amount akin to Dave Gilmour of Pink Floyd. White also uses low-quality instruments to force him to play differently or work harder. White makes this graphically clear by indicating that if it takes him three steps to get to the organ, then he would move it four steps away in order to make himself work harder.

Contrary to popular opinion, constraints are useful for creativity in all walks of life. Isambard Kingdom Brunel would have not built the Great Western Railway without feeling frustrated that he could not get to Cornwall quickly, and having the vision that passengers could travel from London to New York on one ticket bought at London Paddington Station.

It is important to separate what I call 'real constraints' from 'imaginary ones'. A real constraint might be a law of physics, an imaginary one simply an assumption, such as a way of doing things that has become a habit or paradigm within an industry. In my own experience, I led a team responsible for developing the world's first AIDS treatment. A real constraint was that of time. We needed to collapse the traditional drug development process time to bring the drug to market as quickly and safely as possible. At that time The Wellcome Foundation was renowned for its expertise in making tablet formulations and this would have been our 'paradigm response' to the situation. In the event, we elected to formulate the product as a capsule, something we were totally inexperienced with, but which would deliver the quickest and safest route to market and the patient. This committed us to a rapid learning programme of work to develop the product. In doing so we eliminated the artificial constraint of 'we always do it that way'.

For many years, I've used the model of a 'fried egg' to help people understand the essentials needed to specify a problem or opportunity that is amenable to ingenious thinking. I was delighted when Charles Handy wrote me a personal letter to tell me that he had thought of something similar for his book *The Empty Raincoat* before settling on the doughnut model. Our fried egg model requires there to be enough 'thinking space' between 'the demands or goal' and 'the constraints' to provide an arena for productive creativity – 'the choices' or what a mechanic might call degrees of freedom. It is also a very handy model for helping leaders think through tough decisions. Too little choice and we have no room for creative input (boiled). Too much choice and we have what we will describe as a 'wicked problem' in Chapter 3 (scrambled).

At a personal level, Sir Richard Branson's dyslexia seems to have acted as an important constraint around which he has developed new choices. As a result of the condition, he has always needed other people to address specifics on his behalf. This has resulted in him becoming someone who develops deep levels of trust and who is great at delegation. Necessity has literally become the mother of invention for Virgin.

Ambiguity and certainty

Sigmund Freud pointed out that neurosis is the inability to tolerate ambiguity. The ability to tolerate (or even relish) ambiguous situations is a quality that consistently marks out creative people from the pack. They often do this by having an innate curiosity for the unknown or unknowable situations, rather like great scientists. This differentiates them from others who prefer to resolve the situation (for example by accepting a compromise). It is possible to cultivate the habit of perceiving a situation or idea in a number of self-consistent but habitually incompatible frames of reference. If these can be held for an extended length of time, there is a higher probability that a novel idea will emerge from the tension that arises from the ensuing cognitive dissonance. This is especially important for people working on strategic problems or ones that are inherently complex and connected in nature.

One example of how you can make this idea into a practical strategy is the so-called 'too difficult' in-tray as practiced by Sir Trevor Jones. I used to work for Trevor at The Wellcome Foundation, a philanthropic pharmaceutical company which was devoted to medical innovation and curing the world of tropical disease. Trevor had a 'too difficult' in-tray, for ideas that people had submitted that could not be implemented due to various issues including timing. He systematically recycled the items in the 'too difficult' pile so that they could be launched when timing favoured their introduction as an intrapreneur. It is the systematic nature of his strategy and the recognition of the importance of time and timing that turns the approach from something based purely on luck to that of 'planned luck'.

Dissonance and consonance

Cognitive dissonance in business is a term coined by Leon Festinger, used to describe the state of holding two or more conflicting thoughts together simultaneously. In music we can easily understand the idea of dissonance when two notes produce an unstable tone combination. Simply stated, they appear to grate on the ear. In the West we are mostly used to music that adopts the major, minor or blues scales. Indian music tends to use different scales to those traditionally used in Western music. Take a listen to George Harrison's song 'Within You Without You', Lou Reed's 'Metal Machine Music' or some Indonesian Gamelan music to hear musical scales and tones that some consider dissonant to Western conventions.

Dissonance at work is the silence in the meeting when someone suggests something that is outside traditional thinking patterns. Sometimes it can be heard through people talking about other people as mad, bad or evil outside the meeting. Dissonance in business costs millions through wasted time, missed opportunities, inadequate follow-through of ideas and so on. Gerry Johnson (1987, 2007) articulated the problems associated with cognitive dissonance at work and the concept is particularly relevant when attempting to get people to accept new ideas and to embrace change.

I have spent a lot of time helping people use dissonance in business in order to create strategies that set their enterprises apart from the crowd. This is a strategy that has helped companies such as Unilever to succeed, for example in their use of fuller-figured women to promote beauty products, which challenge conventions in this area. Consonance is often better when we wish to fit novel ideas within a particular mindset or paradigm. Just think about advertisements for products that you like to see how consonance comforts in the persuasion process for many people.

Creativity Strategies

Sarah Winmill – On detachment

I find it is mundane tasks that give me my most creative moments. I am currently writing an academic paper and it is no coincidence that all my washing is up to date!

I sort the washing, crate a load in and set it running, knowing that it now gives me approximately 60 minutes to make progress with reading and writing. A buzzer sounds to bring me away from my desk and I take the washing to the garden to hang out. I find the repetitive physical task of hanging things out requires enough thought to clear what I have just been looking at but leaves enough space for my mind to wander creatively. This, coupled with the change of scenery and/or fresh air, will often result in greater creativity and productivity of thought than continuing at my desk. I also note that I take a metaphoric step back from my work during this interlude, checking I'm on the right path, and will often adjust my approach when I return to my desk once the next load of washing is running.

Sarah's insight is one that many others and I myself recognise. For me it is a train journey where I know I have limited time to get things done and am somehow detached from life's pressures. In fact I have written parts of this book on repetitive train journeys. As a 'heuristic', Sarah's methodology also aligns amazingly accurately with what we understand about what works from eminent Neuroscientist Dr Daniel Levitin.

It is really important for leaders to find ways to listen to ideas that seem dissonant to currently accepted views of your business strategy. Try to practise curiosity on a daily basis and delay evaluation of ideas for as long as possible, so that you can put distance between the novelty and a rational evaluation of the potential feasibility and impact of the idea.

Combinatorial creativity

Whilst it is possible to use each of the states we discussed separately, often a creative state comes from the combination of a number of individual principles that mimic the unconscious recipes of naturally creative people. Why not try some combinatorial creativity by mixing up the principles we have discussed to find out what works for you? For example, consider '*detailed naivety*', where you actively and deeply engage with a problem or opportunity as if you were a complete novice, or '*interactive detachment*', where . . . well what do you think?

1. Seven creativity principles		
Bisociation and focus	Solitude and gregariousness	Constraints and freedom
Detachment and attachment	Naivety and expertise	Ambiguity and certainty
		Dissonance and consonance

For example, combining naivety with expertise leads us to the example of 'liquid paper'. Bette Nesmith Graham was a secretary who discovered a way of covering up mistakes by observing how sign writers did this and scaling the process down using water-based paint and a small brush. After five years of working with her son's chemistry teacher she perfected the formula for 'liquid paper'.

Combination requires that we add two diverse elements together. It is essentially an additive strategy. Later on we will consider the concept of 'mathematical creativity', where we use all four principle mathematical operators to help generate better ideas: plus, minus, multiply and divide.

The 3B's of creativity

No doubt you have heard of the three B's of creativity, i.e. the Bed, the Bath and the Bar. Empirical evidence suggests that lots of people get their ideas in these places and the background reasons may lie in creative states such as detachment, solitude and so on. In the case of the bar, alcohol shuts down our ability to censor unusual ideas. In extremis, it also shuts down our ability to remember what we thought so a plan for recall is needed for this method!

Sir James Dyson's approach

James Dyson commented on his own approach to creativity in our interview:

> It is hard not to be in the right frame of mind at Dyson. I am always inspired when in our RDD department. Being around so many creative minds, I am constantly thinking of new ideas. I work very closely with the engineers – I watch every project develop. And it's exciting. Our engineers are guided by problems and the frustration they cause. This means they develop solutions that actually work.
>
> When I go home I can't help but think over what I've seen. I sketch new ideas and changes to designs. It is the same when I read the James Dyson Award entries from around the world. These inventions, like Dyson, solve everyday problems with some truly breathtaking solutions. Take the MOM incubator, it allows premature babies in the developing world to have a chance in their early hours and days. Or Bump Mark that tells consumers when their food is going off thereby cutting reliance on ineffective food labels and reducing food waste.

Reflections

Creativity can be developed like any other personal quality and there is a contribution to be made by 'givens' such as luck and personality. However, it is insufficient to rely on serendipity and genius in the world of work if creativity and innovation are to be distributed throughout your BBE.

Creativity tools and techniques are simply the explicit recipes of 'what works' and are often composed of a number of the underlying states. Many times extremes work such as being completely immersed versus fully detached. Mediocre states do not generally produce the free radical chemistry necessary to spark ideas together.

Once we understand where our own creativity comes from, we can set about creating the conditions where we can put ourselves in creative states when required to get the best out of our minds and those of others we collaborate with.

Many natural creative states are combinations of the fundamental building blocks and you are encouraged to experiment with combinatorial creativity to find your own 'sweet spots' and routes to your 'creative core'.

Chapter 2

Creativity and you

The mind's inclination often follows the body's temperature
Commonly attributed to Galen, Greek Physician
and Philosopher, AD 129-c200

Psyche, bile and skulls

Psychology has its roots in ancient Greek culture through the letter Ψ and the word psyche, meaning life. Aristotle perhaps deserves the credit for his synthesis of psychology with a philosophy of the mind, but psychology did not really become a discrete discipline until the ninetenth century. One of the earliest insights into modern day psychology came from Rene Descartes, who introduced the idea of dualism, essentially separating the mind from the body. Up until that point, much of our thinking about the mind was based on the assumption that the mind and body were in some way unified. This produced medical 'remedies' for mental conditions based on the four humours – black bile, yellow bile, phlegm, and blood, such as blood-letting, applying hot cups and so on. It is only since the enlightenment, with improvements to scientific methods and our understanding of anatomy that we have begun to understand and attempt to qualify and quantify the psyche. However, the legacy of the four humours lives on in some of our thinking, language and even in products on shelves in high-street pharmacies and our descriptions of people as 'sanguine', derived from an excess of blood.

In 1908, Frank Parsons pioneered what we have come to regard as the world of psychometric testing. He asked people 116 questions about their goals, strengths and weaknesses. He also measured their skulls, bringing whole new meaning to our concept of a Brain Based Enterprise (BBE). He believed that people with large foreheads were primed to become lawyers or engineers. If, however, your head was of an 'animal type' you would be best suited to manual work. It was a start, but perhaps we have made some progress since . . . So, we begin with some qualitative approaches to creativity with which I have found great utility over many years. None of these require you to measure your head, administer emetics, or apply leeches to your body . . .

Four P's of creativity

One of the formative moments in my decision to leave a well-paid job to start a business was my attendance at the flagship Open University Business School MBA programme 'Creativity, Innovation and Change'. This was a work of pure joy, written by Jane Henry, John Martin and David Mayle. I loved the programme so much as a student that I made it my ambition to become a tutor on the MBA so that I could really learn. Since this epiphany I have devoted much of the last 20 years to help others create ingenious solutions to VUCA-(**V**olatile, **U**ncertain, **C**omplex and **A**mbiguous) shaped problems. Jane, John and David articulated a model of creativity in this exceptional programme, which uses four 'P's' to describe key habits of creative people. The model needs no adjustment over time and I've summarised the essences here:

Positivity – The consistent habit of seeing problems as opportunities. The ability to recover rapidly from setbacks and tolerate criticism. An unwillingness to let obstacles impede progress. Positivity is different to the notion of unbridled optimism, a disease that stops people applying any level of critical thinking to a business opportunity. This partly accounts for the extreme failure rate of start-up projects and entrepreneurial activity. I notice that this disease grips some people in business, where nobody is allowed to say anything that could be perceived as critical or 'negative'. This will lead to tears in my opinion. There is a huge difference between an optimist who examines the realities of a situation and someone who blocks out such things as we shall learn from the example of John Otway in Chapter 5.

Playfulness – Drawing on the resources of childhood by taking risks, using fun and humour in thinking resulting in flexibility of thought and deed. It involves feeling comfortable outside the mainstream of thinking and action. Playfulness can be both physical and mental. For example, many mechanical engineers play with objects to find new ways to design them. In other cases, thought experiments are more important as exemplified by Albert Einstein when musing on what it would be like to travel on a beam of light. In some companies, sometimes banter is a source of mental play when there is less opportunity for practical experimentation, as I discovered in a London reinsurance company. They told me that humour was their only escape route from the mind-numbing effects of the job into new ways of thinking.

Ken Kutaragi nearly lost his job at Sony Corporation when he worked for Nintendo in his spare time developing what became the Sony PlayStation. Kutaragi found a product champion in the form of Norio Ohga, Sony's CEO, who recognised his creativity when most of the senior management team saw his project as a distraction rather than a serious piece of new product development. By 1998, the PlayStation provided 40% of Sony's profits. This is playfulness turned literally into profits.

Passion – Driven by a consuming purpose. An obsessive will to achieve your goals. Some people prefer to use the word 'purpose' to passion. For me, passion differs from the idea of a manic obsession with a goal in the respect of having a focus rather than a single aim. This is a subtle, but important, distinction.

Persistence – This is the difference between the saying 'If at first you don't succeed, try try again' and saying 'If at first you don't succeed, try something different until you succeed'. Pure persistence is the business equivalent of head banging in rock music, which usually leads to a headache. Flexible persistence is the hallmark of successful innovators such as Trevor Bayliss, Marie Curie and Sir Richard Branson.

For those that enjoy rules of thumb over psychometric inventories, the 'four P' model can be used as a crude but effective compass to pinpoint where you, your team and enterprise sit on the various axes. We are confounded with quantitative analysis these days. There is nothing wrong with some good old-fashioned empiricism, especially when the qualities you are attempting to measure are not themselves entirely scientific. Next, we look at some quantitative approaches to the measurement of creative potential.

Four P's applied at Dyson

The Dyson Story is a case of the four P's in action. The breakthrough of the Dyson vacuum cleaner was its ability to outperform other cleaners by virtue of the fact that the suction performance remains the same regardless of how much dust has been collected. This was achieved by removing the bag and replacing it with a cyclone system to separate dust particles down to 0.1 micron. Like many innovations, the origins of the Dyson can be traced to the inventor's frustration with the constraints of existing vacuum cleaners:

> I noticed that the cleaner wasn't sucking, so I took the bag out and emptied it. But it still didn't suck.
>
> James Dyson

On further investigation, James Dyson found a thin layer of dust on the inside of the bag. After dismantling the machine, he realised that the airflow that goes through the cleaner had to go through the pores of the bag. This problem became the stimulus for the development of the Dyson Dual Cyclone vacuum cleaners. The time from conception to launch was 15 years, and from launch to commercial success another ten years. During the development phase Dyson produced 5,127 prototypes, using the Edisonian method of only making one change between tests so that he could perfect the invention. This is persistence in a bottle!

Breaking barriers to market entry

Experts proved to be a constant source of frustration. In 1982 a large American manufacturer would only meet James Dyson if he agreed to sign over the rights to anything he revealed to them in conversation. Ten years after, the Secretary of State for Wales rejected Dyson's application for a development grant, insisting that if there really were a better type of vacuum cleaner then one of the big manufacturers would already be making it. It took continuing persistence to eventually find a manufacturer and a bank loan of £600,000 from Lloyds to get the invention to the market place.

The poverty of market research

Market research suggested that the clear dust collection bin was not desirable. This was based on the thought that people would not like the dirt being visible in case neighbours saw how much dirt had been picked up in their homes. Dyson ignored this information and was correct to do so. Market research cannot always adequately predict what the customer wants. Leo Fender, Steve Jobs and others have also shunned market research in favour of intuition and insight. We revisit Dyson later in this book to gain some personal insights into leading an enterprise where innovation and creativity still thrives.

Playfulness – From the nursery to the boardroom

Michelle Zal is a volunteer reading mentor for national charity Beanstalk, supporting struggling young readers. By day she works in the Chartered Institute of Personnel and Development (CIPD). Michelle sees parallels in her work with children and the boardroom.

Children who struggle with reading fall behind their peers. In many cases this impacts on other areas of their learning and social development. The first thing we do is to find what the children love and develop their reading skills from there. Out go graded school books, and reading schemes. And in come whatever makes the children laugh and enjoy. Success rates are high. Reading begins to feel like fun again and the children engage.

At the CIPD, we're working to embed a more open and creative culture. Physical changes around the building include the introduction of an innovation zone with circular seating and beanbags, informal breakout areas, and a less formal dress code. It took far longer for behaviours to change. This goes to show that it is easy to change the physical environment but behaviour is what counts for an enterprise to become more creative and innovative. For me there is a direct parallel in what happens in the nursery and the boardroom in terms of encouraging playfulness.

For some time it felt awkward because the content and style of our meetings felt incongruous with the setting. But gradually behaviours started to change, as we felt more empowered to take risks. People are getting more creative with their ideas, and if it isn't perfect, or we get it wrong, it doesn't matter.

At nursery, children are natural risk takers, who learn from exploring and playing. Playfulness is just as important for big kids in the workplace. A creative and playful culture creates risk and innovation, and more enterprises need to learn from nurseries.

Psyche-metric

A great deal of research in the twentieth century has focused on the question 'Can you measure creativity?' More important questions for the twenty-first century are 'Should you measure it?' and 'If so, when?' Psychologist J.P. Guilford was one of the first people to conclude that IQ tests did not measure creativity. He also coined the phrases 'divergent thinking' and 'convergent thinking'. 'Divergent thinking' is thinking that comes up with no holds barred insights to open-ended questions. Convergent thinking narrows the field to a single answer for each question, commonly associated with IQ tests. So, if we are to use psychometric tests for creativity, we need to look in other places and recognise the strengths and limitations of such things. John Cleese refers to these as 'open' and 'closed'.

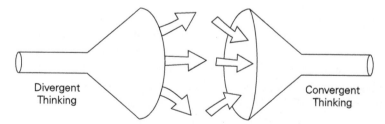

Divergent
Thinking

Convergent
Thinking

Cleese points out in his lectures on creativity that most people spend most of their time in the closed mode and this has a purpose. For example if you are leaping a ravine, the moment of take-off is a bad time for brainstorming alternatives. But many other situations demand the use of open mode. Both open (divergent) and closed (convergent) abilities are required. Divergent thinking is essential to the novelty of innovative products services, whereas convergent thinking is fundamental to appropriateness, decision making and action. Many innovative thinking techniques are designed to achieve these thinking dimensions, either separately through 'staged' methods or simultaneously through 'all together now' approaches. We examine these in Chapter 4.

To adapt or innovate? – that is the question

Creative people are sometimes viewed as being connected with 'wild' ideas that are not seen as relevant to immediate concerns or opportunities. However, innovation in business can be minor as well as major. Innovation can manifest itself as incremental continuous shifts in the way products and services are designed, produced and delivered rather than breakthrough innovations like the steam engine. Professor Michael Kirton developed a continuum of styles, ranging between the creative behaviour of people he called **adaptors** and those he termed **innovators**. The Kirton Adaptor-Innovator inventory (KAI) gives a bipolar measure of innovative thinking style, typified as follows:

Individuals are categorised along a scale, which follows a normal distribution from 32 points to 160 with an average of 96. People with a

Adaptors	Innovators
Provide enough ideas based on original problem and original likely solutions.	Provide lots of ideas, many of which may not address the problem.
Develop ideas that are more readily accepted by most people.	Reconstruct or reframe problems and provide less expected and potentially less acceptable solutions, which challenge accepted practice.
Are likely to provide a more in-depth search of one or a few ideas.	Present many less carefully worked-out formulations.
Seek a solution within the structure of the problem and in ways tried, understood, safe, sure and predictable.	Present ideas that may be far away from the prevailing paradigms which are likely to be more strongly resisted.
Develop ideas with minimal risk and maximum continuity and stability.	Develop riskier ideas.

score lower than 96 are classed as adaptors and those above 96 innovators. Broadly speaking:

Adaptors habitually try to solve problems using rules
Innovators bend or break the rules

Both are required for successful innovation, yet Kirton pointed out that there is potential for conflict in groups where individual KAI scores are greater than 20 points apart. This does not mean that these situations should be avoided since conflict is valuable for creativity, but it needs good management. Change agents and leaders may well have a 'displaced' score for success (e.g. an adaptor in a group of innovators and vice versa). This may help to explain the feelings of loneliness experienced by such people in a team if they have no other sources of emotional support as a minority figure. One criticism of Kirton's model is that there is a social desirability bias associated with being called an innovator, when adaptive behaviour is also innovative. This arises from the use of the term innovator as one of the two types. Adaptive and innovative behaviour can also be inferred from observation of people in business and public life. Examples include:

Richard Branson, who, despite the wide variety of his business ventures and his ability to gain publicity for his ventures well above the size of the Virgin empire through carefully executed stunts, could be said to be adaptive in nature. The principle behind most of his ventures is that of improving an existing product or service. This is particularly relevant in industries where advantage can be gained through calculated risk taking, shortening the physical or psychological distance from the customer, or improving delivery speed. Branson has transformed insurance, air travel, rail and a number of other industries crying out for a customer front end. There are exceptions to every rule and Virgin Galactic is perhaps a more radical and aspirational innovation!

Jimi Hendrix is still considered to be one of the greatest guitar players in the world, more than 40 years after his premature death in 1970. Talking with Bernie Tormé, guitarist for Ozzy Osbourne and Deep Purple's Ian Gillan, confirms the view that Hendrix had more than just guitar technique:

For me, Jimi Hendrix epitomises innovation in rock music still. His willingness to explore sounds that were way beyond those being used by his contemporaries at the time still stands up to scrutiny. He had a playground approach to using equipment and effects that was totally alien at the time. He also fused styles in ways that others would not dream of.

Bernie Tormé, personal interview 2013

Hendrix is an archetype of an innovator, someone who fused together musical ideas to come up with something totally novel. Jimi Hendrix fused the blues with soul, funk, hard rock and psychedelia in a heady cocktail, whereas many musicians stay within a musical genre. By comparison, Eric Clapton has stayed within the blues genre, sticking closer to this genre and consequentially bringing it to a wider audience. This is the behaviour of an adaptor. If Hendrix worked in an enterprise, chances are he would be the head of exploratory Research and Development, whereas Clapton would be in charge of the 'Right First Time' programme!

The musician George Clinton is another 'synthesiser', fearlessly fusing musical genres in ways that others fear or may not even consider. George is mentioned alongside James Brown and Sly Stone as the key influencers in the development of soul and funk music and is the second most sampled artist in the world, his music having been used as the template for Hip Hop. Speaking to George, he is unafraid of mistakes, seeing these as opportunities to learn, exemplified by a story he told me about the creation of the song 'Atomic Dog'. Check our accompanying website to find out more about this and other examples of the use of mistakes as spurs to creativity.

Steve Jobs, who started the Apple Corporation, a runaway success, was reputed to be enthusiastic, hard working and full of ideas. But he was restless, easily bored and blunt to the point of tactlessness. All these elements are characteristic of a high innovator, although being an innovator does not have to mean a lack of interpersonal skills. We need both innovators and adaptors to produce sustainable innovations that will not fade away: the innovators to produce the hard-to-copy ideas and; the adaptors to help bring the ideas into a practical market focus. So, if the Adaptor-Innovator inventor tells us about one specific aspect of innovation potential, what do the more general psychometric inventories tell us?

Myers Briggs Type Indicator

The Myers Briggs Type Indicator (MBTI) measures preferences relating to Carl Jung's theory of personality types, according to four bipolar types.

---

1. Where do you prefer to focus your attention? The EI scale

E – Extraversion	I – Introversion
Focus is on the outer world of people and things	Focus on the inner world of reflection

2. How do you acquire information? The SN scale

S – Sensing	N – Intuition
Focus is on the realities of the situation, careful with detail	Focus on the big picture grasping overall patterns

3. How do you make decisions? The TF scale

T – Thinking	F – Feeling
Focus is on objective decision-making, analysing and considering	Focus on person-centred values, seek harmony

4. How do you orient to the outside world? The JP scale

J – Judging	P – Perceiving
Focus is on structure, planning, Regulation and control	Focus is on organising. understanding, flexibility and spontaneity

---

This produces 16 different 'types' (e.g. ISTJ, ENFP). As with the Adaptor-Innovator inventory, huge differences in type have the potential to grate on each other if they forget that different concerns derive from different working styles. Where differences are accommodated, each type usually benefits from working with people with opposing preferences. In such circumstances, each type will attend to areas that the opposing type is inclined to forget or minimise. A truly great team accommodates the weaknesses of individual team members by compensating for gaps. The following table gives a simplified view of type conflicts and synergies as they relate to innovation and creativity:

Conflict	Synergy
S finds N: impractical, hard to follow.	**S needs N:** to prepare for the future, offer practical ideas.
N finds S: materialistic and pessimistic.	**N needs S:** to remind them of facts, be realistic, have patience.
T finds F: illogical, over-emotional.	**T needs F:** to connect with feelings, persuade, reconcile.
F finds T: critical, insensitive.	**F needs T:** to be tough and weigh costs and benefits.
E finds I: withdrawn, cool.	**E needs I:** for reflection and depth of understanding.
I finds E: superficial, intrusive.	**I needs E:** to make contacts and take action.
J finds P: disorganised, irresponsible.	**J needs P:** for adaptability and information gathering.
P finds J: rigid, inflexible.	**P needs J:** for organisation and for completion.

Innovators vary widely in their MBTI types. It is estimated that James Dyson is an ENTP, Sir Richard Branson an INFJ, Steve Jobs an INTJ, Albert Einstein and Frances Crick have INTP profiles. Clearly there is no 'type' that makes an innovator and this goes to show that personality profiling is just a part of what goes to make the unique entity that is you. Over recent years the 'big five' has gained in popularity. We next take a look at this.

The Beatles, complementarity and conflict

The Beatles are a great example of complementarity and conflict in terms of creativity and teamwork. John Lennon was thought to be an 'enthusiast' (ENFP) whilst McCartney a 'harmoniser' (ISFP) with George Harrison being a 'conceptualiser' (INTP) and Ringo being an 'activist' (ESTP). There is, of course, some disagreement as to where each of them sits as your type varies over time and it is rather difficult to assess John and George these days. In any case, it is interesting to note that all of The Beatles occupied essentially minority types, especially George Harrison who conceived of the idea to produce large-scale concerts to highlight world poverty issues long before Bob Geldof got on the case with Live Aid etc.

Personality tests do not tell us the whole story and perhaps one of the most important elements of the bond between Lennon and McCartney was the fact that both of them had lost parents early on in their lives which must have given them a deep common bond despite other differences in their personalities.

The Big Five

Whilst Myers Briggs remains the most widely used personality test, the so-called 'Big Five' has emerged as the most reliable personality test. The five factors are:

1. Extraversion
2. Neuroticism
3. Openness
4. Agreeableness
5. Conscientiousness

Of these, openness is very important for creativity and this factor is a good predictor of innovative potential as reported in research by Professor Adrian Furnham. Neuroticism and agreeableness are also interesting factors re creativity. Some level of neuroticism is helpful as it can often provide for emotional sensitivity, but too much neuroticism can lead to mood swings and fragile egos. This is the classic stereotype of a creative person: someone who must be wrapped in cotton wool for their own protection and that of others at work. At one extreme, this may account for people's wariness in dealing with such people at work. Although extraversion makes social relationships and networking easier for creatives, it is by no means clear that extraversion is a desirable trait for creative activity as we have explored in Chapter 1. Some people are best absorbed in their own inner world of thoughts. In any case, most innovators have been shown to be introverts; however, in some cases, introverts have taught themselves extrovert behaviours in order to succeed (e.g. Sir Richard Branson).

Implications for innovation and creativity

Creative people generate larger numbers of options and they incubate these options for longer than the average person. Instant judgements are likely to prevent opportunities for inventive search. This has important consequences for the management of creative individuals, since a good deal of management is concerned with decision making and judgement. We introduce the notion of 'convergence with care' in Chapter 4 to describe the relevant qualities that are needed to evaluate novelty.

Whilst we cannot avoid the tendencies of our 'crocodile brains' (the part of our brains which keep us alive through reflex actions and snap decisions) we can minimise their worst effects by the application of conscious routines. For example, individuals with strong judging characteristics can minimise the effects of instant judgement by starting projects earlier and leaving space for the fermentation of ideas, making decisions at the last possible moment and deliberately ensuring that those options have been fully considered before reaching those decisions.

There have been numerous critics of the Myers Briggs Type Indicator, mostly based on the bipolar nature of the various dimensions and the variability of results when taking a re-test. Yet as an approximate guide to how people are, their strengths and weaknesses, I find it to be of value in terms of giving insight into people who may have a low awareness of what they are like. All psychometric tests are valuable, provided they are used properly.

Some psychometric inventories are mainly aimed at the enterprise level; this makes them useful when comparing your own style and contribution to the enterprise. I particularly like that devised by Mark Brown, author of *The Dinosaur Strain*. His approach is called the Dolphin Index and I have used it to good effect in companies like Pfizer to help shape the culture and climate.

The Dolphin Index

> The world is made up of extraordinary people. Don't waste your time being normal.
>
> Sir Richard Branson

The Dolphin Index www.dolphinindex.com measures the creative climate of an enterprise and allows individuals to compare themselves with the enterprise. I spoke with Mark Brown, about the development:

> In the bad old days we sometimes succeeded as creativity and innovation facilitators, but we failed too. A client would ask us to help engender greater creativity and innovation in their enterprise. So we worked to skill individuals and teams with creative mind-sets and a bag of proven innovation tools. Sometimes success, sometimes not. Why?

In the early 1980s Mark came across Professor Göran Ekvall's seminal work on how the climate of an enterprise nurtures or kills off creativity and innovation. Projects often failed with those clients whose climate was uncreative. Those who had creative climates were often more successful. Mark started with the question, how to both accurately measure and then improve the climate for creativity. He developed Göran's work and, in the late 1990s, created the 'Innovation Climate Questionnaire', later renamed the 'Dolphin Index' (to contrast the idea of a stuck-in-the-mud dinosaur versus a lively, agile and creative dolphin).

The Dolphin Index has passed through three factor analyses and now has 68 questions. Respondents who score his or her enterprise as having a more creative and innovative climate also see themselves as more committed to the enterprise and feel more inclined to be creative and innovative at work. The index comprises thirteen dimensions:

Dimension	Definition
Commitment	The extent to which people are committed to the enterprise and work is viewed as stimulating and engaging.
Freedom	High-freedom work environments are those in which people are empowered to make their own decisions (e.g. about prioritizing their work). In low-freedom environments there is close supervision.
Idea support	Organisational support and encouragement for the development of new ideas and suggestions for improvements.
Positive relationships	Extent to which there are positive, trusting, friendly relationships between people, rather than negative (e.g. hostile, conflicting).
Dynamism	Refers to whether work is exciting and dynamic, or static and boring.
Playfulness	Refers to levels of light-heartedness and fun in the workplace. Work environments low on playfulness may be seen as dour and humourless.

Idea proliferation	Extent to which other people in the work environment are perceived as having innovative ideas about their work.
Stress	High-stress work environments are where other individuals are observed to be highly stressed and dealing with heavy workloads.
Risk-taking:	High risk-taking environments promote the speed at which new ideas are implemented. Low risk-taking environments make excessive use of formal rules and procedures.
Idea time	Extent to which employees perceive that there is time for developing new ideas.
Shared view	Extent to which there is open communication between more and less senior employees. Work environments where there is an 'us' culture rather than an 'us and them' culture.
Work recognition	Do people feel that they receive credit and praise for their achievements? Or do they feel undervalued?
Pay recognition	Refers to satisfaction with pay and conditions. Do people feel fairly remunerated for their work? Or at worst, feel exploited?

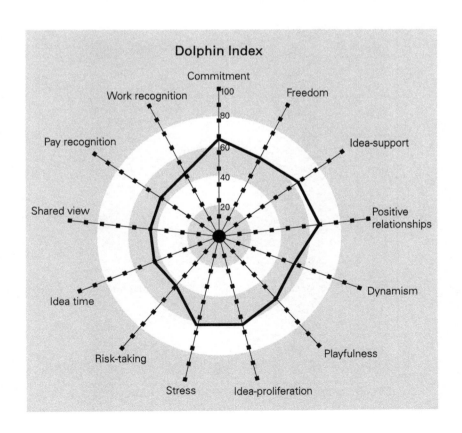

The higher score on each dimension, with the exception of 'stress' where a moderate or lower score is better, the more creative you perceive the climate of your enterprise to be. The diagram shows the UK norm for both large and smaller organisations across private, public and voluntary sectors and international data are available on the index. Later analyses of the thirteen dimensions also revealed two higher order factors of how 'daring' and 'caring' the organisational climate is.

Clients can, therefore, place their enterprise in one of the four quadrants. Mark starts by asking the client what they would hope the different parts of their enterprise would score. He then obtains a robust and representative sample of employees' views on the Dolphin Index to see the gap between the wished for and the current climate. This is what he terms the 'Dolphin Shift'. He gives feedback to the client, including any

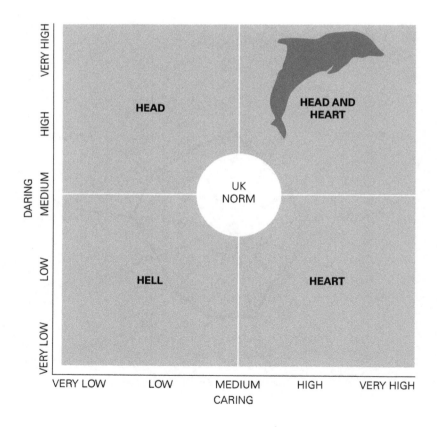

analyses if requested, for example cutting the data by age, gender, location, function, job type, level, length of service, educational background etc. Along with these results he offers multiple detailed, targeted recommendations to shift the culture. The client can implement these recommendations themselves or use other agencies, depending on the need. Mark observes:

> Whereas in the past the core concepts of innovation climate and culture were often not even on management's mental radar or 'dashboard', the Dolphin Index enables managers and directors to convert the qualitative concept of innovation culture into a quantitative measure that can be monitored, benchmarked and managed. In the bad old days we sometimes succeeded, sometimes we failed. Nowadays we succeed more often.

Mindfulness, thinking and decision-making

> It is our choices, Harry, that show what we truly are, rather than our abilities
>
> *Harry Potter and the Chamber of Secrets*:
> Copyright © J.K. Rowling 1998

The practical value of knowing ourselves, our strengths and weaknesses, often comes down to the decisions we make. After all, a key facet of leadership is about making great decisions. When making decisions on novel ideas we face high uncertainty of the outcome and the journey towards that outcome. This places additional strain on our decision-making faculties and requires us to take additional steps to ensure we do not make 'mindless decisions' with disastrous consequences. We discuss 'convergence with care' in Chapter 4 to extend this line of thought. Bias is an important factor in such decisions. If you have ever made a detailed checklist of requirements for buying your ideal home and then been influenced positively by the smell of fresh coffee or baked bread upon entry, or adversely influenced by small children placing dangerous objects under your feet during your visit, you could be slightly less rational than you think. Of course, the same processes take place when big decisions in business need to be taken. We are all subject to bias and there have been numerous experiments that demonstrate this fact. You might like to try out the mind game that follows on the next page with a friend.

Under time pressure bias tends to be exacerbated and most businesses are run under resource constraints. In such circumstances people tend to make emotional judgements rather than purely rational ones. Some of the most common biases are:

Recency – The tendency to overemphasise events if they come to mind easily. Recent, familiar and vivid events tend to come to mind more easily and we thus overestimate their frequency. Examples include the likelihood of accidents from dramatic plane crashes, terrorist incidents, the 'Titanic' and so on.

Confirmation – The tendency to stick with our initial judgements, noticing confirming evidence and dismissing information that does not fit our beliefs.

Hindsight – The tendency to believe that we were more certain about judgements that we were initially, leading to overconfidence in our own judgements.

The systematic practice of the group of strategies that have come to be known as mindfulness can help to minimise bias. These include things like taking periods for calm reflection, meditation, breathing exercises, walking at one level and engaging the rational mind when examining alternatives using some of the tools we discuss under the category of 'converging with care' in Chapter 4. In essence, great decisions require an appropriate balance of what Nobel Prize winner Daniel Kahneman calls 'thinking fast and slow'. As well as mindfulness, great leaders eliminate or minimise obstacles to innovation and creativity in their enterprises. We examine this next.

Decision-making and bias

A rare disease has swept through a community, affecting 666 inhabitants. Experts suggest two programmes for tackling the disease.

- Programme 1 will save 222 lives.
- Programme 2 has a 1/3 probability of saving 666 lives and a 2/3 probability of saving no one.

Take 30 seconds to decide which programme you will adopt. Then try this second example:

A rare disease has swept through a town and has affected 666 inhabitants. Experts suggest two programmes for tackling the disease.

- Programme 1 will result in 444 deaths.
- Programme 2 has a 1/3 probability of no one dying and a 2/3 probability of 666 deaths.

Take 30 seconds to decide which programme you will adopt.

The outcomes from programme 1 in both examples are the same. Both programme 2 examples also produce the same outcomes. Yet many people make 'non-logical' judgements based on some simple but powerful assumptions:

- We tend to prefer life to death, even if we plan to return to the planet!
- We tend to prefer certainty of outcome to uncertainty.

Adapted from my work with The Open University MBA programme.

Removing obstacles to creativity

Enterprises and the individuals within them often think about adding things to the daily grind in order to improve performance. Addition is only one of the four primary mathematical operations we may use to affect change. Sometimes all that is needed to spark a little creativity is to remove or use the obstacle that presents itself. We can extend this idea to the strategy I call 'mathematical creativity', which simply asks:

- What can be added to the situation?
- What can be subtracted from the situation?
- What can be multiplied in the situation?
- What can be divided in the situation?

Here are some common obstacles to creativity and some suggested antidotes.

Environment

The right space and surroundings can make a difference to some people's ability to create. Some extreme examples of people who manufactured a personal environment that inspired them include Schiller, who filled his desk with rotten apples. Dr Johnson surrounded himself with a purring cat, orange peel and tea. Kant worked in bed at certain times of the day, with the blankets arranged around him in a way he had invented himself. These are mostly impractical for business life as they will quickly gain you social disapproval however much fun you might have! Acceptable business versions of these antidotes include going for a walk at certain points during the day, playing sport or music, bringing creative artefacts to the office to provide some points of focus or distraction and having 'field days'. This is where you choose to go to out to the country to (literally or metaphorically) work in a field! Subtraction yields ideas about minimalism, removing clutter that stands in the way of focus and finding environments where stillness and solitude can be enjoyed.

Time and timing

Alex Osborn, who coined the term brainstorming, insisted that a minimum of 30 minutes should be allocated to a brainstorming session to allow participants sufficient time to reach a point of psychological safety and 'escape velocity' in order to suggest something genuinely novel. Modern-day pressures tend to compartmentalise people's time into ever-smaller chunks, with the result that they do not have enough 'immersion time' in a topic with disastrous consequences. If innovation matters, then quite simply (and to quote Nancy Kline) you need to find 'time to think'. Time management strategies and practices are highly relevant. I've written on this subject for Sir Richard Branson and on the accompanying website for this book.

Then there is the question of timing. Are you a night owl or someone who needs to work under pressure and so on? As we have already discussed, sometimes all that is needed is to find the right time for expansive thinking, whether you are awake or perhaps even asleep. Some of us need lots of incubation time to ferment our ideas; others are motivated by urgency and tend to perform well when there does not really seem to be enough time to ferment an idea. Identify peak times when you are at your best for idea generation and improvement. Allocate these times for those activities and play to your strengths.

Premature evaluation

People who make snap judgements are prone to 'premature evaluation'. This can arise in a pressured work environment or from personality traits such as high judging scores in Myers Briggs. Antidotes to snap judgements include:

- Mindfulness approaches as we have discussed previously.
- Use of decision-making routines and processes that install the required incubation time for novel ideas.
- Asking others to evaluate ideas rather than doing it yourself, effectively a 'divide' strategy.
- Good judges build in conscious routines for proper evaluation of alternatives before choosing.

Selective listening

Selective listening is another obstacle. This includes listening beyond the headlines, questioning to gain insight into fragile ideas. Antidotes include:

- The use of processes (e.g. Appreciative Inquiry (AI), David Böhm's Dialogue).
- Learning language and questioning patterns from disciplines (e.g. Neuro-Linguistic Programming (NLP)).
- Using a detached facilitator or mediator to ensure all ideas are fully explored and group dynamics are managed.

Confidence and capability

I have often visited companies that claim not be skilled in the art of creativity and innovative thinking. On further invesigation, it is more often about the confidence to be creative rather than skills and capabilities per se. In some cases, the corporate culture is not sufficiently accommodating of individual creative thought. In other words, what appears to be a capability gap is really about beliefs, either individually (confidence), or collectively (culture). If confidence is at the heart of the creative obstacle, training will not affect overall capability levels unless it also addresses individual confidence or the culture within which people can offer their ideas.

Assuming that there is a genuine capability gap and that the gap may be closed through learning, some self-service options for overcoming personal capability obstacles include:

- Develop your skills at mapping uncharted territory and complex problems by learning to 'doodle'. Resist the temptation to organise your doodling at first, perhaps letting your random thoughts incubate in a drawer for a few weeks.
- Develop the systematic habit of looking for connections between diverse issues. For example pick a random word from an encyclopaedia and attempt to link it with the first e-mail of the day.
- Set out to learn a new creativity technique every week. The website that accompanies this book has some support in this area.

Ambiguity intolerance

If we prefer certainty over ambiguity, this limits our abilities to devise alternatives when faced with a need to choose differently. Leaders believe that there are very few certainties in life and that we must learn to live with ambiguity (indeed to work with it) in order to succeed. We might not learn to love the unknown as leaders – after all the job of leaders is to make the unknown knowable – but we can learn to tolerate ambiguity through what K. Anders Ericsson called 'deliberate practice' (1993, 2009). We discuss ambiguity further when we examine 'wicked problems' in Chapter 4.

Fear of failure

This is one of the biggest obstacles to novel activity at work and we give this special attention later in this book. Eminent psychologist and author Professor Adrian Furnham suggests two antidotes:

- Don't give up: Persistence is the key. Most attempts fail. Breakthroughs are rare.
- Take a risk: Fear of failure, humiliation, teasing and abuse are natural enemies of creativity. Play with hunches and tentative ideas. Break the rules. Take courage.

I'm not creative

Whether you believe you are creative or not you are right.

If an absence of creativity is wrapped into your very identity, beliefs or soul, this is perhaps the most powerful obstacle of all as it is likely to manifest itself through your everyday behaviour and possibly 'infect' others. There are four things you can do about this:

1. Change yourself.
2. Change the situation.
3. Accept the situation.
4. Leave the situation.

We can change our beliefs by modifying our behaviour and watching them follow some time later or we can try on a new set of beliefs. Some practical antidotes include:

- *Act as if you are creative.* This involves modifying your impression of the truth for enough time so that you can test whether your behaviour changes. A practical strategy involves a decision to be creative at the next meeting requiring this quality and then following through with action.
- *Work with others* who do not have the particular obstacles that you possess and elect an 'official conscience' to scan the obstacles and flag them up if any materialise.

An interview with Sir James Dyson

I asked James Dyson to reflect on obstacles to innovation. Here is what he said:

Every new idea and innovation is exciting but testing is crucial. Dyson engineers spend 30,000 hours a month testing machines to make sure they are happy with their performance and reliability. If a product isn't reliable then no matter how good it is there is no point in it. I always tell my engineers to work iteratively. Make small changes at every stage, so you know exactly what works and what doesn't.

You can see this coming through in our latest V6 cordless machines. This new range has been subjected to an extensive physical testing regime, comprising over 550 tests replicating human usage lasting some 50,000 hours at the hands of some 120 engineers and robots not to mention being dropped over 5,000 times onto hard floors to make sure they are reliable as well as powerful.

Reflections

Creativity arises from adaptation of existing ideas or more radical leaps forward. Much everyday innovation arises from adaptive thinking rather than fundamental breakthroughs.

Our four-stage model of creativity (four P's) can help you understand where effort may be best targeted to enhance creativity.

Personality inventories such as the Adaptor-Innovator inventory, the Myers Briggs Type Indicator and the Big Five can help to find your preferences and then manage your strengths and weaknesses with respect to creativity. However, when used inappropriately, psychometric tests may themselves become obstacles to creativity.

The Dolphin Index offers a way to characterise a BBE's climate for creativity, or part of it, giving leaders the opportunity to work on specific areas of their profile, making creativity and its conversion to innovation more reliable.

The systematic practice of the suite of strategies that have come to be called mindfulness can help to minimise our frailties as human beings by delaying early judgement and bias. We need conscious routines to help us make great decisions rather than relying on our crocodile brains.

Once you have identified the major causes of the obstacles to creativity, it becomes much easier to devise a strategy to minimise or eradicate the obstacles. Subtraction and division are powerful mathematical creativity strategies for dealing with obstacles, sometimes more powerful than addition or multiplication.

Chapter 3

Creative leadership

I suppose leadership at one time meant muscles; but today it
means getting along with people

Mahatma Gandhi

From dog walking to fog walking

In the industrial age, it could be argued that the job of leaders and
managers was that of dog walking, following a prescribed pathway

HIGH   UNCERTAINTY OVER ENDS   LOW

UNCERTAINTY OVER MEANS — HIGH / LOW

1
WE KNOW WHERE
WE ARE GOING

WE KNOW HOW
TO GET THERE

2
WE DO NOT KNOW
WHERE WE ARE
GOING

WE KNOW HOW TO
GET THERE

3
WE KNOW WHERE
WE ARE GOING

WE DO NOT KNOW
HOW TO GET THERE

4
WE DO NOT KNOW
WHERE WE ARE
GOING

WE DO NOT KNOW
HOW TO GET THERE

with a team of obedient servants. Discontinuity and disruption in the environment tends to make the job of leaders and managers more like fog walking. The notion of 'wicked problems', originally coined by Rittel and Webber in 1973 describes the nature of problems and opportunities that are termed 'VUCA' (i.e. **V**olatile, **U**ncertain, **C**omplex and **A**mbiguous) in nature. Along with my physicist friend Dr Alan Drummond, we developed a quasi-analytical framework to help leaders decide just where one should place one's emphasis when dealing with uncertainty.

Quadrant 1 problems are 'tame' and simply require good management using rationality, computation or experience. Simply stated, when someone asks you to work out your tax return, you should reach for an

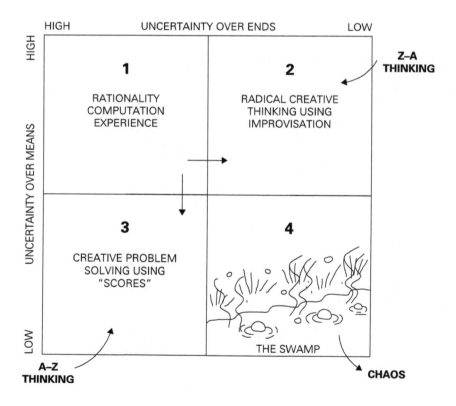

accountant or a calculator rather than a focus group or a week-long appreciative enquiry event. Quadrant 2 problems have an uncertain destination and require the development of a clear vision, which is a function of leadership. Once one direction of travel is clear, many people can and will then engage with that direction. Typical examples would include the determination of a new vision or business strategy. Quadrant 3 problems have clear ends but an ingenious route to reaching the destination has not been identified. They require the identification of novel routes and journeys towards the goal sometimes via an open search (where there are few constraints) on other occasions via a closed search (where a specific zone for divergent thinking has been selected) in a particular domain. Typical examples would include the development

of new products or marketing extensions to existing products and services. They are the realms of systematic problem solving using sequential divergent and convergent thinking, which we examine in Chapter 4.

Quadrant 4 problems are genuinely 'wicked' in nature and require clarity in terms of ends and means to gradually tame the uncertainty. Examples include world peace, transport in large cities, and restructuring the European Union. Leadership is about applying strategies that systematically reduce the area of quadrant 4, also known as the 'swamp'.

A brief leadership history lesson

Ever since Sun Tzu wrote *The Art of War* some 2000 years ago and then *The Prince* by Niccolò Machiavelli around 500 years ago, views about leadership have continued to change and develop. We started to study leadership systematically around 100 years ago. This started with the idea that certain traits were more or less suitable to be a leader, much in the same way that psychologists used to believe that the shape of people's heads would determine their suitability for brawn or brain based work. Basically the idea was about nature (i.e. you could only be a leader if you had the right genetic material). There was nothing you could do about it if you did not have the right traits.

During the twentieth century, we passed through several other phases of thinking on the subject. In the early 1900s, Taylorism or scientific management dominated, which suggested that work could be organised for the workers. Henry Ford exemplified Taylorism. He organised his factories for maximum efficiency, where work was highly proceduralised, people had tightly defined job roles, which they stuck to, and so on. Later on, the notion of situational leadership emerged from Hersey and Blanchard et al. This was followed by a bundle of theories that emphasised the human being as the epicentre of what a leader could reasonably achieve. The emphasis was on the idea that a leader could adopt a particular style and flex that style, almost at will. This has continued into the twenty-first century via people such as Daniel Goleman, whose ideas about emotional intelligence. Authenticity is seen as a major idea in modern leadership thinking, based on the idea that it is better to be yourself with skill rather than attempting to fake a style. If you do not have what it takes for a particular situation, current thinking on leadership suggests that your best decision is to acquire or delegate a particular leadership and management task to others. In the last 20 or so years, the task of leadership has also shifted focus towards the management of complexity, uncertainty and the unknowable through the seminal work of Ralph Stacey and Dave Snowden's Cynefin framework.

To add further confusion, the use of archetypes tends to polarise people's ideas as to what good leadership and management is, from Atilla the Hun to Richard Branson, from Margaret Thatcher to Jim Hacker, from The Prince to Prince and Prince Charles and so on. The metaphor of war is prevalent, yet modern business is not a battle, only in the sense that we must battle to collaborate in order to win. What then lies behind the art of leadership?

Roots of leadership

Leadership relies on power, influence and authority and it is useful to start with some definitions of these terms:

Power is the ability of a person or a group to influence other people or groups.

Influence is the process of affecting what another person or group does and/or thinks.

Authority is the right to exercise power.
The wise leader knows the differences and acts accordingly.

Elegance in leadership arises from the use of the minimum amounts of all three of the above means of getting things done (i.e. what are the necessary and sufficient conditions for obtaining the desired result?). Influence rather than dictatorship is the most legitimate mechanism of getting things done in Brain Based Enterprises (BBEs), although it is more costly in time. Paradoxically, directive leadership styles can be effective with creative people, but that leadership may only be directed towards questions of **ends** (destinations) rather than *means* (journeys).

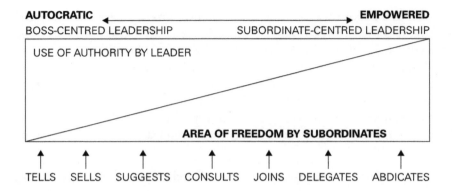

Professor Charles Handy wisely says that the smart leader sets out the goal but then lets people bring their own talents and passions together to realise it. The exact choice of leadership style in a given situation should be informed by the prevailing culture, the expectations of those led and the urgency/complexity of the task. In practice there are many styles of leadership available and the successful leader is either a master of these or knows how to fill in the gaps through delegation. Tannenbaum and Schmidt's model of leadership style has stood the test of time and summarises the '50 shades of leadership' style well.

The elegance principle is of great importance in leading BBEs. Just because a leader may be capable of telling someone to do something does not mean they should if they are to engage their brainpower in the delivery of that task. In general, leading innovative enterprises requires a shift to the right of this continuum. At a practical level, ask yourself:

What leadership style does the situation require of me?
Can I do it?
If yes, get on with it.
If no, find someone who can.

Power consumption

The effective leader uses the minimum power necessary to achieve their goals or what I call 'low power consumption'. Power comes from a variety of sources. Some are given by the enterprise and others have to be earned:

Position power – Your title and the benefits it confers on you from the point of view of decison-making etc.

Resource power – Resources that you hold, such as money, time, access to people, often associated with your position, again given to you by the enterprise.

Social power – Your access to networks of people who can make things happen. When people talk of networking they are discussing social power. Social power is not how many connections you have on social media. It is a combination of numbers x quality of those connections and relationships.

Expert power – For example, a particular scientific discipline or a process expertise such as creative problem solving or a specialism in a particular medical field. Key opinion formers generally have expert power as a major basis for their influence platform.

Personal power (i.e. charisma) – The quality that makes people want to do things for you, for no other reason than it was you. The jury is out as to whether you can develop charisma rather like one can buy beauty products at the pharmacy or whether it is an innate quality. I am of the view that, like any muscle, if you have basic competence, then deliberate practice will indeed develop that muscle (i.e. your personal power). People are finely tuned to detect inauthenticity in leadership and soon spot if your charisma is skin deep. Trust is intimately connected with authenticity and we discuss this subject later in this chapter.

Information power – Either tacit or formal information. In the information age, there is plenty of data but rather less quality information and great leaders know the difference between 'drowning in data' and 'swimming with information'. We return to this theme in Chapter 9.

In flatter structures, the use of power arising from social networks, expertise, charisma or information has greater value, as these are *earned* by the individual rather than *given* to the individual by the enterprise. As enterprises collaborate with people they do not own, the tectonic plates of power, influence and authority start to shift in unknown directions and we can no longer rely on the more usual methods to get things done. How then might you learn to flex your leadership muscles effectively and ethically to influence with integrity?

Deliberate practice – Flexing power, influence and authority

You might like to try this simple six-step exercise to rehearse yourself through the value of this construct, or work it through with a colleague or friend.

1. Think of a specific situation where you want to be more influential.
2. Identify your **major** power sources in this situation using the six power sources that we have discussed.
3. Identify the **major** power sources of the key stakeholder(s) in the situation.
4. Identify a **valid** behaviour that will increase your influence in this situation: What do they value that you can provide? This is the creative step. Ashby's law of requisite variety provides us with the insight that the individual with the greatest flexibility of thought and behaviour can (and generally will) control the outcome of any interaction. Not all sources of power are effective though. For example inappropriate use of charisma can be annoying for other people or even dangerous for the user when it is used to influence someone who only has position power.
5. Develop a strategy to put this into action. Practise by acting it out with a trusted friend, colleague or coach if the situation demands that you get it right first time.
6. As a reflective practitioner, learn from the experience in terms of how you could use your power sources more effectively in other 'difficult' situations.

Modern thinking on leadership does not just talk about being effective. We have reached the age where business ethics are not just a 'nice to have' add-on to the social responsibility section of the company accounts. Responsible leadership can make a difference to your enterprise's ability to prosper or die in the glare of social media, as United Airlines found out. In a famous incident United destroyed one of their passenger's guitars and failed to set in place an equitable response to his attempts to complain. After Dave Carroll wrote and recorded a song about the incident on You Tube and the song went viral (it currently has over 15 million views) United's share price fell 10%, costing the company $180 million. We shall see that responsible leadership can also affect the upside.

Responsible leadership

Marcus Aurelius, Emperor of Rome (AD 161–180) observed that foresight is needed and it is necessary to look to the end as a leader. Long-term foresight is frequently driven out by the short term in an age where leaders are continuously 'on stage', their every move watched by social media, the press, shareholders and staff. Their actions are therefore scrutinised to unimaginable levels and people are pretty good at spotting contradictions and discontinuities between what they say and what they do. It is in essence the age of the responsible leader. The leader is responsible for setting a direction that excites others, rather than bland 'mission' statements.

In practice this often involves the ability to be 'specifically vague'. Specific to give a focal point for action. Vague to allow individuals some freedom to engage heads, hearts and souls. Leaders must learn to walk the line between these polarities. They can also act as idea advocates, sensing and moving ideas around the enterprise so that they attract resources and gain acceptance. In walking the talk, leaders need to be a living, breathing example of the notion that failure is a learning opportunity and encourage appropriate levels of risk taking in the enterprise.

Leaders build teams with high levels of trust. This includes the ability to have conflicts and recover from them. They create 'psychological space' within the enterprise to teams by giving freedom to 'bootleg' and providing encouragement, mental and physical resources to spend on speculative projects.

Leaders are fluent in a range of leadership styles, from coach through counsellor, conflict generator, comedian to hero. More importantly they have the ability to move rapidly from one style to another, taking their audiences with them without losing credibility.

The following cameo illustrates the responsible use of leadership to influence the culture of a whole enterprise. The example comes from Nadine Hack, CEO of beCause, a world leader in responsible leadership (see www.because.net). Nadine has worked with Nelson Mandela, Barack Obama and a host of blue chip companies including Coca Cola and Johnson and Johnson to help them maintain a focus on world-class leadership practices.

It's well known that our children learn from our actions, not our words. The admonition 'Do what I say, not what I do!' never has worked even for the least clever child. The same absolutely holds true for how we, as leaders, inspire authentic, purposeful leadership by embodying it ourselves.

I have found that self-awareness is the most fundamental dimension for this. Can you look into your own mirror with clarity and honesty about what examples you are setting on a daily, if not hourly, basis? Are you being open, transparent and do you bring your whole self to the table, including your vulnerabilities and shortcomings?

Paul Polman, Unilever CEO, recently acknowledged that he and his executives did not have all the answers when they launched their Open Foundry in which the company essentially outsources sustainability by inviting the public to 'collaborate, experiment and pioneer the future with us'.

This is consistent with Unilever principles that I've experienced since I worked with them on a multi-sector partnership with Unicef, Maharastra Government and the Synergos Institute to address childhood malnutrition in Maharastra. This involved extremely hard work to find common ground amongst a broad coalition of stakeholders that wouldn't readily trust each other. We developed trust through a series of unconventional meetings where we shared stories and vulnerabilities to develop unbreakable bonds between partners. Unilever went well beyond other people's expectations, refusing to settle for cosmetic aid packages and insisting on a systemic approach over several years to address the problem.

My colleague Cortney McDermot adds to the question of what Professor Charles Handy calls a 'proper kind of selfishness':

> Steve Jobs focused on the experience he would want as a consumer. Tony Hsieh created the environment he would want as an employee. MLK held a nation spellbound with what he would want as a citizen and as an individual. If we lead from purpose instead of profit, evolution will ensue. If profit precedes purpose, extinction will be the result. We're often told that strength means something very different but my experience is that the strongest among us are willing to be candid about our weaknesses. In fact, that very act inspires a deeper level of trust and respect among those we lead. And, in doing so, we also empower them to take leadership in areas where they might have greater competency than us.

My other colleague Gary Hirshberg, Chairman and Founder, Stonyfield Farm, in his book, *Stirring it Up: How to Make Money and Save the World* demonstrates how companies can work to save the planet, whilst achieving greater profits and satisfaction, and how we can all use the power of conscious consumption to encourage green corporate behaviour. His company, Stonyfield, makes organic yoghurt and were pioneers in responsible business in the 1980s, using local sourcing and CSR approaches long before the term was invented. Stonyfield was so successful that the company was recently acquired by Danone. Hirshberg made more money from acting responsibly, not less. For example, by making yoghurt cups from plants instead of petroleum and many other practices that were not only responsible but profitable.

Nadine's insights are backed up by hard data. Barbara Brooks Kimmel undertook an extensive study of the value of trust in her book *TRUST, Inc. Strategies for Building Your Company's Most Valuable Asset*. The five-year study took 2000 of the largest US-based public companies and showed that America's most trustworthy companies have produced an 82.9% return versus the Standard and Poor's 42.2% since 2012. The balanced scorecard that goes to make up the FACTS® framework stands for **F**inancial stability, **A**ccounting conservativeness, **C**orporate governance, **T**ransparency and **S**ustainability.

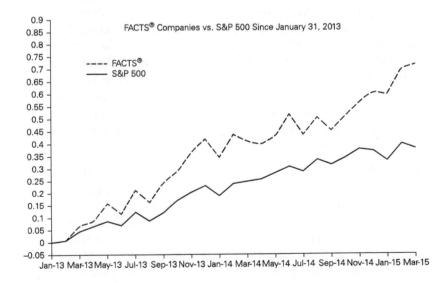

Nadine points out that responsible leadership requires a tremendous level of self-confidence: not a phony aura of confidence but a genuine soul sense of what we know, what we don't; who we are, who we're not. She reflects:

> In my growth as a leader over many decades, I found that these moments which I call 'sacred intimacy', and are completely appropriate in a professional context, allow for extraordinary transformation. As leaders, we all are trying to get other people, usually many of them, to do multiple things that are extremely challenging. Do we give them enough authority and autonomy to really achieve what we're asking for? Or do we find that threatening? And, if the latter is the case, then why is that? Are you willing to do the soul searching to find the answers? Or do you choose to stay in the protective territorial mind-set that says I gain my power by always being in control and zealously guarding everything that I know? I've seen that if you give away non-physical things: knowledge, power, contacts, etc. you are never diminished. You still have those things and someone else does too: exponential growth for which you are respected.

> When coaching senior executives about giving others the ability to achieve, I use the simplest analogy of a parent whose toddler is just learning to tie their shoelaces. You're late for work: your first impulse is to rush in and do it for them. But, if you just wait until they do it . . . you never have to do it again. You're liberated and they've just moved to another developmental stage. We constantly hear and say the buzz-phrases: co-creation, collaboration across silos, build capacity, but we often hesitate from actually engaging with others in the open, candid way that would enable those concepts to come to life. Think about what is holding you back. Find a small thing you can do differently to start to build 'muscles' in your undeveloped realms.

> Let me be clear: I do not mean become someone other than who you truly are; I do mean stretch your repertoire to include a broader spectrum. But, before you can do that, you must acknowledge to yourself where you might need stretching. For me, it's patience. I'm fast and to the point: not everyone can respond to that well. So, I continue to work on calibrating accordingly. I work on that and many other things that would make me more present, more

trustable, more my full self. I feel freer each day to acknowledge how and where I can grow whilst I also know how to genuinely own the ways in which I am gifted. I continue to search for the space between feeling overly inflated with self-satisfaction at one end or completely unworthy at the other.

Beyond our ideas of right-doing and wrong-doing, there is a field. I'll meet you there

Rumi, Thirteenth century poet

Or, in the warped words of Lou Reed: *I do me better than anyone else*

(Paraphrased in Johnstone 2005)

Nadine Hack's long experience and reflections are matched by wider analysis. The Huffington Post reported on the gap between values and behaviour in 2012, that 75% of US working adults found that the most stressful part of their job is their boss and that this values-gap costs businesses $300 billion per year. So there is a real premium in getting values aligned with behaviour. Some businesses have managed to engage employees through simple yet timeless sets of values that we have described as specifically vague, in the sense that they are meaningful to the majority, yet they can be interpreted to local contexts and particular situations. Far from being bland mission statements, they set the enterprise apart from its competitors. Johnson and Johnson remains a standard bearer in this respect via their Credo, which sets out some simple yet powerful principles to live by.

The Johnson & Johnson Credo

The culture, business philosophy and stakeholder priority for the Johnson & Johnson global business are outlined in the Credo, written in the mid-1940s by R.W. Johnson. It is a graphic reminder of Nadine Hack's principles.

Our Credo

We believe our first responsibility is to the doctors, nurses and patients, to mothers and fathers and all others who use our products and services. In meeting their needs everything we do must be of high quality. We must constantly strive to reduce our costs in order to maintain reasonable prices.

Customers' orders must be serviced promptly and accurately. Our suppliers and distributors must have an opportunity to make a fair profit.

We are responsible to our employees, the men and women who work with us throughout the world. Everyone must be considered as an individual. We must respect their dignity and recognise their merit. They must have a sense of security in their jobs. Compensation must be fair and adequate, and working conditions clean, orderly and safe. We must be mindful of ways to help our employees fulfil their family responsibilities. Employees must feel free to make suggestions and complaints. There must be equal opportunity for employment, development and advancement for those qualified. We must provide competent management, and their actions must be just and ethical.

We are responsible to the communities in which we live and work and to the world community as well. We must be good citizens – support good works and charities and bear our fair share of taxes. We must encourage civic improvements and better health and education. We must maintain in good order the property we are privileged to use, protecting the environment and natural resources.

Our final responsibility is to our stockholders. Business must make a sound profit.

We must experiment with new ideas. Research must be carried on, innovative programmes developed and mistakes paid for. New equipment must be purchased, new facilities provided and new products launched. Reserves must be created to provide for adverse times. When we operate according to these principles, the stockholders should realise a fair return.

An important test of a value statement is its use in critical moments in history. In Johnson & Johnson's case the Credo was a vital ethical reference point in the 1982 Tylenol crisis, when one of the company's products was tampered with. The company withdrew all supplies of the product and did not relaunch it until tamper evident packaging was available. This took the company a considerable length of time. It voluntarily incurred substantial financial losses in order to protect the public safety and gained significant long-term trust as a result.

Strategies and tools for leaders

I am firmly in the camp that says that leaders must have basic competence in their art and that training and learning tricks will not deal with basic deficits in the leader's abilities to lead. I also believe that leadership muscles may be developed like any other muscle, by learning new knowledge, enhancing skills and developing values through deliberate practice. For this to happen, leaders must be open and receptive to learning individually and collectively. Here is a roundup of some useful elements to augment a leader's repertoire:

Essential knowledge

If the half-life of knowledge is in free-fall whilst the amount of knowledge available to us is rising exponentially, a key decision for leaders is where to place their time in terms of learning new knowledge. It is a mistake in most cases for leaders to concentrate on 'meta level' knowledge such as leadership and business at the expense of some specific knowledge in their chosen specialism. One needs to be T-shaped to command some credibility with those you lead, although it is unlikely you will ever become a better subject expert than those you lead. After all they are investing many more hours of deliberate practice than you are likely to be able to give. To be a better leader, you do not have to be a better technician, but you must maintain an interest in the technical aspects of those you lead if you are to lead with integrity and trust.

Flexing your skills

Amongst the suite of leadership skills that have utility for consultation, delegation, decision making etc. I would include the disciplines of Emotional Intelligence, Transactional Analysis and selected approaches from the field of Neuro-Linguistic Programming (NLP).

The term **Emotional Intelligence** (EI) was popularised by Daniel Goleman. Simply stated, it involves being a master of your 'internal intelligences', which Goleman called self-awareness and self-management and your 'external intelligences' or social awareness and relationship management. Although the approach has its critics in academia it has huge amounts of face validity in terms of what good, bad and ugly leadership looks like. It is simply not sufficient to have internal mastery of yourself if you

	PERCEPTION	BEHAVIOUR
	INNER	SPACE
SELF	**SELF AWARENESS**	**SELF MANAGEMENT**
OTHERS	**SOCIAL AWARENESS**	**RELATIONSHIP MANAGEMENT**
	OUTER	SPACE

EMOTIONAL INTELLIGENCE UNPLUGGED

have no idea of your impact on others or what to do about it. In an age where much formal intelligence or IQ is widely available on the Internet, the leader needs to be able to use that intelligence to best advantage, whilst having the EQ to manage relationships within, across and outside the enterprise with people they do not 'own' or control.

I observe the highs and lows of emotional intelligence on a regular basis when working with musicians in improvisation sessions. Great musicians are emotionally intelligent. They are masters of 'inner space' whilst they also pay attention on the outside to the other musicians in the ensemble, spotting and responding to subtle nuance and points of inflexion in the music. Lesser musicians often miss these subtle cues from others. I see a direct parallel in the world of enterprise, with great leaders having high emotional intelligence and the lesser mortals tending to live only inside their own heads.

Emotional intelligence also has a darker side. Too much focus on being swayed by the views of others can leave a leader paralysed by indecision and lead to low-level compromises. As in most things the best use of emotional intelligence involves a balance of seeking feedback on your decisions (outer space) but then having to take the best decision for all concerned (inner space), given the demands, constraints and choices available.

Transactional Analysis (TA) identifies a model based on a number of 'ego states' that people 'adopt' at various times:

- The controlling parent – tells, lectures, disciplines.
- The nurturing parent – encourages, protects, shows warmth.
- The adult – encourages responsibility taking, rational, non-judgmental.
- The free child – is spontaneous, fun-loving, uninhibited, thinks laterally.
- The adapted child – is obedient, does what it is told, may be angry.

Although it is dangerous to overgeneralise, creative leadership requires the predominant use of the 'nurturing parent', 'free child' and 'adult' states. Many leaders see the process of leadership as drama and knowing when to use each state is a key skill. The degree of flexibility required to 'jump between states' can confuse followers who would like their leader to be the same at all times and the most effective leaders find ways of signalling state changes. In my life as a leader I used to invite my team to my house where I would cook them a ten-course Chinese meal (nurturing parent), then play organised games, involving fancy dress and musical improvisation (free child). None of this was contrived by consultants selling a team-building package. These team events were clearly flagged as being separate from work, where my predominant style was that of adult for getting things done and nurturing parent for solving problems.

Neuro-Linguistic Programming (NLP) is perhaps a controversial discipline, which has its fans and haters. I am someone who sees both ends of this debate, having studied from the 'academic' end of the subject via John Seymour through to the 'rock concert' end of the continuum through people such as Anthony Robbins and Paul McKenna. I find that NLP offers some pragmatic tools for personal development amidst all the hullabaloo that surrounds the discipline. Used with heart, it offers a range of strategies and approaches to handling difficult leadership challenges. In essence, NLP offers you a set of strategies for using your brain (neuro) to communicate (linguistic) in ways that offer you and others better choices (programming). The word programming can be considered divisive until you realise that successful influence is two-sided (you and the other person/people involved) whereas manipulation is one-sided. Successful leaders influence with integrity. You will find a wide palette of NLP strategies and skills on the companion website that accompanies this book, including:

- Gaining rapport with people with whom you have no natural bond but with whom you must collaborate.
- Developing potent goals that drive you and others towards a shared purpose.
- Becoming a super listener, even when no words are spoken.
- Mind reading, even when someone is a closed book or a good poker player.
- Using what NLP calls 'perceptual positions' for creativity, i.e. 1st, 2nd and 3rd positions.
- Changing viewpoints, behaviour and beliefs using the art of reframing.
- Using the Disney Creativity Strategy alone or with teams as a design strategy for innovative thinking sessions.

Values that support innovation and creativity

Whilst you can learn knowledge from courses, seminars, the Internet etc. and also skills to some degree, the development of values and attitudes comes about through deliberate practice and experience. As we saw earlier in this chapter, the values-gap costs businesses dearly and we are becoming more attuned to switch products and services when values are not matched by actions. MBA innovation and creativity academic Jane Henry and Professor Charles Handy suggest that innovation and creativity in business needs four underlying values. I have found these compelling, instructive and durable over 20 years of consulting, coaching, teaching MBA executives and working with people the world over:

Curiosity – The systematic habit of asking great questions, testing boundaries around problems/opportunities and exploring the big picture and the detail. Artists and scientists often have this quality in great supply, some business people less so.

Love – Using a nurturing approach to leadership, participative approaches to generate ideas, and making connections between other people's ideas to build/develop innovations. Love is a word used by companies like Innocent Drinks and Metro Bank to describe their culture. If love is too emotive a word to use in your enterprise, try care instead.

Forgiveness – Includes ambiguity tolerance, the encouragement of mental play and the ability to build on ideas rather than knock them down. A graphic example of this occurred when Virgin Atlantic decided to do a promotion based on the Austin Powers movie 'The Spy Who Shagged Me' with billboards featuring 'Virgin Shaglantic'. Virgin's brand executives were not consulted on the basis that they would have almost certainly said no to this. Instead, forgiveness was asked instead of permission.

A sense of direction – Having a sense of a goal or mission, an explicit or understood process for generating, improving, evaluating and implementing ideas and the ability to learn and improve. The skills of direction setting are most important for managed creativity and are often those most absent from artistic creativity. It is this set of values and associated skills that help convert creativity into innovation.

These values subdivide into three making a total of 12, explained in detail in the table that follows:

Twelve values for innovation and creativity demystified

Value Group	Value 1	Value 2	Value 3
Curiosity Curiosity is the basic creative engine, with forgiveness and love making it possible.	**Adopt a set to break sets** The endless drive to break your own fixed patterns and mind sets, challenging not just your own ideas but also your own ways of having ideas.	**Explore the givens** We pay most attention to things that are changing, therefore it is important to examine the 'stable irrelevant background'.	**Broad picture, local detail** This involves general reconnaissance and focusing down on details. These two processes depend on one another: understanding generates questions and questioning generates understanding.
Forgiveness It must be made acceptable for people to try things out that do not initially work.	**Value play** There is a developmental continuity between children's play and adult innovative thinking. Play does not have to be overt in nature but can also be internal.	**Build up don't knock down** Often described as learning to say 'yes, and' rather than 'yes, but' by adding something to the idea.	**Live with looseness** Neither innovative thinking nor the issues that demand it are tidy or controlled. Therefore you need ways of 'forgiving' confusion, uncertainty, contradiction and so on.
Love In this context love means 'unconditional positive regard' or trust.	**It is already there, nurture it** Whilst training can develop your capacity for creativity innovative thinking is a natural if fragile state. This might mean removing blocks and barriers to innovative thinking and then letting it happen.	**Involve others** Requisite variety is necessary for innovative thinking. This arises much more easily from diverse groups where it is common to get 40 – 50 ideas before anyone has even consciously tried to be creative.	**Connect and be receptive** You can use literally anything as a trigger for trains of thought using free association and force fit approaches. We can also include intuition under this heading.
A sense of direction Innovative thinking needs steering via a process that respects both the destination and the journey.	**Know what you really want** Clarity about what you are trying to do and really wanting to do it are important. This involves 'taming wicked problems' and ensuring others believe that solving the problem is worthwhile.	**Cycle often, close late** Since you cannot keep everything in your head at once, it helps to have successive diverge/converge cycles. It also helps to keep your options open for as long as possible.	**Manage the process** This includes: Having an explicit process of divergence/convergence; sustaining the flow/ facilitating; stop when appropriate; choosing the right methods; consider interpersonal factors.

Be a reflective practitioner

Constantly examine what you are doing and question/improve how you set about encouraging innovative thinking in yourself and others.

I regularly use these as the design thinking principles for managing climate in groups. This is explained further in Chapter 9.

Pfizer – The twelve values in action

The Pfizer Process Development Centre (PDC) has embedded innovation and creativity at a deep level within its culture, climate and leadership, such that it is now part of everyday life. Liam Tully, head of the PDC, tells the story.

I sensed the need to make the PDC an international centre of excellence around 2007. To produce great chemistry requires great minds that can work together effectively and we set about developing a team of people with the best creative and analytical minds that we could achieve. It has kept us ahead in many ways ever since and we are now recognised the world over for our expertise and ingenuity in process chemistry. To achieve this we conducted an 18-month programme of personal and team development in creativity and innovation with Human Dynamics. Our programme was designed to be drip-fed into the PDC over a period consistent with the adoption and utilisation of the knowledge and skills rather than sending the team on a training course, which would be forgotten the next day. Alongside the development, our facilitator made visits to the site and provoked us with live projects and topics of interest and concern. The use of real life as a source of learning made the development stick much better than fictional approaches.

As well as the acquisition of a comprehensive repertoire of strategies and techniques for creativity, we took very seriously the importance of establishing a culture and climate where innovation and creativity are business as usual. It is a function of leaders at every level to set that tone and we set about making some adjustments after taking stock of the elements that go to make up a climate where innovation and creativity flourish. The repertoire of around 20 strategies and tools for divergent and convergent thinking designed for us by Human Dynamics also allowed for people with different styles to access creativity from rational to more intuitive approaches and tools that were good for solo use to others for team application. An early result from the programme was when we applied some of the tools to redevelop a synthetic route, which had been overlooked in previous discussions. The programme has been sustained for eight years, which is unparalleled in the world of business consultancy. I would say that the longevity of the programme comes down to three things:

- The programme itself was not prescriptive and this allowed people to choose the most useful elements, which produced ownership.
- We ourselves then adapted and added to the store of knowledge and skills, which maintained engagement.
- Ultimately the programme found an internal champion, who has become so good at this that he now travels the world, transferring the skills to other units at a strategic level.

Implications for leaders

To encourage innovation and creativity, the psychological environment must be right: in other words your behaviour as a leader. The twelve values for innovation and creativity provide a practical checklist to help leaders see where most attention is needed. Try assessing your personal strengths and weaknesses using the framework.

A little attention to the physical environment can make a big difference in terms of innovative thinking. It is not all down to behaviour. Just as it is possible to show someone you love them by the way you arrange a dinner date or special event, so leaders can show their love by taking care of the environment in order that others can maximise their contribution.

The consistent practice of being a reflective practitioner (also referred to as mindfulness these days) separates the sheep from the goats in terms of a leader's ability to consciously learn from their experience. To gain deliberate practice in the twelve values, here are three relatively safe ways to learn:

1. Develop your talent for acting. Stand in the mirror and act as though you are externally sober whilst feeling internally delirious and vice versa. Watch the 1950's films 'It's a Wonderful Life' and 'Twelve Angry Men' to learn about the importance of authenticity and principled leadership.
2. Go to the theatre, the opera or a rock concert to learn about the dramatic elements of leadership. Leaders need both substance and

style. Assuming an authentic core, the next level of influence is to ensure that your message is received and embraced by those who must act in accordance with it.

3. Set aside 5–10 minutes at the end of each working day to reflect upon what has gone well and what could be improved. Make excellence and improvement a personal habit. You might like to combine this with a walk in the park as suggested in Chapter 1.

Reflections

Leadership cannot be separated from management. Great leaders must manage and great managers must lead.

Economy matters for leaders, in terms of using the minimum amounts of power, influence and authority to influence others in any situation. The effective leader operates using the principle of 'low power consumption' to avoid the abuse of power.

In BBEs, leaders need to lead through power sources that they earn more than those they are given. Leadership using position and through wielding resources is the tool of last resort in such enterprises.

There is a real premium on responsible leadership. Estimates amount to a doubling of the return to shareholders in terms of an ethical and sustainable approach to trustworthy leadership.

Whilst leaders need to have basic competence in a suite of knowledge, skills and values required to lead effectively, it is possible to develop capacity and capability as leaders.

It is important to act in accordance with values that encourage creative thinking and its conversion into innovation. Values in action separate great enterprises from a regression to the mean.

The deliberate practice of reflection can help leaders shift their enterprises from regression to the mean towards greatness.

Chapter 4

Tools for creativity

Why brainstorming doesn't work

When you invite guests round for dinner, you create a setting where people will feel relaxed. It is all about what you do beforehand. Choose the menu to keep final inputs to a minimum. Get all the ingredients ready. Set that table. Look in control, whatever is happening around you. It is the same if you are to undertake a brainstorming event. Preparation really is the mother of brainstorming. Part of that preparation comes down to the physical and emotional setting. If you lead a BBE, providing people with the means to do brainstorming properly is essential.

You might think that getting the setting right is really easy. Well, it is if you put the work in. Yet, I often notice that even great companies fail to put in small increments of effort to get the best out of their people. What, then, is the anatomy of a great brainstorming session? It is all about the right people, the right environment, and the right topic. We looked at the people in Chapter 2. Continuing with the environment, this has both a symbolic and practical value:

Symbolic value: Using a room that is not associated with work or offsite can help provide the necessary sense of detachment. This also offers benefits in terms of fewer interruptions. Of course, such things can be engineered into the workplace. A sense of psychological safety must be also generated and environments can provide this in part, alongside the skills of a great facilitator.

Practical value: The physical environment should allow for:

- Plenary activity focused on the facilitator to set the scene, co-ordinate ideas for maximum efficiency and consolidate thinking.
- Brainwriting activities, which need the whole group to be seated around a table. Dyads or triads working in small clusters. Space for solo work or private thinking activities.

- Amongst the resources you might have available are coloured pens, Post-it notes, random stimuli, catalogues and magazines, trigger pictures, white boards, clever IT smart boards and so on. Some fiddle toys can help some people. Background music can excite the mind. Avoid over exciting it. Music has different effects on different people and a small percentage find it hard to concentrate when there is background music.
- Hygiene factors – Never underestimate the importance of food and drink to maintain hydration and engagement.

Once you have prepared the stage, the topic and the sequence of thinking styles must be prepared.

Taming wickedness

We examined the notion of 'wicked problems' in Chapter 3 where we classified business problems and opportunities along two axes according to the degree of uncertainty of ends and the means of achieving the ends. Here are some of the strategies, which help to address such topics. Quadrant 2 problems require what I call a 'Z to A' approach (i.e. the clarification of the destination or ends and then working backwards to the present state).

Quadrant 3 problems are more amenable to systematic divergent and convergent thinking – what I call an 'A to Z' approach. Quadrant 4 problems require an iterative 'pincer movement' (Z to A and A to Z) to grapple with the various uncertainties in terms of ends and means. These are the sort of topics that keep people awake at night and which require the greatest level of skill in reaching sensible resolutions.

Talking with Dr Patricia Seeman of the 3AM group, we notice that sometimes people apply the 'wrong tool for the job'. For example, lengthy brainstorming sessions (Quadrant 2) are used to solve 'Quadrant 1' problems like 'How do we compare with competitors?' when a little bit of benchmarking or the use of an expert would do. Or people try to treat Quadrant 4 problems as if they are tame issues, which invariably frustrate their resolution.

Although business issues do not neatly fall into boxes, the use of the matrix flags up roughly where on the radar screen you are. This helps leaders eliminate the wrong approaches and focuses debate where the issue is, depending on uncertainty levels. This can be a considerable help. The leader's task then is to deploy the right tools for the job. The result of any good innovative thinking session is to systematically reduce the area of Quadrant 4, or to drain the 'swamp'. Thus the job of leaders is to make the unknown knowable by expanding the area of Quadrant 1.

Smart thinking in black and white

There are plenty of proprietary processes to guide systematic divergent and convergent thinking, some of them made more complex than they need to be by enthusiastic business consultants. However, they boil down to the three-stage model, depicted below, which involve successive phases of divergence (open mode) and convergence (closed mode).

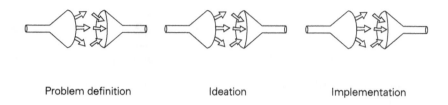

Problem definition   Ideation   Implementation

In some cases, problems and opportunities are best solved using a forward motion, or what I termed 'A to Z' thinking. When the 'destination' for your thinking is initially unclear, there is a case for some kind of reversal of the process, or 'Z to A' thinking, starting with the end in mind. Classic brainstorming starts in the middle, on the presumption that the topic is clear to all, yet that is not always the case. Through long experience, it is best to look at every case on its own merits. Whatever you do, it is vital to be clear on the goal.

There are several versions of any given problem: the problem/opportunity as *given* (PAG); and the problem/opportunity that comes to be *understood* (PAU). An initial exploration of the topic provides a host of benefits later on in the process:

- To understand how the big picture and the small details are connected.
- To separate what matters most from the background.
- To separate what is important from what is urgent so that long-term strategy can be balanced with short-term expediency.
- To identify real versus imaginary demands, constraints and choices.
- To know what success and failure might look like.
- To identify the most elegant points of entry into the topic (i.e. those which are both the most effective and efficient routes to start working on the topic).

Once we have established what the real problem or opportunity is, it is then time to apply some divergent and convergent thinking techniques. Here we sample a range of these methodologies.

Diverging with flair

A well-constructed divergent thinking session improves the *efficiency* of ideas (i.e. how many novel ideas are generated in the time available). It also improves the *effectiveness* of idea generation (i.e. the degree of purposeful departure from current thinking and paradigms). Not all divergent thinking sessions require radical ideas, so there is no implied suggestion that wackiness is a feature of effectiveness in idea generation, even though you must sometimes leave 'planet earth' to return with new insights. Effectiveness can better be evaluated by the degree to which the ideas are novel, appropriate and feasible.

Brainstorming

Is it an insult to mention brainstorming in a book like this? Not really. I've seen brainstorming done so badly over the years and read plenty of articles saying that 'brainstorming doesn't work'. The two issues are related. Brainstorming doesn't work when it is done badly. It is worth returning to Alex Osborn, who coined the term, to seach for clues on how to make brainstorming work. The aspects of Osborn's work that have been long forgotten by busy managers are:

1. Diversity – A good brainstorming group comprises novices and experts and both are valued equally as a prerequisite for thinking.
2. Preparation – People need some idea as to what they are being asked to focus on **before** the event. This allows for what Wallas calls 'incubation' **not** premature evaluation. At the event ensure that a problem/opportunity statement is developed that allows sufficient space for inventive thought. Warm people up: remind them of the 'rules' for divergent thinking: no criticism; build on ideas; no self or other censorship; aim for maximum participation.
3. Time to think – Run the session for a bare minimum of 30 minutes, preferably longer. This ensures that there is sufficient time for the group to reach what I call 'escape velocity', where genuine novelty takes over from re-rehearsing ideas, which the team are already familiar with. It is rare for groups not to need some kind of activation to exorcise pre-existing thinking.

Brainstorming can provide a large number of ideas in a short space of time and it is easy to use. **Brainwriting** is a variant that helps quieter individuals in a group. It gains contributions from each individual in the group on cards, which are exchanged in an ideas 'pool'. I often combine approaches to ensure we reach the whole group.

Imagine you want to improve the **effectiveness** of your brainstorming and the **efficiency** of the process. Several methodologies boost classical brainstorming (i.e. to go further and faster in less time).

Reversal

In situations where people find it hard to produce ideas, the technique of reversal can be used to overcome the blockage. Typically, reversal produces wilder ideas than conventional brainstorming. For example if the opportunity statement was 'In how many ways may we improve the image of the department in the eyes of key customers?', one reversal would be 'In how many ways might we seriously damage our reputation with key customers that would lead to a long-term memory of the department as worst in class?' Once a range of perverse ideas has been developed the team then examines each idea to see if they suggest more appropriate ideas for the original problem/opportunity.

The act of reversal tends to make the issue frivolous and therefore encourages the playfulness dimension of climate. This seduces participants into productive conversation. It is also good in situations where the group is stuck on pre-existing ideas, since it tends to place distance between the issue being discussed and reality.

We developed an approach based on reversal called 'Bitching with Attitude' to help companies with 'overly positive cultures' to release problems which otherwise would not be aired due to unspoken censorship. It proved to be a major improvement through its simplicity and the process, which legitimises dissent. Simply stated, you ask people to moan about some issue that is affecting them with the associated rule that if they moan (the bitching part) they must also suggest an antidote (the attitude part). My colleagues in Pfizer modified the name to 'whinging with attitude' to avoid unintentional offence to bitches, although I had never intended the term to refer to dogs or gender! In my experience, everyone is capable of the cathartic state to bitch about something that bothers them. The important point is to get past this state to doing something about it; this is where innovation lies.

Tools based on bisociation

People who like puzzles find games that force fit related and unrelated elements together compelling. I designed this one for a 48-hour innovation 'hack-a-thon' with a telecoms company.

1. Set up a puzzle of 3–4 issues that are potentially related, but for which no obvious relationships exist. For example: new products, unknown markets, technologies, unknown competitors etc.
2. Draw a series of triangles between the issues (or quadrants if you want to make it more difficult).
3. Discuss each alternative combination in depth until you find a range of alternative ideas that seem appealing. If none appear after some time, change the relationships until you succeed in generating some fanciful ideas that have potential utility.

Although this approach appears deceptively simple, it was responsible for generating ideas that were judged to be worth more than £100 million per annum for the telecoms company.

A second tool based on bisociation is the so-called SCAMPER method, beloved by the 3M Corporation as an innovation tool. SCAMPER is a checklist of words that are used to stimulate thinking through making forced relationships between the issue and one of the checklist words. The SCAMPER mnemonic stands for:

- **S**ubstitute
- **C**ombine
- **A**dapt
- **M**agnify or **M**inify
- **P**ut to other uses
- **E**liminate or **E**laborate
- **R**earrange or **R**everse

There are other innovative thinking checklists such as: the **4W's** and **H** list – **W**hat, **W**ho, **W**here, **W**hen, **H**ow; the **CREATIVITY** checklist **C**ombine, **R**everse, **E**nlarge, **A**dapt, **T**inier, **I**nstead of, **V**iewpoint change, **I**n other ways, **T**o other uses, **Y**es! Yes!

Other ways to induce bisociation include the Catalogue Method, Blindfolds and the Random Walk, which proved to be one of the defining moments of an event we staged for a major pharmaceutical company.

Random walk – Without concern for your current problem, go on a walk and find an object that interests you. Spend some time with the object, reflecting on its physical attributes etc. Return and refocus your attention on your problem, looking for ideas from your object.

Blindfolds – Blindfold some of your participants, turn them round a few times, ask them to focus on the thing they first see when you remove the blindfolds and then take the blindfolds off. Use the observations as stimuli for a discussion, then refocus on the problem at hand, looking for ideas from your 'excursion'.

Tools based on projection and fantasy

Superheroes uses the principle of projection and fantasy to encourage people to see things from other perspectives. It requires you to adopt the persona of a superhero. In this context this could be someone with 'relevant' qualities (e.g. an expert problem solver or creative genius) or just any old hero (e.g. a superstar, fictional hero, or icon of some sort). It matters not who you pick apart from the fact that you will be comfortable 'being them for a few minutes'. Simply stated, ask people to get into role and then from that perspective to offer views on the topic of interest without concern for their practical value. Costumes may be used although the decision to dress up is a personal one.

The **Disney Creativity Strategy** also uses projection. Walt Disney was said to think that three roles were necessary in the production of a great film: The Dreamer; the Critic; and the Realist. He would visit production team meetings, assess what was going on and supply the missing ingredient. The Disney method emulates this basic concept.

Dreamer: This is the visionary big picture role. The person who has no boundaries, limitations or restraint. Ask yourself 'What do I really want, in an ideal world?'

Critic: This is where you test the plan, look for problems, difficulties and unintended consequences. Think of what could go wrong, what is missing, what the spins-offs will be. Remember that a critic is someone who evaluates – not just criticises. Ask yourself 'What could go wrong?'

Realist: This is where the plans are organised, and evaluated to determine what is realistic. Think constructively and devise an action plan. Establish time frames and milestones for progress. Make sure it can be initiated and maintained by the appropriate person or group. Ask yourself 'What will I do to make these plans a reality?'

The process can be used sequentially or in parallel, by having individuals or groups of people allocated to each state. Edward De Bono's 'Six Thinking Hats' works along similar lines although it is more complex and requires the wearing of hats. I have seen this approach fail due to poor facilitation resulting in people feeling self-conscious about wearing the hats. All these methods rely on good facilitation if used in teams.

Tools based on dissonance and catharsis

Metaphor This works by creating distance between the problem and the ideas generated. For example, some people suggest that a career is like a journey. If the journey is taken as the metaphor, it is then possible to generate ideas about how to have a good journey, such as taking frequent refreshment breaks (personal development pit stops), sightseeing in unusual places (networking outside your comfort zone) etc. Ask 'what is the problem like?' and develop a series of metaphors. Using one or more metaphors, generate ideas around achieving the metaphor. Examine all ideas for their relevance to the original topic and creatively draw relevant parallels with the real topic under scrutiny.

As Gareth Morgan points out, a good metaphor has some overlap with the original problem (e.g. like a Venn diagram with overlapping areas) but is sufficiently different to provide some creative tension (e.g. Earth and Mars have certain features in common). If the metaphor appears too distant from the problem, people tend to detach from it, as though the idea has come from 'another galaxy'.

Corporate jesting This builds on the natural states of catharsis and insight that occur when we move from the sublime to the ridiculous. Laughter is a powerful tool for innovative thinking. A colleague of mine used to be the 'corporate jester' for British Airways. His job was to provoke the board to escape habitual thinking where this was not helping to solve certain important strategic problems. BA has an engineering-influenced culture (necessary if you want to land planes safely), but tends to apply engineering-style thinking to all problems, even those of a strategic nature. So they needed a disruptive force within the top team. He existed in this role for many years, until, like a real court jester, his jokes stopped being funny and he was 'corporately excommunicated'. Unlike the middle ages, he lives on . . .

There are several routes into jesting, from which you may make up your own cocktails, ranging from the relatively safe to the extreme:

- Tell irrelevant jokes about the problem.
- Tell relevant jokes about the problem – a bit like an alternative comedian with an MBA! This is a bit more dangerous for the novice.
- Use magic, mime or dance etc. to suggest new interpretations of the problem and its resolution. Not for the faint hearted!

Dialectical enquiry This uses creative conflict to help identify and challenge assumptions to create new perceptions. The facilitator forms proposal, counter-proposal and review groups. The review group contains the topic owner.

The proposal group develops a plan, compiling a short list of key assumptions underlying the plan; this is given to the counter-proposal group. The counter-proposal group endeavours to develop a counter-plan, looking at each assumption, breaking them down, to invent a plausible counter-assumption, and using it to surface new data, re-interpret old data, and devise a counter-plan. The review group is presented with both plans and data and assumptions are presented. The group considers the strengths and weaknesses of each plan. A facilitator maintains goodwill and prevents the competitiveness becoming destructive. The review group are looking for further unmentioned assumptions that may be central to the theory behind the problem.

The total group now work together. Led by the review group their aim is to generate a list of agreed upon fundamental assumptions and the generation of a new plan. All the assumptions that featured highly in the debate are pooled. Unacceptable assumptions are weeded out, and where necessary, competing assumptions are either re-worked so as to be acceptable to both sides, or simple tests are devised to decide between them.

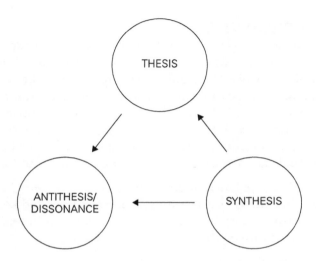

Converging with care

It is one thing to diverge with flair, quite another to converge with care. Careless decision making can invalidate even the best innovative thinking through the use of 'business as usual' criteria to evaluate novel ideas, which by their very nature are untried and untested. That is not to say that innovative ideas should not be pressure tested. Indeed they must if your company's risk profile is to be met. They must, however, be treated differently to existing business propositions, otherwise most, if not all, will be screened out by the process. People may then judge brainstorming to be a waste of time as 'you end up back at the beginning'. You know when you need to converge with care when people say things like 'I think my idea is the best', 'Why bother brainstorming, I think we all know the answer?', 'We haven't a clue what to do' and so on.

Good convergence methodologies allow for the organisation of ideas and the flagging of similar or duplicate ideas. They encourage a rational appraisal of the ideas down to a manageable number without losing essential novelty. They may also allow for combination of interesting ideas into a more coherent approach that hangs together and ultimately, if you need to agree an outright winner, to pick the winning option. They broadly divide into thought organisers and decision-making frameworks.

Thought organisers

It is said that we are only capable of holding 7 +/– 2 items in our conscious mind at a given time. What happens when we have 150 ideas from a brainstorming session? The dumb move is to discount the 150 and go back to the idea you first thought of. The smart money is to use a thought organiser. You know when you need to organise and group ideas when people say things like 'We have idea overload – I'm going to lunch', 'I can't see the wood from the trees', 'There's so much stuff here that I think we should adopt the idea I thought of in the first place' and so on.

Examples of thought organisers include: Mind Mapping, Fishbone Diagrams, Laddering, Rich Picturing, Relevance Trees and LogoVisual Technology (LVT), some of which we discuss later on in this chapter. Others are dealt with on the accompanying website.

Decision-making frameworks

Voting This is, quite simply, what it says. Having listed all your ideas and agreed some sensible ground rules for choosing, give each voter a number of stars and let them stick them, one at a time, on their favourite ideas. Depending on the nature of the group, the facilitator may allow individuals to place all three stars on one idea or insist that a maximum of one star per person be placed on a given idea.

The technique is simple, structured, participative, fast and can give a rapid evaluation of a large number of ideas. Although simple, groups have a habit of making this process more complicated. Particularly if open-ness is a problem, a 'closed ballot' may need to be arranged. The other potential pitfall lies in the phrase 'sensible ground rules'. It is a waste of all your innovative thinking if 'business as usual' criteria are used to evaluate novel thinking. For this I recommend the NAF approach.

The NAF approach This is a development of a simple voting approach of scoring/assessing potential solutions to a problem or opportunity. High (H), medium (M), low (L) or numbers between 1 and 10 may also be used to rate ideas if a higher level of discrimination is required. The NAF criteria are:

- *Novelty* How novel is the idea?
- *Attractiveness* How attractive is this as a solution? Does it completely solve the problem? Or is it only a partial solution?

- *Feasibility* How feasible is the solution to put this into practice using existing resources or ones that can be acquired?

Grids are a useful way for narrowing options down typically using two or three dimensions such as impact versus ease of implementation and so on.

Paired comparison analysis is a much more complex approach if a completely rational comparison of alternatives is needed and an outright winner required. The method allows you to compare the importance relative to one another of a set of options. Since it is complex, it tends to eliminate the tendency for the 'crocodile brain' to intervene in the decision making process. We describe the process on the accompanying website.

Decision trees can also provide a systematic and logical approach to identification of options for convergent thinking and making key choices when many options exist.

Creativity Strategies

Convergence, Haiku and Health

I've always loved poetry, ever since hearing a recording of Dylan Thomas reading 'And Death Shall Have No Dominion' at the age of fourteen. It has been my ambition to try and introduce some of that passion into my work.

Opportunity found me when I was asked to facilitate a session involving NHS managers and community groups around leadership. I could have opted for PowerPoint but it was just after Christmas and my wife had bought me a book of Haiku poetry. So, rather than fill their heads with mine and other theorists' ideas I tasked the group with defining, in a Haiku, what leadership meant to them. There was initially a stunned silence and some quizzical looks and glances between people. One brave person asked 'So you want us to write poetry?' 'Yes!' I said. Immediately the energy levels in the room rose. The end results were stunning! Much crisper than the normal 360-page white paper.

I have since used this technique on numerous occasions and every time it produces results, which are both unexpected but also very powerful. For me it shows that, given the freedom and the space, people can produce wonderful things when given constraints and asked to simplify.

Paul Deemer, NHS England

Evaluation

Visit the accompanying website for more techniques for divergence with flair and convergence with care, such as:

Methodology	Suitable for divergence or convergence?	Suitable for individuals or teams?	Best for incremental or radical creativity?	Requires facilitation or self service?
Brainstorming and brainwriting	Divergence	Either	Either	Facilitation
Reversal	Both	Either	Radical	Either
Puzzles	Both	Either	Either	Facilitation
SCAMPER	Divergence	Either	Either	Either
CREATIVITY	Divergence	Either	Either	Either
Force fitting	Divergence	Either	Radical	Either
Superheroes	Divergence	Teams	Radical	Facilitation
Disney Creativity Strategy	Both	Teams	Either	Facilitation
Six Thinking Hats	Both	Teams	Either	Facilitation
Metaphor	Both	Either	Radical	Either
Corporate jesting	Divergence	Either	Radical	Either
Dialectical enquiry	Both	Teams	Either	Facilitation
Voting	Convergence	Either	Either	Either
NAF criteria	Convergence	Either	Either	Facilitation
Grids	Convergence	Either	Either	Facilitation
Paired comparison analysis	Convergence	Either	Either	Facilitation
Decision trees	Convergence	Either	Either	Facilitation
Complexity mapping	Rich picturing	Boundary relaxation	Synectics	Bionics
Laddering	Bunches of bananas	Morphological analysis	Village People	Mind mapping
Q-sort	Snowballing	Commitment charting	Implementation checklist	Force field analysis

The techniques we have sampled are rather like the 'sheet music' of divergent and convergent thinking. As with music, 'sheet music' will take you so far on the road to greatness. True masters of the art use imperfections and mistakes in order to reach beyond 'painting by numbers'. With deliberate practice you will reach a 'free improvisation' approach where you master your own strategies and techniques for specific occasions.

Creativity and enterprise at Virgin – Not only free improvisation but also technique

I asked Sir Richard Branson to reflect on whether he believes that creativity is something that can be learned through study, practise or technique, or whether you either have it or you don't. He wisely uses the full range of strategies available to him, both those coming from your genes and from formal development.

People often wonder whether entrepreneurs are born or made. Whilst I do think that some people have the natural ability to turn their hand to running a business, I still think it can be taught. Entrepreneurship isn't reserved for a certain group of people – we are all born entrepreneurs, some people just forget as they grow up. The same can be said for creativity. We've all sat in meetings where the ideas have run dry and nobody can find a creative solution to the problem. But we've also all probably been in meetings where the ideas are flowing and something amazing has been born. The people in the room, the techniques being used to generate ideas, the mindset of the person leading the project – these are all important factors.

As you become more experienced you'll work out how to get the most creative ideas out of yourself and your colleagues. At Virgin Australia we have an Ideas Lab that sources suggestions from people at all levels of the business. This process allows us to find solutions to problems that arise and also enables us to identify innovation champions – strong performers who are given further training.

Strategies for innovation and creativity

Whilst techniques can be combined by skilled facilitators to deliver innovation and creativity events, an alternative is to use complete strategies that address the same processes. Here are some of my favourite approaches, based on 20 years' experience of working in this area.

LogoVisual Thinking (LVT)

The Centre for Management Creativity in North Yorkshire helps senior managers innovate by helping them to clarify purpose, vision and values as the front end of business plans and change programmes, often compressed into intensive events. Two days of guided interaction aligns minds. The processes are very carefully designed to integrate learning, physically, emotionally and cognitively, in order to systemically change the collective consciousness.

Alongside excellent facilitation and the provision of a microclimate for thinking, the Centre is also itself an innovator in thinking technologies with its LogoVisual Thinking (LVT), which enables everyone to contribute to the design of the outcome. Participation is an essential pre-requisite in terms of ownership of the results of any innovative

thinking process, as realised by companies such as TNT, Yorkshire Water and Alstom.

LVT is a special kind of visual thinking in which ideas are presented as moveable objects that can be manipulated to explore their relationships. This encourages enquiry, enables people to make sense together, revealing inherent patterns. It challenges people to shift the logical level of thinking so that, with the understanding gained, they are better able to decide, plan and act. Ideas written on magnetic hexagons (magnotes) become shared material from which new meaning can be abstracted from 'old' ideas. As they 'make sense' together, everyone learns. They improve their thinking, iron out misunderstandings and build relationships.

Anthropologist and systemic thinker Gregory Bateson points out

> Structure is the algebra of that which is to be described; It is always one degree more abstract. Structure presumes a gathering and sorting of some of the infinite details, which can then be thrown away and summary statements offered in their place.
>
> Bateson and Bateson, 2004

What Bateson wrote in the 1980s foreshadows LVT in which details are gathered, organised and then epitomised so that one can set aside the detail to work at a more abstract level. LVT is algebraic thinking. The next stage, ring composition, goes further, being a device to reveal higher order structuring.

Around the core process, other approaches are brought into the relationship according to client need. For instance, Boal's theatrical techniques or outdoor experiential learning, blended with inputs to challenge mindset, leadership development exercises, group work, collage, constellations, reflections and meditations, all carefully orchestrated to achieve the desired output. Meals, background music and the environment itself are vital parts of the process. We have already discussed this subject in Chapter 3.

We discussed the notion of convergence with care earlier. This is something that centre director John Varney sees as a vital 'secret of success'.

When we cluster ideas in LVT we try not to categorise but attempt something more subtle. Categorising aims to sort information according to similarity, enabling us to retrieve it by following logical trees, as in a filing system. In LVT we have a different purpose – to break free from past logic to allow novelty to emerge. Hence our conceptual clustering is more intuitive.

What is more, instead of merely naming the clusters we write epitomes. Epitomes 'stand for' the detail contained in the cluster and give it substance. This is a very important and challenging aspect of meaning-making, requiring that we 'under-stand'. (Under-stand has the same meaning as sub-stance). The move from clustering ideas to exploring how epitomes relate, is a change of logical level.

LVT thus provides us with an epistemological process that facilitates the creation of new knowledge.

> John Varney, the Centre for Management Creativity
> (www.high-trenhouse.co.uk)

Whole system interventions

A number of café and town hall-style interventions have grown up over the years to provide the opportunity for large numbers of people to physically collaborate on topics of mutual interest or concern such as Large Group Interventions, Appreciative Inquiry and Real Time Strategic Change (RTSC). Of these, the approach known as Open Space Technology (OST) is especially worthy of note due to its propensity to release creativity and self-directed change. Open Space Technology operates on five principles for self-directed participation and one simple rule:

1. Whoever attends are the right people.
2. Time and timing are irrelevant.
3. Wherever it occurs is the right place.
4. Whatever happens is what was meant to happen.
5. When it's over it's over and not before.

The simple rule is the 'law of two feet'. If you find yourself in any situation where you are neither learning nor contributing use your two feet and go somewhere else. One of the hallmarks of OST is that the purpose of the meeting emerges rather than is given. This is both its greatest strength and potential weakness for people that do not enjoy self-organisation. When done well, the amount of commitment to what emerges from an OST event is unparalleled. Like most things, it comes down to the preparation.

Developing mastery

Whilst proprietary tools are ideal for many situations, a lot of people ask me how I design events. The answer essentially goes back to the states we investigated in Chapter 1. I consider three prime factors when designing an approach or tool for use in a specific situation:

1. The task under scrutiny (the degree of wickedness).
2. The people, their 'types' and expectations etc.
3. The context (environment, time and so on).

For example, our design of 'puzzles' for the telecoms company was based on two key considerations: that the people attending were engineering types and were broadly the sort of people that liked solving complex puzzles; and the design must be able to cope with a range of factors that could be permutated together. I'm pleased to say it was the most successful tool in the suite we provided for this particular summit.

On another occasion, we had to design an approach for a pharmaceutical company that was trying to look for new product development strategies. We had fairly logical people and the environment was highly regulated. For this I designed the '8I' checklist, which included two provocative I's – the words *Illegal* and *Immoral*. By asking the group to focus their attention on illegal and immoral ideas to start with, we broke several taboos in the group and generated a great deal of absorbed playfulness. Later on in the process, we 'backed off' the extreme ideas so that they would meet legal and ethical constraints. In doing so, we produced a series of genuinely novel ideas that extended the patent life of the product under review for several years to come.

Mastery comes from experience and trying new things, rather than simply repeating familiar recipes. It is important that you find an arena of practice to hone your skills and experience if you wish to become a master of innovative thinking. Another aspect of mastery is the gentle art of facilitation, which makes the difference between good and great.

Russian ballet dancer Anna Pavlova understood the relationship between technique and mastery when she suggested that we should master technique and then forget about it and be natural. Techniques alone are often insufficient to create the conditions where thinking outside the box occurs naturally. One response to this is to introduce explicit procedural rules such as our structured innovative thinking process approach. Another is to employ the services of a skilled facilitator. The difference between an amateur and a professional facilitator is in the following areas:

A professional facilitator has a wide repertoire of techniques and approaches to draw on, plus an underlying understanding of their theoretical operating basis, so that the right tools for the job can be assembled together. They are also a process efficiency expert. If time is at a premium, a skilled facilitator will be able to get to the heart of the matter much more quickly than an amateur. They have the ability to apply techniques in a seamless way. This often means 'bundling' techniques together to reach different people and providing 'scaffolding' to support 'challenging' topics and complex methods. They also look after the group climate. This includes relationship building, reinforcing progress, handling the unexpected, finding acceptable ways to confront undiscussible issues etc.

This story perhaps explains the vital and often hidden work that a skilled facilitator will do as compared to that of a novice.

A day in the life of the facilitator

Julie starts her day at 5.00 am. After all, she has a 50 km journey to the client's site. On arrival, Julie finds that the e-mails she sent regarding room layout and other important details have been mostly ignored. Just as well that she got there by 7.15 am. Julie fixes the various items that seem unimportant to the event organisers (but wonders why they asked her to e-mail all of this in the first place).

The client (Johnny) throws in some surprises. Of the 20 people invited, eight of them have been sent to another meeting. 'No matter' says Johnny, 'I've invited a collection of office staff that might enjoy the meeting, even though they have no real interest in or knowledge of the topic under review. You did say it was important to have naïve people in the room, and these people are quite stupid really'. Johnny did not send them the invite, which explained the reason for the event and what was expected by the end. Julie smiles and sighs inside. 'Ah well, this is why they hired me', she says to herself. Julie reminds herself of some useful knowledge she picked up when working in an improvisational theatre company. If an unplanned obstacle, such as a chair, appears on stage, the rule is to make sure that you 'use the obstacle'.

She quickly introduces herself to all, explains the purpose of the day and what is expected of them before the start time. At the start, she asks for one or two members of the group to explain the purpose of the day to the newcomers and asks the newcomers to ask questions until everyone is at the same level. Not only has she 'used the obstacle', but the exercise reveals that some of the previously invited people had not read the invite anyway! Two administrators have sociology degrees and had wanted careers in marketing and sales. The team learns that the uninvited guests have real value to add.

Reflections

BBEs must have a flexible repertoire of strategies and tools for divergent and convergent thinking to keep their enterprise alive, awake and agile.

You can save the amount of time and energy invested in resolving a VUCA problem or opportunity by spending time understanding the issue under study. Sometimes a clearer understanding of the issue reveals the answer without the need for brainstorming.

Brainstorming works when it is done properly. It does not when done badly. It is all in the preparation and in the hands of the facilitator.

You may increase the effectiveness and efficiency of innovative thinking by supplementing classical brainstorming with a suite of tools and techniques that help you go further and faster.

The hardest part of any innovative thinking process is convergence with care. A careless approach to convergence will invalidate all the useful innovative thinking you have done, so approach it professionally. This means giving appropriate care to fragile embryonic ideas rather than judging them the way we evaluate 'business as usual'.

As well as tools and techniques, there can be a case for using whole-system strategies for creativity and change. LogoVisual Technology (LVT) and Open Space Technology (OST) are just two such strategies for engaging larger groups of people in divergent and convergent thinking processes.

Techniques are nothing without excellent facilitation. A great facilitator will help you glide towards answers to wicked problems without seeming to need any techniques for divergence and convergence at all. Like all great professionals, a great facilitator makes it look easy.

Chapter 5

The F word: Failure and success

People who don't take risks generally make about two big mistakes a year. People who do take risks generally make about two big mistakes a year

> Peter Drucker, Innovation and Entrepreneurship, 2006

If you are an entrepreneur and your first venture wasn't a success, welcome to the club

> Sir Richard Branson

F2L not F2F

Failure is sometimes considered the ultimate sin in some businesses, yet if you or your enterprise is to innovate, you must also accept that some of your first attempts to succeed will end in failure. Henry Ford's first two ventures into automobiles failed before he started the Ford Motor Company in 1903. Coca Cola started life as a patent medicine in 1886. The greatest brains in a BBE occasionally make mistakes and failure should provide opportunities to learn (i.e. Fail to Learn (F2L)) and not an opportunity to repeat the mistake (i.e. Fail to Fail (F2F)). Is it then possible to predict when something is going to fail before embarking on a project to design and develop a new product or service innovation? At an absolute level, the obvious answer to this is no. Otherwise there would be no failures in the world of innovation! Nonetheless, there are some fairly reliable reasons behind many failures and it is well that we learn from them, so that we may apply the reversal technique to avoid failure. In particular, Everett Rogers' list of factors affecting successful diffusion of innovation offers us some foresight in terms of making sure we do not miss the obvious points that lead to failure. To improve on the chances of innovation success, ensure that your innovation meets these criteria:

Relative advantage – The term relative advantage is important in so far that the innovation may not need to have a unique selling point as long at it offers an overall relative advantage. The relative advantage may be expressed as functional, emotional, spiritual benefits or all three modes (i.e. head, heart and soul). According to marketing guru Phillip Kotler, we now exist in a marketing world where people expect their products and services to meet people's values as well as the more traditional 'features and benefits' approach. Just think of the examples – James Dyson launched his revolutionary Dyson vacuum cleaner by making it a talking point at fashionable cocktail parties rather than just organising an 'engineering in plastics convention'. Ask yourself these questions:

- How does my innovation demonstrate superior benefits, in terms of head, heart and soul for the end user or consumer?
- What secondary gains will follow from adopting the innovation?

Compatibility – A common reason why innovation fails to reach the market or percolate into popular use over time is the issue of compatibility. Even the mighty Google managed to ignore the compatibility issue when they launched Google Wallet, a digital app that would replace your wallet ... except you still needed your wallet! It is estimated that this has cost Google more than $300 million so far. A more successful application of compatibility was the Sony Walkman. The CEO of Sony realised that the Walkman was a new item and that it did not fit into people's 'sociology'. Sony designed shirts that included a pocket for the Walkman and made it a fashion accessory, thus eradicating the problem and moving into the shirt market at the same time! Ask:

- How is this innovation consistent with current thinking or practice within its paradigm?
- Is the innovation a better way to reach a mutually desirable outcome?
- Can the innovation be memorably named or packaged so that it is easily accepted?

Compatibility is terribly important in the field of software and computer system development. Ignore it at your peril.

Simplicity – A common problem with inventions that do not turn into innovations is the fact that they are only understood by the people who made them. If an innovation is perceived as complex, it is likely to be rejected by a large proportion of the population. Kodak exemplify simplicity in action as early as 1888:

> You press the button and we'll do the rest
>
>   Kodak advertisement 1888

Tim Smit, CEO of the Eden Project in the UK (see www.edenproject. com) has transformed the fortunes of the West of England through the creation of a monument to sustainable creative growth. Tim's background is in the music business, having written songs for Barry Manilow and produced music for Motörhead. Tim uses a great deal of learning from his time in the music industry to inform his approach to business development. He describes his approach to marketing the Eden Project in the same way that you go about designing an album sleeve, using a simple narrative that other people can fall in love with. The album sleeve here acts as a useful constraint to prevent more lengthy and complex explanation. Simplicity of the story is essential to get engagement. Gerald Page-Wood also understood this long before the marketing gurus wrote their books, with his fantastic 1919 slogan for Hoover 'It beats . . . as it sweeps . . . as it cleans'. Ask:

- Is the innovation easy to understand by people outside the enterprise?
- Can the innovation be communicated in less than 30 seconds, or seven words?
- Can the innovation be simplified?

Trialability – Some new things need to be tested by people before they will adopt them. Imagine you had been offered a revolutionary way to clean your teeth. You might want to see a prototype before committing to a purchase. Ask:

- Are there means for the adopter to try out the innovation in part before deciding to adopt the innovation as a whole?
- How might uncertainty be reduced concerning new elements of the innovation?
- How might you encourage early adopters to try out part of the innovation?

Observability – Especially in the case of intangible services, observability of the innovation is a problem. Just consider telephony, electricity and Internet services. Usually we only know that these things exist when they are absent. Turning off the supply is hardly likely to endear you as a customer to your preferred electricity supplier. Making an innovation visible, audible, touchable and possibly smellable and tasteable are important to convey the experience to early adopters. Ask:

- Can the innovation be made more visible? How?
- How might I best communicate the innovation?
- How might I engage all the senses in the communication process?

> **SUCCESS FACTOR #1**
> Make sure your projects or ideas are passed through the checklist of relative advantage, compatibility, simplicity, trialability and observability to improve the chances of successful innovation diffusion.

At a personal level, some inventors and innovators are prone to ignoring such wisdom to their ultimate peril. We examine Sir Clive Sinclair next and John Otway later on as examples of wonderfully creative people who perhaps have not made such great innovators.

Personal factors
Dangers of the Midas touch
Ancient Greek philosopher Democritus warned that it was better to correct your own faults than those of others long before we gained any formal understanding of the psychology of success and failure. Sir Clive Sinclair was celebrated as one of the UK's best-known millionaires, building his empire on the Sinclair range of home computers. Spurred on by this, he developed the Sinclair C5, an electric car for commuters with exceptionally green credentials, intended to gain interest from car and bicycle users. The car received poor reviews based on safety concerns, a maximum speed of 15 miles per hour, short driving range and poor weatherproofing. It ended up appealing to neither segment, mainly because of its lack of sociological fit, failing several of Everett Rogers' tests. It would seem that Sinclair suffered from a degree of hubris, assisted by his early success, thinking that more or less anything he put his name to would sell. As Democritus would have counselled, this is a dangerous mindset since it is plain to see in hindsight that some of the

limitations of the Sinclair C5 were obvious deal breakers for many of the people whom he wished to target.

SUCCESS FACTOR #2

Never lose touch with reality. Cross-check your dreams with enough analysis to gain a reality check from time to time when starting an enterprise.

Next, we examine stories that show how failure is a marvellous opportunity to learn, if only we are capable of seeing the unexpected result rather than the goal we were seeking.

Seeing round corners

Doug Morris, CEO of Sony Music, talked with me about the importance of 'seeing round corners' as a core skill of his most successful music business executive hires. The discovery of Viagra and its successful delivery to the market place is also an exemplar of innovation from an unexpected result – or what could easily be termed a failure. Several people were involved in the innovation process and the story of Viagra may be summarised through the special contributions that they made.

Ian Osterloh, who originally synthesised the drug (sildenafil citrate) is a quiet character who would not be used to 'shouting from the rooftops' about his invention. It is a testimony to a company that does not just listen to the 'loudest voices' that Ian's discovery was picked up and resourced.

The drug was originally developed for hypotension, but proved to be ineffective for this condition. So it was essentially a failure with respect to its intended target therapeutic condition. During clinical trials on the product, the nurses noticed that the drug had a side effect in the form of penile erections. Many companies would have failed to see the significance of side effects that were not directly concerned with the primary therapeutic target for the drug. Pfizer took the nurses comments seriously and investigated further.

The third innovative step came when Pfizer took a calculated risk in the marketing arena. Diana Bell became product champion, gaining acceptance for the product and allowing Pfizer to enter the market in what was essentially unknown territory. In essence, this is a story about looking beyond failure, listening well and taking calculated risks. Were it not for these qualities, we would probably not have an effective treatment for erectile dysfunction.

| **SUCCESS FACTOR #3**
| See beyond the goal. Successful innovators remain open to the
| unexpected.

Institutionalised innovation

Failure, triumph and success

Barry Furr at Astra Zeneca distinguishes between 'failure', 'triumph' and 'success' in scientific Research and Development (R&D) when I spoke with him some years back. Failure involves incompetence (e.g. omitting key experiments) and should be dealt with, based on the fact that the company expects its scientists to be working at the highest levels of professionalism. Success and triumph give meaningful answers to the hypotheses and questions asked. Success arises when an experimental result leads to a decision to abandon a project and stop investment. This is an important result for both the scientist and the company. Triumph arises when a decision leads to the final result. Both success and triumph are rewarded, if not in identical ways. We saw how the development of the periodic table was characterised by 50 years of incubation before Mendeleev came up with a model that fitted the facts. Getting it wrong, or what Furr describes as success, is very much part of getting it right or triumph, on a grand scale in this example. Sir James Dyson gives real insight into the importance of failure in our interview with this continuously creative entrepreneur:

Failure at Dyson

At Dyson we solve problems. Our technology and the engineers behind it are at the heart of the company. Every morning I head down to our Research, Design and Development lab to review their ideas and discuss how we can make our technology better. I encourage failure – it allows you to think and do without restriction. And getting something wrong often leads to getting it right. It's the Edisonian approach, and an approach I took when inventing the first ever bagless vacuum cleaner – 5,127 prototypes and only the final one worked.

A great example of how failure can create success is the Dyson Airblade hand dryer. Engineers were working on a project which included the use of air knives. Whilst conducting research and making prototypes, an engineer realised that high velocity air literally scrapes the water off your hands. And so the idea for a Dyson Airblade hand dryer was born. After nearly three years' intensive R&D by a team of 125 Dyson engineers and an investment of £40m we now have a range of Airblade hand dryers – technology that solves the problem of energy hungry, poor performing conventional hand dryers. The range includes the Dyson Tap, which means you can wash and dry your hands without even leaving the sink.

At Dyson we consider failure as a good thing; it's a way of learning quickly and understanding why something doesn't work. This mindset is instilled in every member of the Dyson team from day one. At Dyson we believe in iterative thinking; make small changes and rigorously testing to see where the faults are. That was the philosophy for our first DC01 and it's the philosophy for all our machines. Take the 360 Eye for example. In 2001 we almost launched a robot vacuum but shelved it, the technology wasn't advanced enough. It had 70 sensors and 3 computers – bulky and inefficient. Since then a team of 200 Dyson engineers have spent the last 14 years and over £200 million to create our Dyson 360 Eye including over £28 million worth of research and development on the latest generation of the Dyson Digital Motor. It shows that we only launch a new machine when it is absolutely right.

W.L. Gore is another privately held company that has built its business on calculated risk taking over 57 years. One of Gore's maxims for experimentation is what it calls the waterline. It is OK to take a risk that 'punches a hole in the boat', as long as that hole is above the waterline. On those occasions where the decision risks the enterprise, then the expectation is for staff to consult others before taking the risk.

SUCCESS FACTOR #4
Reward and recognise good tries (successes) that lead to new insights or changes in direction in a project as well as the final triumph.

It is one thing to create a business that innovates, such as Sinclair and Dyson. How do you do this over more than 100 years in a corporate context? We now move up a scale to the 3M Corporation, which has innovation written into its very DNA.

Frogs into princes

You have to kiss a lot of frogs to find a Prince

3M slogan

Perhaps one of the most glorious examples of failure turned to triumph comes from the 3M Corporation. 3M famously started their enterprise as the Minnesota Mining and Manufacturing Company, having bought land for the purpose of mining carborundum. They quickly discovered that the mountains had little carborundum in them and had to quickly adapt in order to survive. That DNA of creativity has been passed on through many generations in their innovations, ranging from sandpaper to the Post-it Note™. 3M is over 100 years old, with global sales of $31 billion in 2014. It innovates with products that change the basis of competition. This involves a double leap forward. In practice this means that 3M has a high product turnover, yet it is immensely successful and is one of the most admired companies in the world. Examples of its success in double leap competitive advantage include products in the fields of adhesives, abrasives, electronics and software, light management, microreplication, nanotechnology, nonwoven materials, surface modification. Here are just some of 3M's innovations:

- The world's first waterproof sandpaper, developed in the early 1920s.
- Scotch brand pressure-sensitive tapes.
- Scotch® Cellophane tape for box sealing. Soon hundreds of practical uses were discovered.
- Dry-silver microfilm was introduced in the 1960s, along with photographic products, carbonless papers, overhead projection systems and a rapidly growing health care business of medical and dental products.
- Markets further expanded in the 1970s and 1980s into pharmaceuticals, radiology, energy control, office products, and globally to almost every country in the world.

- In 2004, sales topped $20 billion for the first time, with innovative new products contributing significantly to growth. Recent innovations include Post-it® super sticky notes, Scotch® transparent duct tape, optical films for LCD televisions, and a new family of Scotch-Brite® cleaning products.

Wynne Lewis, R&D director at 3M, points out some of the factors that make the company successful:

> We allow up to 15 per cent of employees' time to be dedicated to projects that aren't yet adopted by a 3M business. It is part of a culture that recognises that unexpected outcomes are an inevitable part of the innovation process, so you need to create time and space for exploration.

> Sometimes things don't work as expected – you kiss a frog, it stays a frog. Other times, though, you discover something that takes you down a path with a prince at the end; a breakthrough product or technology that has the power to disrupt the way things have traditionally been done.

> Collaboration is another key attribute in 3M employees. If a customer comes to one of our people with a problem, is it really likely that individual will have all the expertise and skills to come up with a solution single-handed? It's a long shot. Surrounding yourself with the people who have that knowledge and ability is a key step towards solving whatever issue is presented to us.

Christiane Gruen, 3M's managing director recalls that much of its success comes from having good management principles and practices. William McKnight, established the McKnight Management Principles in 1948. These are durable to this day, offering a subtly different view of failure and the management of creative people.

> Management that is destructively critical when mistakes are made kills initiative. And it's essential that we have people with initiative, if we are to continue to grow. Failure is a word we tend not to use as we think more in terms of "learning experiences". This isn't some fluffy tree-hugging philosophy where "nobody's a failure". It is recognition that if something doesn't quite work out as you expected, you might have learnt nothing more than not to try it again. It is more likely

though that you discover something that takes you down another path – and who knows where that might lead to?

One example of 3M's innovations is that of microreplication. This is the art and science of applying to various materials an engineered surface microstructure or topography with precise dimensions and configurations. An example of a particular application of microreplication technology is 3M Scotchlite Diamond Grade Reflective Sheeting. Visually, this is three times brighter than the traditional glass-bead products. It is based on cube-corner or prismatic technology instead of glass beads. Each square inch of Diamond Grade sheeting contains about 7,000 unique prismatic cubes. These improve the reflection of light even if a sign is located at a severe angle to oncoming headlights. Highway engineers call this 'capability angularity'. Angularity is important because older drivers need more light to see at night; also because the headlights of trucks and autos are not at the same height. Angularity is a feature of Scotchlite Series 980 Conspicuity Sheeting. This product is used to outline the shape of tractor trailers for highway safety. The film reflects at angles to almost 90 degrees which means trucks can be seen whilst making a wide turn or reversing out of driveways. Turning and reversing are when most truck-auto accidents occur.

The story began in the early 1960s. 3M wanted to expand their sales of overhead transparencies and supplies by reaching into the important education market. Microreplication technology began when Roger Appeldorn, an optics scientist, developed an innovative plastic fresnel lens that was light, cheap, easy to make and made possible the first practical overhead projector. Grooves in the plastic and reproducing them were key to this invention. It replaced heavy glass lenses that were very expensive to make. The new machine established 3M's position as the leading maker of overhead projectors and supplies. From that base, Roger and others looked into the interesting phenomena that occurred when microscopic changes were made in the surface structure of materials. That led, first, to light pipes and what, today, is our most highly reflective highway sign material as well as other product areas.

SUCCESS FACTOR #5
Build in time for experimentation if you want to innovate.

Another corporate company that tolerates failure within its culture is Virgin and this ethos comes directly from its founder Sir Richard Branson. In the exclusive interview for this book, I learned a great deal about the background to this serial entrepreneur which shapes the culture in some 400+ enterprises.

Entrepreneurship, failure and success
Like a virgin

> Nothing will stop you being creative so effectively as the fear of making a mistake.
>
> John Cleese, keynote address

In Virgin's case Richard Branson says he has lost count of the times he heard that his new ideas would not succeed. Having won a prize for my work on leadership I learned from Richard that we shared parental encouragement to always keep trying, albeit not the same thing over and over. In Richard's case he says:

> My mother taught me that I should not focus on past regrets, so with regards to business I don't. My teams and I do not allow mistakes or failures to deter us. In fact, even when something goes wrong, we continue to search for new opportunities.

Some of Virgin's most famous failures include Virgin Cola and Virgin Brides. Virgin Cola launched in 1994. In Branson's book *The Virgin Way* he comments that:

> When trying to promote anything in the US one really has to "Go big or go home" – well, we went big! . . . I drove a vintage Sherman tank down Broadway . . . heroically smashing through a giant wall of Coke and Pepsi cans.
>
> Sir Richard Branson, *The Virgin Way*, 2014

On this occasion Richard's underlying modus operandi of 'playing David to Goliath' did not succeed. Coca Cola engaged their massive distribution machine to ensure there was no room on the shelves for Virgin's product, Coke was discounted massively and Virgin retired injured. The key point here is the idea that success recipes work for a set of reasons and therefore transplanting a recipe (the David and Goliath approach in this case) does not always work in a new set of circumstances. We explore the concept of 'creative swiping' rather than 'copy and paste' in Chapter 10 as a way of adapting one approach to new circumstances. As I write this, Virgin have just introduced a superb piece of branding innovation via their 'Sex Pistols' credit card. We will see how this fares in the battleship grey world of banking in due course. I asked Sir Richard Branson what his greatest failure was, what he learned from it and how he ensures that others in the Virgin Group tolerate mistakes and failures:

> We've had our fair share of failures over the years but it's not something that worries us, if anyone tells you they haven't then they're lying. Failure needs to be embraced as it's going to happen if you're willing to take risks – the key is ensuring that you learn from your mistakes. An example I often give is that of Virgin Cola. Whilst we usually look to enter an industry and disrupt it, offering consumers a better product or service, we didn't really have anything superior to give them on this occasion. Virgin Cola was a good product, but so is Coca Cola, and we soon found out that our presence in the market was not welcomed by our competitors, who pulled out all the stops to drive us out of business. When British Airways tried to do this with Virgin Atlantic we were able to stand our ground, our customers wanted to stick with us as we were offering something truly different – the same cannot be said of Virgin Cola.

> We learned a big lesson by going through this process. We also unearthed some great talent that went on to work on many of our other projects. A failure can give you more than a success sometimes.

SUCCESS FACTOR #6

Never give up. This relates to the notion of flexible persistence in Chapter 2. If at first you don't succeed, try something different.

For the lone entrepreneur, collaboration skills with other corporate bodies become vital if your idea is to turn into an innovation. They frequently hold the keys to large-scale finance and other resources necessary to play effectively in the innovation game. Anna Hill gives valuable testimony to this when discussing a long-term collaboration with several large government agencies involved in the aerospace industry. For her, the risks of not succeeding put her entire enterprise at risk and the project is on the edge of a fiscal cliff as I write this book.

Lost in space?

> Instigating change is never easy – but neither was going to the moon!
> Anna Hill, CEO, Space Synapse, personal interview

Space Synapse is a digital space education and space awareness games company, fusing software innovation, creativity, space science, space exploration experience, and simulation with a rich network of social relationships for immersive and online participation (see www.earthrider.eu). The company aims to communicate the human experience of space exploration and development, democratising space and environmental engagement.

Co-founded by Anna Hill and Frank White in 2012 as a one-stop shop for space education and space enthusiasts to access digital space content with 50% grant support from the European Space Agency (ESA), a grant that took four years to process. In 2014 Space Synapse completed a commercialisation study for ESA. However, despite working for three months alongside a dedicated team on the proposal for the product development phase, funding was withheld in a last-minute U-turn by the UK ESA delegation. At the point of writing, Space Synapse sits on a point of inflexion between failure and success after ten years' hard work. I asked Anna to reflect on the lessons learned so far with a view to tilting the project in favour of success. She said:

> When working with large monoliths, entrepreneurs often need the assistance of a product champion. Having become frustrated with the U-turns and slow pace of Government institutions, I have been working to secure the interest of Sir Richard Branson in the project, given his own interest in Virgin Galactic and his passion for the democratisation of space. Current values in business and finance must shift exponentially to the crowd to facilitate "a magnetic polar shift" that places people, the environment and the sustainability of the planet first. A "people's space movement" is

the best way to achieve this. Sir Richard is one of a small group of people who seems to understand the power of the crowd and the customer in such matters.

Aligning speed between the entrepreneur and the monolith is important. Large organisations often work on long-range plans whereas entrepreneurs take small steps towards a moving target. This can present frustrations on both sides of the partnership. The administrative burden on entrepreneurs to serve their proposals up in weighty documents only to find that the proposal may be shelved or binned presents extreme risks to the entrepreneur's livelihood and ultimately the enterprise.

We shall find out whether Space Synapse succeeds in the coming years. Updates will be placed on the website that accompanies this book.

My personal story of failure

Some years ago, I sponsored an audacious plan to circumnavigate the world on a rock tour, performing at the greatest venues on the planet and taking our audience along. I invested the equivalent of £55,000 of my life savings in order to help a friend to rescue the enterprise. Alas, my involvement came too late. Despite achieving a temporary turnaround in fortunes, it was insufficient to recover the situation. I lost the money and six months *pro bono* effort in the attempt to help my friend realise his dream. I dubbed the project 'The Real Spinal Tap Tour' after the spoof Hollywood rockumentary, partly because of the comedy of errors that ensued. Like most business failures, John Otway's World Tour was a great idea but poorly executed. It is never enough to have a great idea in business. Meticulous execution skills are needed to bring the idea into existence. Here are a few headline mistakes from the project:

• John Otway rejected Sir Bob Geldof as a partner due to reasons of John's ego, losing us access to a worldwide market for the enterprise.
• John's aviation 'expert' booked a jet that was too big to take off from John Lennon Airport in Liverpool!
• We booked the Sydney Opera House and the seven-star Madinet Hotel in Dubai for punk rock gigs. Both venues were blissfully unaware of the PR huge mistake they had made in allowing us to do this!

John Otway is not as famous as The Rolling Stones or U2, so some background is helpful. You can find out more on Wikipedia. John describes himself as a 'cult punk rocker and serial failure' with two hits to his name across a 30-year career in the music business. Quite surprisingly this appeals to a quintessentially English person who likes the quirky underdog. John is an INFP in Myers Briggs term, a hopeless romantic, loveable character but an endless dreamer. John's career is not all about failure however:

- John was offered ten times more money than 'The Jam' in 1977 as an advance by Polydor Records due to an apocryphal appearance on 'The Old Grey Whistle Test', where he fell off an amplifier midway through his performance, injuring vital parts.
- John had two hits – 'Cor Baby That's Really Free' with Wild Willy Barrett in 1977 and 'Bunsen Burner' in 2002, which his fanbase bought into the charts as a fiftieth birthday present.
- John booked the London Palladium one year in advance of having his second hit in 2002 to ensure his fans would support his ambition. John is a fan of the idea 'If we build it they will come'. This strategy rarely works . . .

John Otway's great strength is his staying power in an industry where longevity is usually measured in months. He is, therefore, a great creator but rather less of an innovator, with a long trail of ideas that failed to succeed. He capitalised on this 'core incompetence' by writing a self-effacing biography with the subtitle 'Rock'n'Roll's greatest failure'. His World Tour concept can be reduced to a 'recipe'.

Take one fading rock star
+ Add a big idea
+ Execute the idea well
= Rejuvenate the star's fortunes

The big idea was to charter an Airbus, fill it with rock'n'roll adventurers and take them on a once-in-a-lifetime trip around the world. The itinerary started at Liverpool's Cavern, then on to JFK to perform in Madison Square Gardens, to Caesar's Palace in Las Vegas with kitsch one-hit disco wonder act The Cheeky Girls. Across the international dateline to Tahiti then to Sydney Opera House, on to Shanghai and then to the 7-star Madinet Hotel in Dubai before returning to London.

We would also have made a comic film 'rockumentary' to rival classic spoof movies such as 'This is Spinal Tap', 'Waynes World', 'Anvil' and 'The Blues Brothers'. Three hundred thrillseekers would live the rock'n'roll dream on a record-breaking two-week circumnavigation of the world. The project had a budget of £1.5 million and promised to deliver nearly twice this investment for those involved. The venture failed with less than half the seats sold by departure date. Hindsight is a great teacher. Here are some examples of the points of inflexion where things may have been turned to advantage.

Emotional incompetence

It is obvious that selling your product matters a lot. In this case, however, the travel agent John Otway chose (we'll call him Mark) managed to lose sales from fully paid-up passengers. Some might say this was somewhat careless! However, the ability to choose people who are genetically unlikely to succeed is one of Otway's less helpful characteristics! You may be wondering how did this bizarre situation occur?

Mark had been drafted in halfway through the project after John could no longer afford to pay his regular manager, Jim, who had already sold half the seats to the fanbase. Mark took the project on to protect his travel agency from the Internet invasion. It became apparent that he neither understood, nor had any interest in the unique qualities of the John Otway fan base. Mark's first move was to e-mail paid-up passengers with a 33% (£1,000) price hike with no explanation for the reason. Many fans cancelled at this point and they turned against the travel agent. We would never really recover from this decision, as the fanbase are effectively a closely-knit tribe: what one person knows, all the others know instantly. Hindsight is a perfect science and the lessons are plain:

- If you must make a change of this magnitude to just 150 people, do this in an entirely personal way (phone, face-to-face etc.), rather than in an e-mail. Sending 'Dear passenger' e-mails was one of the most stupid moves and ultimately cost us the bond of trust that had been built up over about 18 months.
- Give people good reasons for change and some encouragement to stay on board – literally and metaphorically.

I eventually installed an unemployed drummer with no travel industry experience but who had excellent rapport with the John Otway tribe. 'Al the Drummer' revolutionised sales and even brought back 50% of the passengers we had lost. However, Mark found Al to be an irritating contrast to his own performance and eventually found reasons to 'sack' him, even though he brought back the passengers that the travel agent had lost! Unfortunately John Otway stood by Mark's decision since he does not enjoy conflict or facing unfortunate truths.

The computer says NO . . .

Mark's replacement for Al the Drummer (we'll call him Simon here) did not share his liking for work. A typical day for Simon would involve playing solitaire and installing firewalls and other 'interesting' gadgets. Over time we discovered that he had built the company's 'IT walls' so high that requests to spend £4,000/£7,000 on a world tour were frequently thrown out of the company computer system as junk mail and ignored. You don't need a business degree to see the ultimate impact of this!

When passengers complained about service, Simon banned them from internal chat rooms, thus ensuring that most people were unaware of the lost sales opportunities. However, Simon cleverly made sure he was the equivalent of a blood brother with Mark. This meant that Mark defended Simon's incompetence and disengagement with the project. As a result the enterprise was allowed to continue towards a plateau of mediocrity with the tacit agreement of John Otway. Once again, John was not strong enough to take the tough decisions to turn things round.

It became apparent to all but John that we had run out of John Otway fans with £4,000 or £7,000 to spend on his dream. At this point you can either give up or change course. I had bumped into Sir Bob Geldof and thought there might be a way to co-opt Bob's campaign 'Make Poverty History' and gain a wider interest in the world tour at the same time. Even here, John managed to turn opportunity into disaster. You can find out more about this on the website that accompanies this book.

The world tour was a glorious failure with a number of turning points that were artfully dodged. The biggest lesson for entrepreneurs and anyone trying to make things happen is to spot these turning points along the way and do something about them rather than deluding yourself that a 'miracle' is just around the corner. It was also a case of continual divergence with a lack of 'convergence with care', to make the hard decisions needed to execute the project. My great mistake was in loaning my heart, soul and life savings to a friend. John took IBM's Thomas Watson's maxim 'if you want to succeed, double your failure rate' just a little too literally, bless his creative soul.

SUCCESS FACTOR #7

Creativity without good management can lead to disaster. This relates to the notion of 'A sense of direction' from the list of values that support innovation and creativity in Chapter 3.

Seven habits of highly successful failures

Factor	Description
1. Apply Everett Rodgers' principles	Ensure your innovations provide relative advantage, compatibility, simplicity, trialability and observability.
2. Reality check	Never lose touch with reality when starting an enterprise. BBEs cross check hubris with logic at certain points on the journey to success and are willing to press the stop button.
3. See beyond the goal	Sometimes the outcome you are looking for is not the final destination. Remain open to the unexpected.
4. Reward successes and triumphs	Reward and recognise good tries that lead to new insights or changes in direction in a project.
5. Tinker time	Build in time for experimentation if you want to innovate.
6. Never give up	Be persistent and flexible when things do not turn out as planned. Failure should not be a repetitive strain injury such as the John Otway approach.
7. Manage creativity	Creativity without a sense of direction can lead to disaster.

Part Two
Innovation, creativity and enterprise

Chapter 6

Innovation and enterprise

It's the end of the world as we know it . . .

IBM's New York Stock Exchange survey of more than 1,500 CEOs from 60 countries and 33 industries worldwide reported that creativity mattered more than rigour, management discipline, integrity or even vision to successfully navigate an increasing complex world. Moreover, less than 50% of global CEOs believe their enterprises are adequately prepared to handle a **V**olatile, **U**ncertain, **C**omplex and **A**mbiguous (VUCA) environment. The study went on to report that:

- Top performing enterprises are 54% more likely than others to make rapid decisions. CEOs indicated that they are becoming more adaptive and nimble.
- 95% of top performing enterprises see engaging with customers as a vital strategic initiative over the next five years.

Dr Clayton Christiansen (2013) discusses the need for disruptive innovation, warning us to look in unexpected places for new sources of competition, to the bottom of the market, illustrating his arguments with the example of mini-mills. Mini-mills started by tackling the bottom of the steel market, a 7% margin business whilst incumbents were making 20%. They were largely ignored by the main players. They next crept into the segment with a 12% margin un-noticed. Mini-mills now dominate the market with most of the existing players now bankrupt. It is a salutary tale of what Professor Michael Porter meant when he talked about new entrants and substitution in his famous 'five forces' model. Dr Christiansen points out that if you're coming from the bottom of the market, the leader will tend not to fight but will flee to the higher-end of the market. Toyota did something similar starting with the small car market in the 1960s, un-noticed by the main players. Now Toyota competes with GM. Sir Richard Branson's initial forays into airlines was also ignored by British Airways until he challenged their state monopoly position, by which time he had gained a foothold.

In *The Age of Unreason* (1989), Charles Handy pointed out that discontinuous change requires discontinuous upside-down thinking to deal with it long before Clay Christiansen had formulated his ideas of disruption. Handy argues that discontinuity requires re-thinking the way in which we do things, incrementally building on the knowledge and responsibility of the elders of society. He also questions whether these ways should continue and whether the rules are adequate. It means exploration and experimentation, which are viewed as disruptive and rebellious. However, revolutions unblock societies and galvanise businesses. Handy cites Copernicus, Galileo and Jesus Christ as 'arch-exponents' of discontinuous upside-down thinkers of the past. Freud, Marx and Einstein are more recent examples who along with the revolution of rock'n'roll in the 1950s and then pop music in the 1960s more or less set in motion the decline of jazz and easy listening music, accompanied by the widespread diffusion of electric amplifiers. So, innovation disrupts markets and societies. We begin by looking at how innovation manifests itself.

From the abacus to calculus and papyrus

The word innovation has been devalued by its use throughout society as an approximation for the word 'new'. It is therefore useful to start with some definitions of what innovation is.

Strategic – This includes building and changing a brand, developing the company's competence base or unique position, restructuring the company so that it maintains competitive edge. An example would be the Automobile Association's repositioning as the '4th emergency service' in the UK, which added 2.5 million customers (nearly 20%) to their business. The idea for this change came from one of the staff, which illustrates that strategic thinking can come from anywhere in an enterprise. We examine Innocent Drinks as a supreme example of innovation in branding later on.

Product/Service – This is the exploitation of novel ideas to deliver something of value to the market place, or the reconfiguration of an existing product or service so that it is more in tune with market demand. Classic examples of product innovation include the 3M Post-it Note™ (1977), Papyrus (4000 BC), the Fender Stratocaster (1954), the analogue computer (150 BC) the Bic pen (1950), the bra (fifteenth century), the abacus (500 BC), the Macintosh (1984). Later on in this chapter, we study Metro Bank as an outstanding example of service innovation in a tired and traditional industry.

Process – This is basically a new way to do old things. It is often about incremental or radical change management internally within an enterprise and is often visible through lean programmes and their ilk. Other examples include shortening the distance or number of steps between the enterprise and its customers. In a busy world, shorter and smarter processes have the potential to give your enterprise sustainable competitive advantage. Just think how Amazon captured the world's attention with the 'one click and you're done' promise. This is a lesson yet to be learned in public services where the Internet has tended to extend the distance between the public and the public service. This is often due to the transference of paper-based systems to computer-based ones without a fundamental review of what is really needed. Many times, additional checks and balances are added. Public services are clearly in need of some mathematical creativity, especially the minus and divide operators.

Another way of looking at innovation is to examine it using the reversal technique we examined in Chapter 4, by looking from the end point backwards, at how we measure innovation. We live in an age where lots of things can be quantified and it seems almost irresistible to then measure all the things that can be measured. Yet it is a fundamental mistake to assume that those things that cannot be measured easily are not important to the long-term future of businesses. This is well illustrated by what US Secretary of State (1961–1968) Robert McNamara said in what came to be known as the 'McNamara fallacy':

> The first step is to measure whatever can be measured easily. This is OK as far as it goes. The second step is to disregard that which

can't easily be measured or to give it an arbitrary quantitative value. This is artificial and misleading. The third step is to presume that what can't be measured easily really isn't important. This is blindness. The fourth step is to say that what can't easily be measured really doesn't exist. This is suicide.

It is so important to choose the right measures. A manic obsession on the speed of development for bringing new pharmaceuticals to market in the 1990s caused an inappropriate implementation of business process engineering (BPR) initiatives. This actually increased time to market, the associated costs and reduced the number of launches, an equal and opposite reaction to the intended strategy. Whilst it is generally unrealistic and unintelligent to throw measurement out as a tool, it really matters that you do it well. With this in mind, here are some measures that might be meaningful for innovation in your business to stimulate your synapses and promote thinking about what would best-fit your situation:

- Increase the number of sustainable new product/service innovations per year.
- Increase the number of new markets entered where you could sell existing products/services.
- Increase number of patents registered each year.
- Increase the ratio of employee suggestions: profitable innovations per year.
- Increase levels of customer involvement in product concept and design.
- Increase the value of the innovation pipeline.
- Return on investment on innovation spend.
- Decrease the average time from idea approval to implementation.
- Increase your customer targeting index (i.e. reduce the numbers of customers who buy products and services that they did not really want or need).
- Increase your customer responsiveness index (i.e. reduce the number of customers who are indifferent to products and services they have purchased or used).
- Increase your customer advocacy index (i.e. convert customers who are willing to give passive referrals about your products and services to proactive advocates).

Set some time aside to consider which of these might be most relevant either as they are or in some adapted form. What then are the essential elements that are required to energise your enterprise? How do they combine or contradict one another? As Peter Drucker neatly suggested, what gets measured gets done.

The bare necessities

To be successful, innovation needs the following as a bare minimum:

A market that ultimately needs or wants the product or service

Throughout the ages, marketers have talked themselves into the idea that they can force products into markets without seeming to notice the pretty dismal statistics that surround the idea of 'product push'. Yet, it is also clear that there is very little competitive advantage to be gained from waiting for a need to arise and then filling it unless you can reach the market quicker than your competitors. There's the rub. British sociologist Roy Rothwell described a number of 'generations' of the innovation process:

Level	Example
1 – Product push	Hovercraft, the laser
2 – Market pull	Safety razor, safety belt, the digital camera
3 – Coupling – of R&D and Marketing	Sony Walkman, electric light bulb
4 – Integrated – across supplier chains and those of key customers	Land Rover Discovery, Toyota Prius
5 – System integration and networking – involving the whole business to customer chain	Boeing 777, The Shell Gamechanger Programme, Samsung's Open Innovation Centre

One of the key problems with product push (level 1), is that your customers have no idea that they need the product you intend to foist upon them. The task of market research must, therefore, be to isolate those elements of a new product or service that people really value or will pay for. Since market research is not usually a purely academic exercise, it can also have a secondary goal to educate potential customers about the product or service. This effectively moves them from the 'blind' region of the Johari window 'into the light'. Market pull (level 2) is generally more successful as it starts with a want or a need. The coupling model (level 3) brings together the needs of society with the new technology, product or service. This approach attempts to maximise the strengths of product push and market pull. The integrated model (level 4) moves from a sequential process to one where some stages of the process are conducted in parallel, with the aim of gaining advantage through speed to market. In practice, this might involve starting marketing and production engineering activity alongside the research and development process. Whereas integration is focused on internal processes in the level 4 approach, the networking model (level 5) integrates activity right across the value chain, sometimes known as open innovation. Unilever is a good example of a company that joins up its entire value chain including customers in the innovation process. Crowdsourcing and crowdfunding are essentially extensions of the level 5 approach, using the power of social media to create 'hives' of people with common interests and passions. The Internet has the power to coalesce the 'long tail' of interests from disparate individuals and bring them together in ways that would otherwise not be possible. The accompanying website has examples of crowdfunding strategies that exploit the power of the Internet to reach long tail interest groups.

The merger of form and function

Great design does not just add style for its own sake. A great design merges form and function. The Fender Stratocaster is an excellent example of this merger in action, which we visit shortly.

Coupling of brains and brawn

Even in a BBE, there is often a physical manifestation of a product or service, thus brains must be coupled with brawn, to provide an appropriate balance of intellectual and practical talent. This means that innovation moves from the drawing board to the boardroom using a healthy balance of thinking and doing. The failure of many university-based start ups is often due to the inability to couple thinking and doing or perhaps just over-thinking. Academics do not always make great entrepreneurs or marketers and vice versa. Successful leaders ensure that the balance between thinkers and do-ers is right and that the two are coupled together.

Forgiveness of failure

We looked at failure in Chapter 5. The basic need is to focus on longer-term ambitions and the acceptance that early attempts at innovation will often fail. As David Kelly of innovation consultancy Ideo says 'Fail faster to succeed sooner'.

Structure like a chameleon

Innovation needs an organisational structure that is flexible enough to allow people, money, information and time to flow to where it is needed at the right time. One can never get the perfect organisation structure yet a poor one will impede or even kill off innovation. We look at structural dilemmas in Chapter 8.

Form and function at Fender

Real world design seeks to bring together form and function in ways that emphasise product/service features so that they convert to real and perceived customer benefits. There is often a great deal of redundancy in the design process. For example, one of the key weaknesses of early electric guitars was the fact that the necks warped, causing them to play out of tune. The prevailing paradigm of the major guitar manufacturers at the time was that guitars must be made only from wood for good tone, resonance etc. although Electro, National, Dobro had proven that other materials worked as far back as the 1930s. Leo Fender challenged this paradigm by designing a guitar that was made from two separate pieces of wood (the neck and body). He did the unthinkable by attaching the neck to the guitar using four wood screws, challenging the quasi-religious viewpoint at that time that guitars could only be made by craftsmen from wood.

Fender's two-piece design meant that if the neck warped, it could simply be removed and replaced. At the same time, he introduced an adjustable 'truss rod' along the length of the neck. This effectively provided a steel reinforcement to the neck and made it possible to apply tension there when it started to warp. As a result of the truss rod, the necks hardly ever needed to be replaced. Thus the bolt-on neck was hardly ever needed. Nevertheless, Fender's bolt-on neck became the dominant design for many years to come. He also introduced a number of innovations within the design, such as a contoured body, which gave the guitar a futuristic appearance as well as perfect balance and easier access to higher notes, thus blending function with form.

Later on, a five-position tone switch and tremolo arm was added, which gave the guitar its characteristic 'twang' beloved of groups like The Shadows. It is entirely possible that we would not have had 'surf music' without these innovations. Jimi Hendrix also took the whole business of guitar playing on to a new level using the Fender Stratocaster.

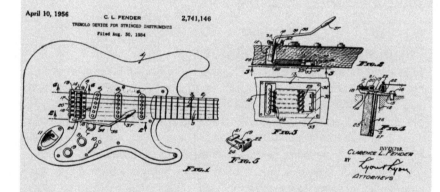

Importantly, Fender introduced these innovations without conducting extensive market research, focus groups and the like, demonstrating that market research cannot always tell you about unknown needs. His designs have subsequently been proved to be intuitively correct for over 60 years.

Whilst there have been many incremental adjustments to the guitar during this time, (e.g. new materials, electronics improvements) few, if any, changes have successfully challenged the fundamental innovations which Leo Fender introduced. Don Randall and Bob Perine at Fender were also supreme innovators in marketing. Their product branding ensured that the Fender Stratocaster has become a sustainable innovation in the face of extreme competition.

Fender organises itself for innovation in a host of ways. I asked Justin Norvell, Vice President, Product Development for Fender to explain more:

Ideas can come from anywhere, and we have a companywide open door policy for all ideas throughout the business – anyone can bring ideas to the Product Design teams, the CEO, etc. We also work in lockstep with the shop floor and R&D, so we all communicate about our ideas and concepts regularly. We schedule 'open research' time for our R&D team and certain staff members are 100% dedicated to pure forward looking research. Artist input is one of the biggest things we do, and this goes back to Fender's earliest days – getting contextual input from professionals and solving problems they are having, or finding sounds they are seeking. In the end it's all about enhancing a musician's toolbox for creativity and enabling that process.

Fender also encourages innovation through its approach to HR policies:

> Much of our goal setting revolves around innovating, whether that be in business practices, manufacturing or product design. We give regular awards out and recognise contributions for effort. We also evangelise the cultural DNA of Leo Fender and his tireless forward-looking and disruptive work ethic, and strive to carry that maverick spirit forward, so it is indoctrinated into the entire company's fabric.

Fender continues to innovate. Justin pointed out:

> Not every idea makes it to market. We are experimenting constantly behind the scenes. As far as what we have brought to market in the last several years, we have had digital modelling guitars that can change sounds and tunings with the turn of a switch (VG Strat), a guitar that connects to iOS devices, MIDI, USB compatible instruments and more. We are looking to find ways to keep the guitar a relevant tool that interfaces seamlessly with the new equipment people are using. We will always make them the old school way, but we will also keep on top of technology and the way guitar playing evolves. Ten years ago, who would have thought that you could play your guitar through a tablet with our Amplitube app?

Design is itself an iterative process and one modification can have unexpected effects on the overall function of the product or service.

Many design features are therefore redundant in terms of end-user benefits. Just think how many options the average domestic washing machine has versus how many are actually used. A consequence of this is that people involved in innovation must be prepared to let go of things that are found not to contribute to the overall ambition and practical value of the product. In practice this is hard to do, as inventors often feel passionate about their inventions, whereas the needed quality for innovation is a dispassionate view of customer wants and needs. An unemotional outlook is also of value when you are trying to gain acceptance for new ideas within companies. The lessons from Fender may be summarised:

- Great design combines form and function.
- Market research cannot always tell you about new product innovation. Fender did plenty of research one-on-one with dealers, salesmen, musicians, etc. but it did not rely on market research like a crutch.
- Design is insufficient to ensure your innovation diffuses into the market. You need to be great at marketing your products as well.

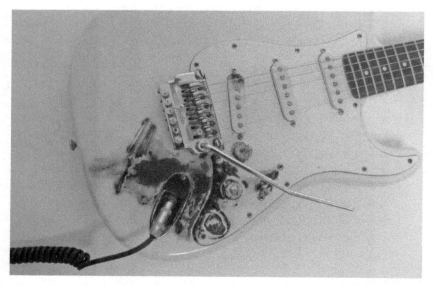

The Fender Stratocaster: indestructible innovation

Dyson: A diverse culture

The business culture(s) must accept and use differences positively. This moves beyond counting quotas of certain types of people and is more about diversity of thinking rather than reporting diversity metrics for their own value. James Dyson pretty much summed up the business case for diversity:

> A common theme runs through all of Dyson is a desire to make something better. Not tinkering or tweaking but creating disruptive technology that will be a game changer. Yes our teams are made up of every conceivable skill set from microbiologists to robotic engineers and sound specialists but they all share the same goal and that's what makes us special. The best example of this is our Dyson 360 Eye. It takes the concept of the Internet of things and blends hardware and software together, combining over a decade of development and research with hundreds of Dyson people from across the business. It works because it has been created by people who all see the same problem but work together to create a complete solution from every standpoint.

Strategic coherence

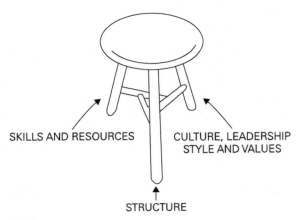

SKILLS AND RESOURCES

CULTURE, LEADERSHIP STYLE AND VALUES

STRUCTURE

A question of balance

An enterprise's culture, leadership style and values, structure, skills and resources must be in balance if it is to thrive in terms of innovation and creativity. A useful analogy is that of a three-legged stool in which all three legs must be in balance if the innovation strategy is to be fully supported. Any changes in one element (leg) of the system must also be balanced by corresponding changes in the other elements. Dyson is a great example of this. Everyone who starts at Dyson makes a Dyson vacuum cleaner in their first few days, which they then take home for their own use. Making staff customers of the end product on day one ensures that they are always focused on the reason they get paid and puts them at the front end of innovation. Engineering and design are not viewed as separate disciplines. Design people are as much involved in testing as engineers are in conceptual ideas. Many Dyson employees are recruited straight from university because their minds are open to new ideas and working methods. This probably originates from James Dyson's own experience as an Imperial College graduate.

Perhaps more controversially, Ryanair also has a completely consistent approach to low-cost innovative product and process strategy, even though their founder Michael O'Leary eschews MBA thinking and strategy consultants, as I found out some years ago! Moreover, the external brand is entirely consistent with the internal culture. Ryanair offers low-cost travel and nothing else to its customers. This attracts both lovers and haters, who are not part of Mr O'Leary's target market. This focus on 'doing exactly what it says on the tin' is modelled internally down to the last detail. They have one aircraft type. Seats do not recline, mainly because broken seats are the main cause of downtime on an aircraft and you cannot afford downtime in a low-cost operation. Some would say that his HR strategy is built on compliance rather than commitment, yet there exists a market segment of people who want jobs where they have an instrumental attachment to their employer. Love him or loathe him, Michael O'Leary should himself have an honorary MBA (**M**ore **B**ullish **A**ttitude) for his meticulous connection of business strategy in the clouds to what happens on the ground.

Both Dyson and O'Leary exhibit a sense of balance in their three-legged stools, even though they are coming from a completely different value base.

Product and service innovation at Metro Bank

Metro Bank (www.metrobankonline.co.uk) in the UK has carved out a niche for itself by making service innovation a major point of differentiation. It is ranked highest for customer satisfaction (93%) in the UK banking sector. In just three years, the bank has grown from 325 to 1,800 staff. I spoke with Danny Harmer, Chief People Officer, about the enormous growth of the bank and the contribution of their people strategy. Metro Bank has an insatiable desire to make its customers the heart of their success. Hallmarks of this are evident in their product and service innovations:

- Open an account in about one-third of the time that it takes in an ordinary bank. Leave the branch with your debit card, chequebook etc. on the day that you apply.
- Open seven days a week, Metro Bank is happy for you to bring your dog to the branch. This strategy produces a disproportionately high affection rate from customers with pets. The cultural message is 'We love you so much as a customer that we love your dog'.
- Metro Bank is obsessed about simplifying banking in an age where the trend is to extend the distance between customers and banks. A true disruptor in the world of financial services.

Supporting heads, hearts and souls

Metro Bank focuses on hiring talent rather than trying to develop it as a general principle.

Rather than trying to train people to smile, why not hire people who smile and treat them well. We hire for attitude and train for skills. We also want people to bring all of themselves to work. We think like a retailer and act like a bank.

One of our maxims is complexity for the few, simplicity for the many. Unlike other organisations we don't have an employer brand and a customer brand, since there should be no difference between the two.

They aim to ensure the hiring process creates fans regardless of whether people end up working for the bank or not. The induction strongly emphasises what the individual can bring to the enterprise. Training is done internally. Careers are structured in three career 'families': customer; leadership; specialist and the company helps people to move around these climbing frames rather than focusing on 'snakes and ladders'. Interestingly, they do not use the nine-box grid as a means of talent management, preferring instead to use talent families to offer people a flexible and inclusive climbing frame of career opportunities rather than 'ladders'.

> The nine box grid really only focuses on the top 5% and can create the problem that the top 5% wait for things to happen and the other 95% leave.

Simplification is a consuming passion. Their annual employee survey consists of thirteen questions whereas the norm would be up to 100. Metro Bank also likes to say yes to ideas and requires staff to check with someone else before saying no to a request.

> It takes one to say yes and two to say no.

Innovation at Metro Bank

Metro Bank uses internal social networks (Yammer) to cross-fertilise knowledge via 'bump ups' (e.g. if you need an answer or an opinion on a new idea). Like all other social media topics, they find their own 'level' within feeds and the bank did not set out a strategy or set of rules for its use. Things which have not captured people's minds have withered. In this respect, Metro Bank conducts its approach to engagement in an emergent and bottom-up way. This is much closer to our biological metaphors of organisation along the lines of how termites collaborate, as we will explore in Chapter 8.

A learning culture

Metro Bank is fanatical about learning from expressions of dissatisfaction. This is a simple enough strategy but one that sets it apart from other companies. This springs from the belief that, for the most part, customers do not complain on a whim. One practical example of innovation is the ability to temporarily block your credit card if you lose it. This compares with the normal situation where if you lose your credit or debit card, the bank cancels the card, so you have to wait for a week for a new one and so on. This came about when the app developers were considering how they could improve matters, having had personal experience of the time and inconvenience of losing credit and debit cards from other banks.

Metro Bank values failure as an opportunity to learn. An early mistake that they made was to offer its customers free banking worldwide. The strategy encouraged an unanticipated set of behaviours based on moral hazard. They attracted customers who only ever used their accounts when travelling abroad and this cost the bank dearly in foreign transaction charges. They continued to offer free banking in Europe and promised to be the lowest cost in the rest of the world.

Deliberate Practice – Designing your BBE

Use the seven points we have discussed and the Dyson, Ryanair, Fender and Metro Bank micro cases to outline a more coherent innovation strategy for your enterprise:

Culture, leadership style and values – The 'way we do things here'.
Structure – Both the formal organisational structure and informal structures (networks within and outside the enterprise).
Skills and resources – The attraction, development and retention of creative talent, supported by knowledge, finance and a climate for innovation and creativity.

Posture to prosper

If the environment is disruptive, your innovation strategy must marry the benefits of planning and responsiveness. Strategy may start with a plan, or posture, but it needs to adapt to environmental change. This need not necessarily be every week, as this is merely strategy as fad following. However, it must at least respond to continual scanning to seize on emerging environmental trends before others can do so. In setting out an innovation posture, it is all about finding a unique position that confers sustainable advantages. Our concepts of combinatorial creativity and mathematical creativity are relevant here, in terms of combining and multiplying capability and capacity to give you a hard to copy offering. A number of individual innovation postures are possible:

First to market – Popular myth suggests that this is the best approach. It is also the most expensive, the most risky and potentially the most rewarding if done well. The Sony Walkman and Direct Line Insurance are good examples of this strategy in practice. Being first to market is only any good if you can capture and keep the entire market through branding or some other barriers to entry.

Fast follower – Fast followers profit from the mistakes of the first market entrant. Provided that the first entrant has not established themself in an invincible position, the fast follower can benefit from having low development costs. One of the difficulties with Direct Line's entrance into the low-cost insurance market in the UK was that their low-cost strategy left them with very few places to go after their initial strong start, and their strategy presented relatively few barriers to entry.

Me too – 'Me too' players offer a modified design at a lower price, designed to undercut the main players. To achieve this, these companies must be able to deliver economies in the manufacturing or service delivery process. This is effectively a 'copy and paste' operation, which rarely leads to market leadership. The range of low-cost airline operators such as Wizzair, Flybe, Germanwings and so on do not have the same brand recognition as Ryanair, who have capitalised on their branding to maintain their position in a price conscious sector of the airline industry. Ryanair serves nearly 10,000 passengers per employee whereas BA manage just around 700.

Niche player – These companies aim to fulfil the specific needs of a particular customer group by offering them tailored products to attract them away from the mainstream offer in a mature market. It can be very successful with the innovation generally being around customer centricity and customisation of the offering.

Alongside the question of posture, we also need to consider the issue of adoption of innovation. Everett Rogers et al. proposed a model for adoption based on the normal distribution curve, which many new products and services must pass through in order to diffuse into a market. The first group of people to adopt the product are called innovators, constituting about 2.5% of the marketplace. The second group are the early adopters (16.5%), followed by the early majority (34.5%) and the late majority (34.5%). The last group are called the laggards. Conventional thinking suggests that you gain access to the innovators who then influence the early adopters and so on. Disruptive thinking on the subject suggests that you may waste considerable energy on the innovators but fail to breakthrough to the early adopters, who tend to be more influential and impact on the early majority. Another factor that may influence innovation diffusion and speed is the positive use of laggards to drive engagement with the late majority. The term laggard implies that such people may never adopt an innovation. A different view of such people suggests that they may simply have good reasons not to adopt the new product or service and, given suitable evidence or experience to overcome their objections, may become advocates who then persuade the late majority. To increase diffusion probability and speed, innovators may squeeze both sides of the adoption curve.

Another concept to consider from the biological meaning of diffusion is the need for a concentration gradient if diffusion is to occur at all. You might want to consider what 'pull levers' can be created to move from one group to another. How can you mix 'segments' so that greater levels of diffusion occur through the effects of a concentration gradient? James Dyson intuitively understood this when he first made his vacuum cleaners talking points at cocktail parties, spreading the ideavirus through social networks quickly.

Unblocking the innovation pipeline

We examined barriers to personal creativity in Chapter 2 and the notion of mathematical creativity. The approach is also useful when examining the world of enterprises and innovation; sometimes it helps to subtract or even divide barriers to innovation rather than adding more things to the mix. An oversimplified view of the innovation process sees it as the conversion of inputs into outputs. We can envision this simplistically as a linear pipeline, perhaps the accountant's utopian dream of innovation, where ideas, people and money enter the pipe at one end and products, profits and sustainability emerge at the other end, without losses in the process. The inputs and outputs would vary depending on the type of company; for profit, not for profit etc.

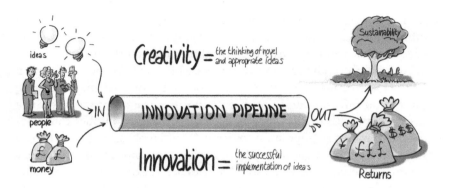

The time spent in the pipeline will vary for different industries (e.g. in software applications it may be months and in the aerospace industry it may be decades). Any shortening of the pipe 'length' or improvements in the number of ideas converted to innovations will produce financial benefit. In not-for-profit enterprises the notion of increased market share or return on investment may be replaced by more appropriate metrics, such as contribution or enhancement of strategic positioning. This 'accountancy' view of innovation is attractive because it is simple, yet the reality is rarely so simple. Innovation is an analogue rather than a digital process; a more appropriate representation of the pipeline is more distorted and probably contorted. Our illustration suggests an engineering metaphor whereas the reality may be more biological in nature, such as an intestine.

In our 'innovation intestine' the variable width represents resource variations: human; financial; technical and information-based. The shape represents the organisation structure. The 'viscosity' of the contents represents the culture, how adaptive and responsive it is and so on. Pressure and suction are functions of leadership and the market demand for innovation. As we mentioned earlier, pull or 'suck' is more effective than push or 'blow'. There can, of course, be further levels of complexity; we will develop these in subsequent chapters.

Using our extended metaphor, innovation effectiveness and efficiency can be increased in the following ways:

Increase the pressure – This is a function of leadership, which we explored in Chapter 3. Pressure in this context is about creating a sense of urgency rather than outright panic (i.e. the difference between creative tension and paralysis). We shall examine this again in Chapter 10.

Increase the suction – This is a function of market forces and may be enhanced by systems that encourage faster innovation (e.g. innovation awards, intrapreneurship grants etc).

Improve the flow – By lowering the viscosity of the contents or widening the pipeline etc. This is a function of culture and climate change, which we examine in Chapters 7 and 9.

Modify the structure – To achieve more rapid results by building fast tracks and using experimental structures to bypass restrictions. Increasing the porosity of the pipeline using open innovation. We explore these options further in Chapter 8.

Improve resource utilisation – By reducing blockages, through using better planning processes such as project management and 'all together now' innovation processes. We explore issues of capacity and capability in Chapter 9.

Proctor and Gamble attempted to unblock the innovation pipeline through a series of reforms to increase the ratio of ideas: innovations, which only stood at 15:100 in the early 2000s. Amongst the reforms they introduced were: structural modifications – smaller dedicated project teams focused on specific projects; development of creative leadership capability through a full leadership development programme; and increasing the suction by encouraging disruptive behaviour and intrapreneurship. Our example of Nokia in Chapter 10 is all about improving horizontal structural collaboration and diluting the 'viscosity' of the culture.

Reflections

Innovation may be strategic, product or service based or process driven. In any case, the goal is to take a unique posture that is hard to copy and which confers sustainable advantage. Combinatorial creativity can foster uniqueness.

The leader's goal is to increase the probability that good ideas will turn into viable and sustainable innovations. The innovation pipeline helps to gain a strategic and cohesive view of the different elements and how they interact.

A BBE balances culture, leadership style and values, structure and skills and resources in such a way that creativity is allowed to emerge. There can be no 'standard' here if you want excellence. Each enterprise needs to adopt a best-fit position that is appropriate to its environment, customers and colleagues.

Once you have identified the major obstacles to innovation, it becomes much easier to devise a strategy to minimise, eradicate or ignore the obstacles. Mathematical creativity can help to deal with obstacles to innovation.

Chapter 7

Building an innovation culture

Cultivating cultures not cults

> The role of a creative leader is not to have all the ideas; it's to create a culture where everyone can have ideas and feel that they're valued.
> Sir Ken Robinson, Out of our Minds, 2011

I was once invited to lunch by Professor Ken Robinson at the University of Warwick, where we talked of creativity, culture and collaboration. It was at a time when Ken had just written his ground-breaking book on education called *All Our Futures*. The essence of Ken's book was that creativity in education was a core skill across all subjects and that it could and should not be confined to the art department. Nor should it be reduced to incorporation via a 'creativity week', but it should be embedded into the very culture of education and learning. Ken left the UK to join the Getty Institute after his book was largely ignored by the government of the day. Nonetheless his thoughts on creative cultures remain relevant and more accessible than most. Culture is a word that has slipped into common usage, but it seems that the word is commonly misunderstood. My local council seems to think that it is about staging rock concerts in the local castle. My arty friends mostly believe it has something to do with the Romans, the Ramones, the Renaissance and so on. The term is also dropped into business e-mails casually, rather like we carelessly sprinkle salt and vinegar on chips. This is neatly illustrated by the following story:

I was invited to visit a large industrial company some time ago. On arrival, the HR Director proudly announced that they were 'doing culture change'. This was clearly why I had been asked to visit so it seemed polite to follow with some good questions such as what the existing culture was like, what he wanted to be different, how that might affect the business and so on. After a rather lengthy pause, he looked at me sternly and repeated in a louder and firmer voice 'We are doing culture change' as if this was quite enough for me to know what he wanted. They do say that there are initially two confused people in any consulting assignment, but I felt this minimalist position was quite impossible. Despite some quite clever prodding and facilitation, it was more or less impossible to get anything vaguely useful out of him so I retired injured, not wishing to take on what seemed like a poisoned chalice. This story illustrates the difficulty experienced by many intelligent people in grasping what culture is and being able to describe their own organisational culture(s). In this chapter, we turn to the culture leg of our three-legged stool, having already examined leadership style and values in Chapter 3. Before we move on, can we learn about creative cultures from jazz?

Cultures and all that jazz

A jazz band is a loose collaboration of individuals who share a common passion and purpose for the music they play. They need no sheet music as they have learned to improvise through thousands of hours of deliberate practice. The band relies on a careful selection of musicians, based on ability and empathy within and on the edge of the band's style. There is scope for musicians to 'blow their own trumpets', whilst recognising the need for the 'solos' to be consistent with the overall musical direction.

The leader helps band members reach new heights of musicianship and sometimes encourages the swapping of instruments to broaden skills. The band is paid on the quality of the group performance although random bonuses are allocated by group consent for outstanding individual contributions to the band's popularity from a 'slush fund'. This builds a genuine meritocracy where co-petition outweighs competition.

The band's repertoire is wide and both well rehearsed and spontaneous, for the performance has both elements of formal musical structure and improvised chaos. There are indefinable moments when the band seems to know exactly what to do to take the music in a new direction that has never been rehearsed formally in a state of what Mihaly Csikszentmihalyi (1990) calls 'flow'.

Although the band get great enjoyment out of playing the music when practising or performing, off stage the members sometimes disagree about issues concerned with music and other matters. In some cases, individual members are not great personal friends, yet this is subsumed to the greater 'task' of the music itself.

Co-petition manifests itself in a positive way, in so far as individual soloists attempt to outdo each other with the aim of moving the general level of performance upwards. Although each person could probably play very impressive pieces on their own, the results from the team are greater than the individual players could achieve alone. The band does compete with other acts for gigs and one of the members carries out the job of getting the band gigs through boasting about the band to club owners.

The jazz band story matches reality. Through conversations with Marcus Anderson, saxophonist for Prince and Sheila E, he confirms much of what I've discussed from his experience of working with some of the world's greatest musicians:

> Although I can read music and therefore understand the "mathematics" of jazz, the real skill of improvisation comes from using your ear/intution, paying attention to the other band members, feeding off them and finding a flow that moves the group performance up to the max.
>
> Marcus Anderson, personal film interview, 2015

The jazz band story illustrates what we shall describe later on as a hybrid between a task and a person culture in Charles Handy's terms, perhaps one of the more fertile cultures for innovation and creativity.

Stuck on you

Metaphor and word pictures are useful means of describing intangible assets such as culture. One such example of the use of word pictures is offered by Simon Heath as a cameo coming up. One such metaphor for culture is that of 'glue'. When viewed in this way, culture has a positive effect in holding the enterprise together and keeping focus on a shared vision. Businesses that view culture as glue tend to adopt processes that are intended to be the enterprise's 'adhesive', such as high profile internal company media, briefing groups, team development activities, values workshops etc. Such cultures can become very 'strong', in the sense that there is a high degree of alignment with the enterprise's values and purpose. They also tend to have a Marxist outlook on organisational purpose, sometimes expecting visible displays of compliance from employees. In extreme cases, staff are rewarded and punished according to how well they live the brand values. Whilst there is nothing wrong with this as an attempt to gain cohesion, it misses out on commitment and engagement, another set of words that are sprinkled around like salt and vinegar, but with little understanding of the differences between basic compliance and full commitment.

There is an alternative, more sinister view of culture as 'glue'. This involves the properties associated with preventing the enterprise from responding to change through becoming 'viscous' or even 'stuck' in a number of unconscious patterns of behaviour. UK high street retailer Marks and Spencer suffered the consequences of having a 'strong culture' when they suffered a serious long-term decline in their fortunes in the early 2000s, by failing to keep in touch with the wants and needs of their customers and assuming that they knew better than the market. In essence all cultures have the weaknesses of their strengths.

Permaculture

Culture is held together by rational and emotional forces, which are powerful and self-sustaining. Therefore, it is a mistake to use only rational means to change culture. The economist Jay Kenneth Galbraith allegedly summed up this dilemma in just one sentence by suggesting that faced with the choice of changing one's mind and proving there is no need to do so, almost everyone gets busy on the proof.

The subject of changing people's ways of thinking has been a challenge from the earliest times. Ancient history is, therefore, an important starting point to inform us about the topic. In 204 BC, the comic poet Naevius was convicted of slander for poking fun at public officials. Later on, Emperor Nero deported critics and burned manuscripts of which he disapproved. These examples illustrate the dramatic results of being found out for thinking differently from the prevailing view.

Culturing Virgins – A strong culture that flexes, adapts and learns

Many innovative companies are inspired by the vision of their leader, but the really clever trick is to transmit and maintain that spirit and culture/ climate as the company grows larger and more diverse. I asked Sir Richard Branson how he keeps the 'Virgin way' alive in some 400 or so companies.

When we started Virgin we were keen to do things differently. We wanted to go into industries and disrupt them, fight for the consumer and offer an alternative to the status quo. We did this in the music industry, the airline industry and countless others. We always thought it was best to ask for forgiveness rather than permission and made some daring decisions. The problem is, the bigger you get the more there is to lose. When you're operating in the banking sector, as we are with Virgin Money, you don't want to be making risky decisions with people's money. However, whilst you may have to respect industry rules and regulations, you should feel free to challenge things that you feel aren't right. It's about protecting the downside and taking calculated risks.

Virgin seems to attract people that share the same vision and that's reflected in the work of all our companies. Whilst we do have a diverse group of companies, there are some common traits and purposes that bind them all together. Our Virgin Money lounges are a good example of this, places where you can go to have a coffee, read the news and do your banking without pressure from any sales people – it was a first for the banking sector. The feel of the lounges is actually rather similar to the Virgin Atlantic Clubhouses, which in turn are like the facilities at Virgin Hotels in Chicago. Three very different companies but when you walk into any of them you know it's Virgin, there's something different and exciting going on. The key thing binding them altogether is the fun, engaged, welcoming staff.

If collective mind-sets or paradigms are involved, the difficulty is magnified. When Copernicus proposed that a rotating earth revolving with the other planets about a stationary sun could account in a simpler way for movements of the sun, moon and other planets, it took 26 years for his account to appear. Galileo also experienced severe problems in advancing the Copernican argument nearly 100 years later on and was eventually forced to disavow his belief by the Inquisition in 1633. The penalties become greater as the degree of cognitive dissonance with the prevailing paradigm increases.

Modern businesses do not have a SID or 'Spanish Inquisition Division' to create leverage for change as practised in the Middle Ages. However, there are powerful psychological and practical penalties for being seen to be a 'Martian' or in 'another galaxy' by challenging the enterprise's status quo. These can include penalties such as downsizing and euphemisms such as being assigned to 'special projects'. It is worth taking a look at the 'Crimson Permanent Insurance' story from the Monty Python film 'The Meaning of Life' to understand the longevity of culture.

Are strong cultures weak?

Traditional thinking on culture suggests that it is a good idea to have a strong culture, but what if that strength prevents the business from responding, adapting and flexing? Alternative responses to the dilemma of having a culture that is strong yet responsive include building a strong culture based on generalised values rather than specifics. This has the strength of being tolerant to multiple interpretations by staff and the corresponding weakness that staff may not identify with any of the expressed values if they are too 'motherhood and apple pie' in nature.

Unilever appears to have got this trick working well to their advantage using just ten characteristics of an organisation culture to guide behaviour. 3M has also achieved the trick of transferring its DNA across more than 100 years of operation, way past the point at which the founders could have passed on its genetic code. Toyota is another example of a company that has built an innovation culture based on a set of generalised values called the 'Toyota Way', although these owe more to a Marxist cultural management tradition than more western approaches to culture. However, Toyota successfully blend control with space for ingenuity, along the lines of our demands, constraints and choices model in Chapter 1.

Visualising cultures

Simon Heath is a corporate artist who works on innovation projects using his skills as a corporate artist. He explains why visual approaches are so important to help individuals, teams and enterprises see the future or simply old things in new ways.

Psychological studies clearly demonstrate the powerful link between images and recall and it is this link that we seek to exploit through graphic facilitation. All too often, people attending meetings are bombarded with reams of printouts and subjected to death by PowerPoint. Graphic facilitation reconnects people with their intuition and other senses through drawing and kinaesthetic experience.

Drawing is particularly powerful when trying to reach for hard to describe concepts like corporate culture, which may be likened to 'nailing jelly to the ceiling'. The powerful psychological principles of fantasy and projection are powerful tools that help people say difficult things through imagery and drawing. On some occasions I operate as a visual interpreter for groups who are trying to articulate such things, leaving them free to devote their time to description, dialogue and decision making. On other occasions, we hand the tools to the client for maximum engagement. One obstacle we are very skilled at handling is the one called 'But I cannot draw'.

We have worked with large companies such as Roche and Johnson and Johnson to help them articulate 'hard to express concepts' such as corporate culture, novel innovation concepts and 'wicked problems'. As with LVT, the use of projective methodologies through drawing allows people to see trapped dilemmas with fresh eyes.

1. Build a strong culture based on a single principle or a few timeless principles. An example of a single principle culture would be one where the number one value is change such as that adopted by Anita Roddick when she started The Body Shop. The strength of such an approach is that the culture is highly adaptable and the associated weakness is the possibility of losing sight of the enterprise's goals. This is the so-called 'Adaptive Organisation'. Such a culture needs a matching structure that allows for extremes of entrepreneurial behaviour, so that new businesses may spring up as autonomous enterprises.

2. Tolerate a weak culture. The strength of this is again adaptation and a key weakness is lack of alignment and motivation due to a diluted identity. Paradoxically, weak cultures can become very effective if they are built around a genuine sense of trust, even if strategic control is problematic.

The innovation pipeline model offers some alternative perspectives on cultural management. We will revisit the pipeline later on in this chapter.

The wind of change

One of the biggest difficulties in defining what the organisation's culture should be like rests with the problem of 'seeing' the culture and its associated strengths and weaknesses. This is because much culture is wrapped up in the unconscious assumptions about the 'way we do things around here'. Just think of wind for a moment. We know when there is a gust of wind or a storm and these phenomena can be described using concepts such as velocity and direction, yet wind cannot be seen directly or grasped. It is, however, possible to see wind through observing its effect on trees and other objects on the landscape. In the same way, it is also possible to see the enterprise's culture through its effect on the things that are visible on the enterprise's landscape:

- The environment – This includes 'high and low profile symbols'. High-profile symbols include the mission statement, company logo, annual report, uniform etc. Low-profile symbols include the stories, myths, slogans, buildings, dress code, furniture and specific jargon that influences the way people work.
- Employee behaviour – Especially when the enterprise faces a critical moment in its history, such as a take-over or financial crisis. This is often most apparent to an outsider such as a consultant or new starter, who has not adopted the habits.

Unblocking culture

In the context of innovation, organisation culture should produce sufficient cohesion of action to speed new products and services to market. In Chapter 6 we likened culture to the viscosity of a fluid in a pipeline. To improve fluid flow in a pipeline in scientific terms you may warm it up, dilute it or make the pipe wider etc. To improve the velocity of ideas along your innovation pipeline, consider the following 'innovation culture changes'.

- *Warm up or dilute the culture* – Creating a sense of urgency, relaxing rules that hinder progress, building trust and greater levels of team cohesion and goal coherence.
- *Add more or different resources* – Such as what Rosabeth Moss Kanter calls boundary crossers and more people who are good at execution to create 'pull' rather than 'push'.

Approaches to speed: Warm up the culture, create pull

At a deeper level, culture involves the values and collective beliefs about the enterprise and its identity. These elements are generally invisible rather like an iceberg, where environmental and behavioural aspects are visible above the water line and everything else invisible. We return to this theme later in this chapter when we look at culture change.

There are at least two camps of people who argue about the relative importance of the visible versus invisible elements. Pragmatists say that behaviour is all that counts and it matters little whether people's values are consistent with their behaviour, since employment is a contract where performance (appropriate behaviours) is exchanged for rewards such as money. Spiritualists say that one can never get excellent performance until people's values are lined up with all the other elements. Such assumptions produce cultural reinforcement programmes where people are challenged to live the company values and where people are expected to sign up to what the company believes in head, heart and soul. Both perspectives are valid. It just depends on what type of enterprise one is working for and the psychological contract that develops.

The gods of culture

Charles Handy in his book *Understanding Organisations* offered a classic set of cultural models that are still relevant and worthy of repetition here. I say this because Handy, above so many other business and management thinkers, has risen well above the need to write such things for their value as management fads. His ideas and wisdom are durable and stand head and shoulders above the vast majority of thought leaders in this area.

Power cultures are frequently found in entrepreneurial companies. Handy points out that if these companies had a patron god it would be Zeus, who ruled by whim and impulse. The power culture depends on a central power source with rays of power and influence spreading out from the central figure. They are connected by functional or specialist strings but the power rings are the centres of activity and influence. Many small entrepreneurial businesses start out as power cultures. Extreme examples of the worst excesses of a power culture is typified by the sort of fake deference to authority that is regularly demonstrated to Sir Alan Sugar on the TV business soap 'The Apprentice' and the Texas oil drama 'Dallas'.

Role cultures are frequently linked to bureaucracies, and the accompanying structure reflects this allusion, reminiscent of a Greek temple. The patron god is Apollo, the god of reason. The role culture has its major strengths in its pillars, which are its functions or specialities. These are controlled at the top by a narrow band of senior management. Some large manufacturing concerns have role cultures, particularly where the environment is stable and there are economies to be gained from large-scale operations. Some parts of universities and many hospitals have role cultures. In spite of the massive growth in expectation by an Internet savvy public, I must report that role cultures are still alive but not kicking in local authorities in the UK. The expectation of rapid, personalised services by a public who expect more from their taxes butts up very badly against the reality of delivery in some cases. In most cases role cultures and innovation are incompatible.

Task cultures are job or project orientated, with an accompanying structure best represented as a net. Some of the strands of the net are thicker than others and much of the power and influence lies at the interstices of the net. Many project-orientated matrix businesses (e.g. software houses, biotechnology companies) have task cultures; this type of culture can be very compatible with a mission-orientated innovation-led enterprise. Our jazz band story illustrates both a task and person hybrid.

Person cultures have the individual as the central focal point. Structure is as minimal as possible and may be represented as a galaxy of stars. If it were to have a patron god it would be Dionysius, the god of the self-orientated individual. It is most commonly found in 'professional' businesses such as consultancies, doctors' practices and architects. This type of culture is increasingly relevant in a society where the individualism is growing and virtual businesses are becoming more commonplace. However, the weakness of such cultures revolves around the fact that the 'nucleus' is each single star player. Cohesiveness can therefore be a problem if the enterprise needs to collaborate and co-operate in order to innovate. If this limitation can be addressed, it may well be the way to go in terms of collaborative innovation.

Inside an innovation hothouse – Psion

When I left university, I was offered a job by Psion, one of the UK's high tech pioneers of the eighties and nineties. Psion lived and breathed innovation and creativity in its culture and climate. It was considered perfectly acceptable not to turn up for work until 11am, as long as you worked correspondingly late in the evening to get your projects done. When Psion offered me a start date of July 1, I wrote back saying that I would like to start on September 1 instead as I wanted to hitch-hike across the eastern provinces of Canada that summer. As an employer, I now understand the slightly grudging tone of the letter I received back agreeing to this change.

When I started work in September, I found that Psion had offered ten graduates jobs, and the other nine had started work on July 1. The others had naturally taken all the best jobs, leaving me with the task of writing the documentation for other people's programs. This is the sort of job that nobody wanted to do. It got worse. A year or so later I got laid off in a 'last in first out' shrinkage. I had invited my boss and his wife round for Sunday lunch at the weekend following the redundancies. He called me and said, in the circumstances he would understand if I told him to make his own Sunday lunch. I said 'come over anyway', and he brought a bottle of wine with him, which we enjoyed as we talked. I told him about the mortgage calculation program which I had written, probably in company time if the truth be known. Mortgage brokers were earning large commissions by mis-selling endowment mortgages to young people like me. I watched one slowly multiply 3 (the multiple of income they would consider) and 20,000 (my income at the time) on a calculator and realised that these people needed help with their basic maths skills.

That Sunday afternoon, encouraged by the wine and my boss, I rang up the office which had sacked me on the Friday and got through to David Potter, Psion's founder. He often went into the office on a Sunday afternoon and when I asked to see him, he paused for what seemed like a long time. I pitched to him my idea of selling my mortgage program for his new range of handheld computers. He laughed and gave me a preferential dealer price and a credit account on the spot. By the Monday morning I was in business as a reseller of Psion's hand-held computers to mortgage brokers. I developed the business into a company called Widget as a distributor for Psion's products. Since that time Widget has developed through selling TomTom's satellite navigation devices, Flip Video Cameras, the original point and shoot hand-held video camera.

Widget started from a culture built on adaptation and thrives by selling goods from a very tightly defined range of suppliers, usually fewer than ten. As well as TomTom, the company has brought products such as Fitbit's fitness trackers and Orbitsound's soundbars to the UK market. It has carried with it the Psion spirit.

Mark Needham, Chairman, Widget www.widget.co.uk

Culture	Strengths in respect of innovation and creativity	Weaknesses in respect of innovation and creativity
Power	Rapid decision making, which means that innovators can get on with their jobs. Respond to crises well. Puts faith in key individuals. Creativity is rewarded to the extent that it makes the enterprise and key individuals in it more powerful.	Finds it hard to exist without the leader. Growth and innovation can present problems if they do not concur with the leader's vision. 'Unfocused' creativity will more than likely be punished.
Role	Produces economies in stable environments. Career tenure and opportunity based on time served. Adaptive innovation and creativity is possible provided that it is disguised in 'rational clothes'.	Resistant to change. Low incentives for mavericks. Slow to change if the opportunity is spotted. Over performance or radical creativity will limit career progression.
Task	Rapid adaptation to change. Good in changing markets. Can release high levels of productive creativity.	Can lose focus if purpose becomes obscured. Can be inefficient. Difficulties with control.
Person	High performance is possible when there is strong alignment of individual/enterprise goals. Can release high levels of creativity.	Control near impossible. Creativity can become internally focused (needs driven).

In many large businesses, multiple cultures must co-exist. GE, under Jack Welch, had a central power culture but managed to grow by giving maximum independence to the individual heads of linked businesses which had task cultures, requiring a common theme of financial results as the only criterion of interest to the centre. As enterprises grow in size, there is an argument for them to develop sub-cultures to enable them to face different markets and customers. The issue then becomes co-ordination and collaboration internally. This requires the use of people who can handle conflict.

Deliberate practice – Metaphors from Mars

If you were to describe your enterprise's current and desired culture (or sub-culture) using a metaphor, what would they be like? What are the critical differences? Visit your enterprise as though you had just arrived from Mars.

What do your first impressions tell you about the culture? Which of Handy's four cultures, or combinations, do you favour?

Myth management

I subscribe to the idea that cultures can and should be managed in order to keep them relevant to the customers and markets that they serve. If this is the case, what needs managing and how do you do that? A comprehensive model that informs us of the levers that can be pulled comes from Gerry Johnson in his book *Exploring Corporate Strategy*. My adaptation of his model is shown below:

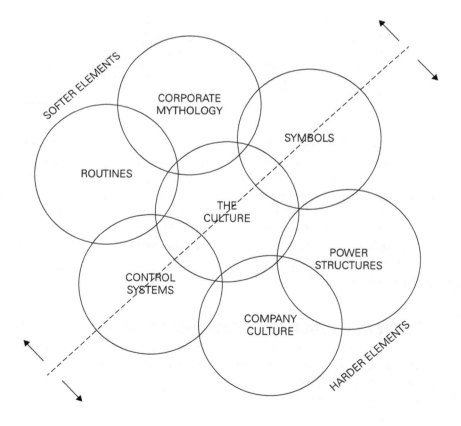

In Johnson's model I have separated those elements I call 'hard elements' from the 'softer elements'. It is relatively easy to move people round the 'chess board' (company structure), reward them differently (control systems) and thus affect the power structures. If this is not matched by corresponding changes to the softer elements such as what the company stands for, the rites and rituals that it believes contribute to success and the stories and corporate mythology, it will be difficult to manage culture. Taking each of these in turn:

Symbols are the visual language of the enterprise – logos, the way people dress, physical manifestations through offices and so on. Corporate mythology is evident through the success and failure stories that the enterprise tells itself, its customers and competitors. Routines are what the daily protocols of acceptable behaviour are etc. Control systems include budgets, performance management, rewards and recognition systems. The company structure is the physical structure of the company and who reports to whom etc. The power structure differs from the company structure in so far as it is the 'underground map' of relationships, networks, who matters and so on. Paradoxically, in an innovative enterprise, the most powerful people may be the information brokers, the gatekeepers to networks etc. and not the people with the longest titles. We have discussed the issue of power in Chapter 3.

Metro Bank, exhibit a collaborative and collegiate approach to control systems via their 'It takes one to say yes and two to say no' policy. High-profile symbols include allowing customers to bring their dogs to the bank. Routines are about a manic obsession with customers and simplifying banking. This is set alongside a fairly traditional company structure with an ingenious approach to career management that allows for multiple power structures. This is a coherent and creative approach to cultural management that has set them apart within the banking sector.

Clash of the Titans

It takes a great deal of courage to stand up to your enemies, but even more to stand up to your friends

Harry Potter and the Philosopher's Stone,
copyright © J.K. Rowling 1997

> Creativity comes from a conflict of ideas
> Donatella Versace, Vice President of the Versace Group

If you are to have sub-cultures in your enterprise, there are undoubtedly going to be times when conflict occurs. There is a school of thought that believes that conflict at work and in life is to be avoided and some people deliberately or accidentally encourage the problems of obedience and blind deference to authority. Obligation is insufficient to generate the required drive and is worse than outright civil war in terms of long-term productivity at work. One of the consequences of developing a collegiate company culture, where positive 'can-do' values are the norm, is that innovation and creativity can suffer due to the implied assumption that conflict is bad. Dentsu, the largest advertising agency in the world, is an example of an enterprise that flourishes on contention. Dentsu's founder, Hideo Yoshida (www.dentsu.com), devised ten precepts which he named his ten rules of the Demon. Rule number ten reads: 'When confrontation is necessary, don't shy away from it. Confrontation is the mother of progress and the fertiliser of an aggressive enterprise. If you fear conflict, it will make you timid and irresolute.'

However, some varieties of conflict are helpful and others are positively damaging. Conflict over ideas and tasks (debates) is productive in the long term as it results in improved innovations and productivity. When it moves towards conflict over personality and emotional issues, there are occasions when this is healthy for the individuals involved. However, it can become a chronic condition, which can lead to decline of the climate and impacts badly on the work group and the enterprise. However, if you are going to run an innovative enterprise, it is implicit that you will need to manage conflict rather than avoid it. I have found the model proposed by Thomas and Kilman (1974) (see www. kilmanndiagnostics.com) to be a reliable and comprehensive set of options for handling conflict at an individual level.

Thomas and Kilman proposed five strategies for handling conflict, according to two dimensions: your concern for yourself (assertion) and concern for others (co-operative):

- **Avoid** – Involves walking away physically or emotionally from a conflict.
- **Accommodate** – Involves smoothing things over for others.

- **Compromise** – Reaching a low level solution for all.
- **Collaborative problem-solving** – Reaching a high level solution for all.
- **Compete** – Involves playing to win.

Contrary to what some people believe, each style has a place in the creative leader's toolkit. Avoiding conflict when competition is required is disastrous; the 'avoid and accommodate' strategies are not 'weak' styles when used properly. Most of us have a preferred range within which we operate and each of the five styles has its own strengths and weaknesses. I did some work for a social services department some years back who admitted they were largely avoiders and accommodators. Whilst this was 'nice' because they never upset anyone, they also admitted that they failed to tackle serious issues because of this tendency. Importantly, without a leader who competed, they would have never secured sufficient resources to deliver their services to children and families.

At an enterprise level, conflict over personality becomes conflict over collective personality (i.e. ideology) and this is where leadership is required to manage conflicts between sub-cultures (e.g. between sales and HR departments) where sub-cultures can be diametrically opposed. Some of the options which leaders use to resolve conflicts include:

- The use of integrators or what Rosabeth Moss Kanter calls boundary crossers. These are people who can talk a variety of 'internal languages' and have wide acceptance across the various sub-cultures.
- Moving people across the sub-cultures outside their professional role to encourage mixing. This is a grand version of what we will discuss under the heading of job design in Chapter 8.
- Accepting that conflict is a natural process that leads to improved ideas and allowing or encouraging it. This is not a passive view.
- Encouraging parallel activities with the intention of raising the general level of creativity and performance. This is akin to one interpretation of the word 'marathon', where two runners would attempt to win so that both competitors would improve their performance. We have also seen that this is the nature of competition within good music ensembles.

- Changing the geographical set-up so that creative conflict is more likely (e.g. by bringing departments with radically different sub-cultures together).
- Using dialogue, appreciative enquiry and other assumption surfacing processes to surface the positive intentions and mental maps of people who are in conflict, so that they can come to recognise the value of their differences.

Reflections

Culture has a powerful effect on the generation of the conditions necessary for innovation and creativity to flourish in a BBE. It can take years to build a culture that inspires creativity and minutes to crush it.

Whilst there is no single preferred culture for innovation and creativity, these qualities are unlikely to survive in a role culture where procedure takes precedent over ingenuity, initiative and inspiration.

It is important to find ways of cultivating a culture without engendering too much permanence in a changing environment. Strong cultures have weaknesses in terms of adaptiveness.

Conflict over ideas is a valuable resource provided it is harnessed and used. The creative leader adopts many roles and is master or mistress of conflict, giving a positive example to others.

The leader's job is to align values, climate and behaviour in a way that delivers the enterprise's goals whilst simultaneously encouraging dissonance with the paradigm. Managing the paradox between goal focus and corporate escapology separates the leadership sheep from the goats.

Chapter 8

Structuring for innovation

You may be capable of great things, but life consists of small things
Tao Meditation, Ming-Dao Deng 1992

The math is not the territory

The role of the future-orientated Human Resources function is not to create organisation charts and two-dimensional pictures of who reports to whom. Rather it is to help design flexible structures and bio-diverse networks inside and outside the enterprise to help it realise its ambitions, whilst holding the enterprise in tension to reinvent itself. Since big ideas come from small teams, a key role in medium to larger enterprises is that of designing things such that it feels small but benefits from the wider resources that are commonplace in such enterprises. None of this is easy. The individual must get used to connecting with people outside their professional comfort zone. Teams must form, storm, norm, perform and reform around shifting priorities. The enterprise must balance the long-term consolidation of its talent with the willingness to collaborate with resources it does not own or control, except in the sense of shared passions and purposes.

I've spent a lot of time in dialogue on the vexed question of structuring enterprises for innovation with MBA colleagues, Dr Stephen Leybourne at Boston State University and Russ Derickson, a PhD engineer, computer genius and jazz musician. Stephen has helped me explore the links between structure and improvisation through his own research on the topic. Russ's insights come from a pure mathematical perspective and have stirred my synapses about the building blocks of organisation structure. They are complemented and helpfully disrupted by the perspectives of Professor Pam Burnard and Dr Julianne Halley at the University of Cambridge. Julianne is a theoretical biologist, ethologist and a musician. We begin with mathematics.

The mathematics of organisation

Organisations started with hunter-gatherer hunting bands. Anthropologists tell us that hunter-gatherers lived in nomadic communities of up to no more than approximately 150 individuals (Dunbar's Number). It is thought this is the brain's cognitive limit on the number of people with whom one can maintain stable social relationships. It would appear that the hunter-gatherers knew this without having done anthropology or social psychology degrees. However, each hunting band within a social order typically was limited to five to six members. In the world of organisations, the smallest team is a dyad with two members.

Team size crucially affects efficiency and effectiveness. For instance, a team of two has one two-way channel. With three members in a team, there are three such possible channels. With four team members, there are six channels. Adding one person to a triad doubles the number of potential channels. With larger team size, the number of potential dyads is N (N-1) ÷ 2.

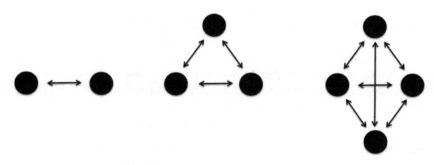

Number of potential dyads as a function of team size									
Team size	1	2	3	4	5	6	7	8	9	10
Dyads	0	1	3	6	10	15	21	28	36	45

As the number of connections grows, communication becomes more complex with both the sheer number of channels and the attendant process losses for each dyad. Larger teams, therefore, have difficulties in managing collaboration. Asynchronous electronic communication only goes so far in addressing the complexity and in some cases multiple communication channels makes collaboration more complex. So, small is beautiful as a fundamental organising principle when designing a large enterprise. Can we break the rule of five to six members? In some cases we can.

Orchestras, factories and some music groups often break the unit size rule. In the case of orchestras, this is mostly because the sub-components of an orchestra (string section, horn section etc.) are often playing the same or similar parts, which reduces the complexity. Other ways to achieve unified performances in large teams include using shared rules of participation. The music artist George Clinton of Parliament/Funkadelic is an archetype in this respect. When I interviewed George for this book I asked how he achieved seamless performances on stage when there are 40 people in the band in a semi-chaotic state of improvisation around a theme. He pointed out that the ensemble works from shared cues, much like a conductor drives an orchestra but it is done in the moment rather than to a predetermined set of operating instructions such as a score. This is much like the operations department of a factory where it is possible to manage larger groups of people provided that people share the cues required to achieve co-ordinated action. In terms of gaining organisation from initial chaos, the approach known as Large Group Interventions is a parallel strategy in business, which produces unity from initial uncertainty of ends and means. As per George Clinton's example, Large Group Interventions operate around a few simple principles and the law of two feet, as we explored in Chapter 4.

With larger numbers leaders must generally make a choice as to whether to address the team using a wheel or all channel communication style.

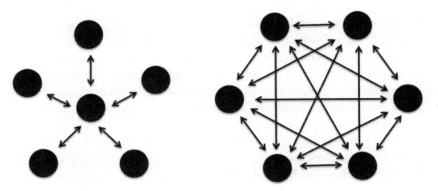

Whilst the mathematics of teams matters, so does the geography. Preston Smith and Donald Reinertsen in their book *Developing Products in Half the Time* studied product design teams and discovered that co-located teams perform much better than remote teams. Furthermore, if team members are more than about 30 metres from each other they may as well be in separate buildings. Studies from the University of Michigan show that if a software development task is divided between two individual programmers working separately, errors in the range of 30–40% occur. If the same two programmers operate as a radically co-located pair, errors drop to only 3–4%. Whilst we may be getting cleverer at asynchronous communications, it seems that we ignore the value of human contact at our ultimate peril in the innovation game. This is something recognised by Innocent Drinks who co-locate people from different functions within their head office. Innocent co-locate mainly to benefit from organic mixing and the diversity of thinking that this produces, rather than for shared project working.

Large does not have to be cumbersome and slow. Virgin is a good example of a business that is large by most people's standards (55,000 people worldwide in 400+ businesses) but which retains an entrepreneurial and customer-focused spirit. HP used principles derived from anthropology and Dunbar's number to maintain a small company ethos inside a large corporate structure. Whenever a unit exceeds Dunbar's number the idea is to subdivide the unit to preserve the benefits of thinking and acting small. Innocent Drinks' approach to the massive growth that it has seen since 2009 has been to replicate its operations as autonomous business units through Europe, guided by its core purpose and careful selection of staff according to its values.

So size need not matter, but it is often true that comfort breeds complacency in businesses as they get larger and more successful. As soon as that happens, someone is likely to enter your market and find a better way to deliver your product or service to a demanding customer. All too often hunger, naïvety and playfulness are driven out of corporate life as structures get larger, with disastrous consequences for the health of the business. So, size need not matter, but culture and climate do. It is what Professor Charles Handy wrote about in his book *The Hungry Spirit*. To grow a large structure, continue to think small if you want to retain nimbleness, agility and hunger for innovation and creativity.

The biology of organisation

I am constantly dismayed at the way in which two-dimensional charts fail to capture the networking, collaboration maps and 'nuance' that make enterprises work. In short they report the 'mathematics' of an enterprise rather than its 'biology'. If we want better organisational structures that flex and bend, we would be better to consider models that are more organic rather than two-dimensional. Having spoken with Dr Julianne Halley at the University of Cambridge, I'm convinced we can learn much more from the world of biology for some provocative insights into organisation and structure.

Termites, bees and earthworms

In the insect kingdom, how do termites build the human equivalent of cities without Microsoft Project, a decision tree or a Gantt chart? How do bees co-ordinate complex affairs without standard operating procedures, lean thinking, Six Sigma and a host of other explicit approaches to organise themselves? Bee colonies have flat structures. There is one boss (who is a woman). The HR (Hive Resources) Department has identified a few specialised roles: workers; drones. No single bee wants to become Senior Vice President of Pollination (SVPP), CEO (Chief Ecology Officer) or Director of HRM (Honey Resource Management). Bees do not have marketing, HR, IT or corporate governance departments or extensive compliance divisions requiring every flower to be checked for PC (Pollen Coefficient). By contrast, humans have not yet managed to make flat organisation structures work as well as bees. We simply must be able to do better than bees with all of our supposed intelligence.

Turning to the animal kingdom, it is possible to accidentally divide an earthworm and the half with the 'saddle' survives. It also makes the earthworm resilient by being less vulnerable to birds. Slightly more optimistically, in the case of plants, Gareth Morgan wrote on the notion of spider plants in his book *Imaginisation* in the 1990s. Spider plants replicate themselves and, unlike the humble earthworm, both plants survive. Some innovative businesses set a lot of store by keeping things small (e.g. by breaking up a unit as soon as it becomes a certain size). In *Maverick* by Ricardo Semler (2001), he suggests that people will only perform at their potential when they know everyone around them – Dunbar's number. Another company has a 'magic number' of 1,200 that signals the need to subdivide a unit. Obviously the actual number depends on a host of factors such as the simplicity of the work, the number of sub-units and the degree to which the work is specialised or standardised.

Designed for life

In 1962, Chandler pointed out that strategy is the master in his book *Strategy and Structure*. Structure is the servant. It should never be the other way round. Or should it? As Tim Smit, CEO of The Eden Project points out

> As soon as people get stuck in roles, an organisation ossifies
> Tim Smit, CEO, The Eden Project, personal interview

The prime factor in designing a structure should be the extent to which it facilitates the delivery of the business strategy. However, this requires that the structure facilitates the delivery of the people strategy, without which there will be little long-term success. It is therefore incumbent on the leader to design organisational structures to serve the strategy and the delivery of that strategy (i.e. the people). Organisation structures therefore need to be designed with care, flair and flexibility, giving consideration to these design principles:

A certain ratio – The number of subordinates directly reporting to a person is affected by the degree to which a given individual's work depends on others. In Brain Based Enterprises (BBEs), one would expect the ratio of subordinates to leaders to be fairly low, perhaps 2:1 at the extreme and rarely more than 6:1. This compares with factory lines where ratios may reach 30:1, using the principles we described before to achieve seamless co-ordinated action.

Height versus width – Whilst the trend is to flatten structures and collaborate horizontally to encourage innovation, an academic study some years back demonstrated that those organisations that had flattened their structures paradoxically had taller hierarchies than before the delayering exercise some years back. This is probably due to a persistent view of careers as a vertical climb. If we are to work in flatter horizontal structures, we must get used to career advancement via 'climbing frames' rather than 'ladders'. Human beings are not bee colonies where 'every bee knows their place' and great companies find ways to square the circle of career ambition versus vertical hierarchies.

Structuring for agility at Virgin

I asked Sir Richard Branson about how he structures the Virgin Group to maintain its agility and freshness. In other words how does Virgin solve the paradox of being large but feeling small? Does he follow Dunbar's Law on size? Do biology, mathematics or both figure in his thinking on organisational design?

This is an issue that we first encountered when Virgin Records began to expand. Things were going well and the number of employees was nearing 100, but we were worried about the organisation becoming slow and cumbersome. I decided to split the organisation in two, creating a new company in the process. We picked talented people from Virgin Records to run the new company and then when the new company approached 100 people we did the same thing again.

This tactic ensured that the companies remained nimble, agile and adaptable. The weight of responsibilities was shared amongst the teams and some great management talent was able to emerge. Nowadays, we encourage anyone who has a great idea for a new project or even a new business to run with it. It's no surprise that many of our new companies and initiatives are started by people already working within the Group.

How power flows – The power that managers possess at each level of the structure reflects the degree to which power is centralised or decentralised. Both have their advantages and disadvantages. Paradoxically, some centralisation is often helpful in innovative businesses, especially around resource power (money, people and time) for example providing rapid response funding for promising projects. The centralisation – decentralisation debate is itself a wicked problem, elaborated by the excellent work of Fons Trompenaars.

Collaboration, collaboration, collaboration – Since organisation structure is intended to facilitate communication, it would make sense to group people together who regularly communicate as we saw earlier. Humans have, however, complicated matters compared with termites and bees, by working globally, working with people they have never actually met and who may not have the same goals and operating protocols. Leading businesses do not merely rely on serendipity to make innovation and creativity happen. They recognise and encourage a nomadic approach to collaboration because people working on the same project need to communicate.

Too many cooks spoil the broth? – Whilst it has been considered desirable for people to have only one manager, this may make the enterprise slow to adapt to new and changing circumstances. In any case, project management in modern organisations means that many people work for more than one boss. However, this requires high levels of skill in contracting over goals and priorities and can leave employees feeling overwhelmed and in stasis due to overload or conflicting priorities. An alternative strategy is for the bosses to co-ordinate their demands, leaving those they manage relatively unfettered by such distractions.

Structuring for innovation

Organisation structure in a BBE is there to facilitate the effectiveness and efficiency of converting ideas into innovation. Consider the following 'innovation bypass operations' to improve the effectiveness and efficiency of your innovation pipeline:

- **Starting later** – Outsourcing non-critical elements of your enterprise's IP. A typical example would be that of a pharmaceutical company that buys promising new drug substances from a contract research organisation, thus avoiding the uncertainty and long timescales and resource commitments of exploratory R&D. This is shown as a trap door into our innovation pipeline below.
- **Short cuts** – To circumvent bottlenecks in the company structure. An example is the use of venture teams and intrapreneurship within the enterprise to work outside the enterprise's boundary.

- **Increase the porosity of your pipeline** – Open innovation weakens the boundary between the enterprise and its customers and partners, allowing ideas to flow from outside and therefore strengthening your access to early stage innovations.

Approaches to bypass: Start later, use short cuts and use open innovation

Structural archetypes

I am not persuaded by the argument sometimes put forward by so-called 'creatives', that structure is unnecessary for innovative enterprises. This requires a utopian view of the relationship between employer and employee, where the employee is self-directed and free from wishes of personal career enhancement etc. This only operates in a minority of exceptional organisations. In any case, people who work in such organisations also need to know what is expected of them even if there is greater latitude in how they go about delivering results. So structure at both a macro and micro level provides important anchor points for many people in terms of understanding their goals and how they relate to others and in co-ordination of effort. A complete lack of structure can lead to creative chaos, where individuals pursue their own whims.

Whilst this sounds ideal for the self-directed individual, it is wasteful and expensive in terms of innovation for the enterprise. It may only be a viable strategy for micro businesses that have no desire to scale their enterprise. Even Google, Virgin and Innocent have structural architectures beyond the cultural illusions that others create for them. We still have the major structural forms and it is worth examining their strengths and weaknesses with respect to leading innovation and creativity in BBEs.

Bureaucracies

A number of clichés apply to the word bureaucracy:

Nothing is impossible until it is sent to a committee.

A camel is a horse designed by a committee.

The word bureaucracy has, therefore, acquired a pejorative quality, where it is associated with red tape and delays rather than the qualities that were originally associated with the word by Max Weber. The classic features Weber mentioned were: hierarchy; clear lines of authority; the use of rules; well-trained managers; career development based on merit; apolitical etc.

As an entirely rationalist approach to building an enterprise, it is hard to argue with the virtue of Weber's original principles, until you realise that some of his principles have been extended beyond the natural limits of what he meant (e.g. excessively tall hierarchies, too many rules). In any case, many enterprises are not rational systems.

So, there is still a place for good bureaucracy in innovative enterprises. The challenge then becomes how to lead creative people in a structured environment and also to use aspects of bureaucracy where these confer advantages in terms of efficiencies without having 'bad bureaucracy' (e.g. red tape for its own sake). Shell are often quoted as an example of an organisation that took bureaucracy too far and one only has to look at some banks and local and national government departments in the UK to find the worst excesses of bureaucracy still alive and dozing. Metro Bank is a shining example of a bank that has a consuming mania with driving out bad bureaucracy to its customers. Ultimately shareholders benefit.

Given that bureaucracy has some positive features but significant weaknesses in terms of what it has come to mean, one adaptive move is to reform the weaknesses of bureaucracy. W.L. Gore has a policy that allows staff to 'sack' their bosses, similar to that employed by Ricardo Semler at Semco. What this means, in practice, is that they can bypass their boss if they feel that they are an obstacle to getting something done. This disruptive facility has the effect of shortening the chain of command so that innovative ideas can have space to breathe.

The Matrix

Matrix structures combine formal reporting relationships within a function, often vertically with task accountabilities, often horizontally. They have become fashionable in the last 20 years or so and tend to increase identification with end results, yet matrix working is not without its dilemmas. At its extreme the matrix is responsible for chaotic meltdowns in the delivery of promises as 'too many bosses spoil the broth'. These typically arise from: an inability on the part of individuals to juggle priorities; lack of good informal contacts with functional managers; corrosive competition for resources, which tends to be bad for the playfulness dimension of innovation and creativity; and dissipation of passion through the reality of individuals reporting to more than one manager. That said, many enterprises now work in matrix structures. If that is the reality and complete reform is not an option, then reforming matrix structures to make them work is a pragmatic ambition.

Autonomies

Autonomy is not new. It was a feature of many enterprises thousands of years before we attempted to formalise them via bureaucratic designs. Not interfering with assets you own in an enterprise is an incredibly easy thing to write in a book but much harder to do in practice. At the time of writing Amazon owns Zappos but has thus far resisted interfering with the way Zappos organises itself (to its ultimate credit). Coca Cola also took a shareholding interest in Innocent Drinks in 2013 but has, so far, resisted interfering with the way that Innocent is structured, cultured or operated. There have been other benefits from the benign partnership. Richard Reed points out that Coca Cola were pivotal in making Innocent Drinks the official smoothie of the Olympics. Zappos and Innocent are rare exemplars of the maxim of 'don't fiddle'.

Novel structural forms

Given that many people still feel the need to report to someone, seek guidance, advice and mentoring, and despite what Frederic Laloux says in his book *Reinventing Organisations* (2014) it seems that we will never get rid of structures and there are only so many ways of arranging your affairs. Even Laloux admits that his so-called 'Teal' organisations may rightly have aspects of 'red', 'orange' practices and so on within them. In such circumstances the best we can do is to reform structures with a view to making them best fit the external and internal circumstances faced by the enterprise. Here are some of the major reforms of existing structural forms.

Intrapreneurship and adventure capitalism

The terms intrapreneurship and venture teams are more or less synonymous ways of promoting entrepreneurial behaviour inside an enterprise, producing fast tracks for innovation within the innovation pipeline. They have these features:

- Relatively small and therefore potentially nimble.
- Full-time membership is essential – floating membership rarely works.
- Set up to take risks that are normally outside the regular scope of the company's mainstream activity or at least speculative ventures.
- May start with a broad objective at first.
- Will have greater freedoms to experiment, fewer rules and possibly a better budget than would be possible as an entrepreneur.
- Responsible for successful development and exploitation of ideas.

Venture teams can be used for whole product/service innovations. The IBM personal computer was the product of a venture team. A smaller-scale example of venture teams in action is that of a social services department that was concerned about becoming more responsive to its clients. A venture team was set up with its own agenda for action and learning and adapting what they learned to their own situation. The team visited a number of establishments, including hotels, to learn where customer service counted most. This would apparently have been considered to be counter-cultural in the formal organisation, demonstrating that what is considered radical crucially depends on the context.

Skunkworks

Skunkworks are a variant on the intrapreneurship model, offering the chance for individuals to form entirely separate organisations inside the corporate whole, protected from the centre and supplied with resources to continue their work without interference. Lockheed Martin allowed Kelly Johnson, Skunkworks founder, to work as an autonomous organisation with a small, focused team. Skunkworks created some of the most innovative aircraft models, including the SR71.

Virtual enterprises

Innovation springs from difference and the Internet allows people to collaborate around the world without having to belong to any formal enterprise, or in extreme cases, without even having met or worked together. Such enterprises require a fundamentally different outlook on how work is conducted. One challenge is how to design enterprises where there are few or no core elements. The advantage is in their ability to allow different parts to operate in completely different structural (and cultural) ways. Outsourcing is a core feature of virtual enterprises and we look at outsourcing as a separate structural reform later on. Examples include Benetton and the music downloading company Bandcamp. Virtual enterprises may hire specialists on an *ad hoc* basis, outsource to a flexible manufacturing firm, use a traditional accounting firm to manage its financial affairs, hire a marketing agency for specific projects etc. Each separate enterprise will have varying contractual and communications requirements with the core enterprise; this requires the leader to be something of a chameleon in managing across cultures and structures.

In structural terms, each separate enterprise must agree to work together to achieve the enterprise's goals. Within these demands, each enterprise is free to structure its activities as it pleases, minimising bureaucratic burdens on the structure. For such businesses to work effectively, there needs to be a clear understanding of the nature of the contract and a bond of trust over those issues that are critical to success. The relationship will vary between the different participating businesses. Whilst there is theoretically no need for the separate businesses to ever collaborate, there may be some significant opportunity costs. There are several options:

- The core co-ordinates everything, operating as a power culture and an information hub.
- The core ensures that the separate businesses come together on a regular basis with an explicit agenda that benefits all participants.
- Peripheral businesses form local arrangements that suit their individual collaboration needs.

Structuring innovation and creativity at Dyson

I asked Sir James Dyson how he sees the future of innovation in terms of the possibilities for collaboration almost anywhere around the globe.

At Dyson we have never been afraid to work with others to create solutions to problems. Take our recent partnership with Sakti3 for example. A company based in the US that has the potential to transform the way we power our new range of cordless machines with the Dyson Digital Motor. The partnership means consumers can have machines that are more powerful and last for longer. Our partnerships are not just limited to private enterprise. I have always believed that young people are the future of invention and that's why the James Dyson Foundation works with over 50 top universities to create the next generation of global engineering and technology leaders who can go on to solve the major problems of the 21st century.

I also asked how Dyson is structured to maintain agility and freshness.

At Dyson we have always been led by our engineers and that remains the case to this day. It allows us to move quickly when our research takes us in a new direction, whether it is our dual cyclone technology or our research into robotics, we aren't afraid to explore new possibilities.

One of the great advantages of being in our research department almost every day is that I see every new idea develop and I continue to work closely with our engineers, which allows us to move quickly from an idea to a working prototype. Dyson has always been privately owned which means we aren't constrained by shareholders – we let the research guide us to create exciting new technologies.

Outsourcing

Outsourcing has often been associated with poor service from call centres with disastrous reputational impacts for companies such as O2 Telefonica and poor delivery reputation from companies such as G4S, Atos, Capita and Serco. When used properly, however, outsourcing can confer significant structural advantages for companies wishing to be nimbler and faster. Effectively outsourcing can provide the opportunity for an enterprise to 'start later' in the innovation pipeline. One question that must be addressed is what can sensibly be outsourced and what remains a vital element of your competitive advantage. Unfortunately, there is no standard answer to the question of what is 'core' and what is 'peripheral' in a given enterprise.

Cantium Scientific (see www.cantiumscientific.com) is a perfect example of an entrepreneurial business that operates as a virtual organisation and which uses networks and outsourcing as principal modes of organisation. Cantium Scientific specialises in the design and development of electronic systems and products to support the needs of science in industry and academia. Cantium's product range includes bioaerosol samplers to detect bacterial and fungal presence in the air in clean rooms, food packaging, hospital, even into space exploration.

Managing director Steve Plumridge organises his entire global operations from a purpose-built cabin at the bottom of his garden, much the same way that HP started life in a shed. Steve's cabin acts as his Research and Development centre and virtual HQ, working collaboratively with customers and suppliers using a variety of cloud-based software tools. With manufacturing fully outsourced to local companies with many components sourced locally, global sales are managed via a distributor network. Importantly, Steve does not outsource the enterprise's brain, maintaining strong links to academia and a network of market sensors, to keep his intellectual capital and market knowledge several steps ahead. He has outsourced those elements of his company's IP that can be sensibly compartmentalised and co-ordinated simply. The relationships between the different parts of the business are managed differently, with some demanding much greater expert input and others left to run autonomously.

Non-structural reforms

If you cannot reform your organisation's structure there are still some time-honoured things you can do as a leader to mitigate the weaknesses of a given structure. They may be unbranded and unvarnished, but they are relatively simple to do and, more importantly, they work.

Job design

Hackman and Oldham outlined five principles for the design of jobs that tend to encourage the engagement and intrinsic motivation required to encourage innovation and creativity at work.

- **Skill variety** – Using an appropriate variety of skills.
- **Task identity** – Being able to see the whole task.
- **Task significance** – The extent to which people identify with the task and its importance to something wider.
- **Autonomy** – Giving some discretion over the way in which work is done.
- **Feedback** – Gaining an idea of how well people convert effort into performance.

In practical terms, these translate into some simple, but effective, strategies. For example: vary work where possible to encourage skill variety; design jobs so that they enable people to see a task through to increase task identity; assign work as a whole unit to enhance task significance; delegate tasks to their lowest possible level to create autonomy and responsibility; connect people to the impact of their work through feedback. Some of the world's best workplaces such as Prêt à Manger use these principles intuitively as they are common sense, although they are not commonly applied. Some of Prêt à Manger's other HR strategies are summed up via the 3R's:

Recruitment: Prêt hires 'oven ready' people with attitude and then lets them be themselves, providing them with autonomy. Most companies hire people for their knowledge and skills and sack them for their attitude. This simple reversal has dramatic effects. Three-quarters of managers are promoted internally; the rest are hired with relevant work experience. Staff have an input on who joins their team.

Rewards: Staff are eligible for bonuses from day one. They also get generous rewards if they receive commendations from customers and mystery shoppers. Rates of pay are better than average in the sector.

Recognition: Prêt throws a party for all staff every six months and has Friday-night drinks once a month. Staff are not subjected to ritual humiliation by having to wear ridiculous uniforms, clean toilets or dress up as mascots.

Collaboration without borders

Bandcamp operates as a virtual enterprise with just 28 staff worldwide as of 2015, offering its customers superior service and clear commercial advantages for the aspiring musician. As a musician on Bandcamp, you gain a minimum of 85% of the income from your music. Your royalty on a £0.99 single can be absolutely nothing on the major platforms, depending on how many other places the purchaser has gone to get your song. The artist gets paid immediately they sell their music. Bandcamp is a great example of an organisational structure which supports its stakeholders rather than stifling them. In contrast, I know some musicians who are still waiting for royalties from traditional music labels some 30 years later! As a result of offering these clear advantages to musicians, Bandcamp is growing rapidly. Amongst the artists that have rejected traditional music deals for Bandcamp are Amanda Palmer and Bedhed. Artists like Thom Yorke, Four Tet and Wolfmother all have their own accounts, alongside notable indie labels like Sub Pop, Ninja Tune, Fat Possum etc. who make music from notable acts like Tom Waits, The Black Keys, Spritualized and so on.

Bandcamp's founder Ethan Diamond had the idea after becoming frustrated trying to buy an album from a local artist from their website about six years ago.

> After many emails, a couple of calls, and several weeks, I got an email from one of the band members with a link that left me with tracks titled something along the lines of 01masterfile.mp3.

He thought that there had to be a better way for any band to be able to sell their music directly to fans. By refusing to copy the prevailing organisational structure, Bandcamp has succeeded. We will see how well they do now that they have the 'opportunity of growth'.

Bootlegging

One of the strategies most often copied to help set a context for innovation is the so-called 15% 'bootlegging' rule, pioneered by 3M and adopted by companies as diverse as Roche and Google. W.L. Gore offers their employees 10% bootlegging time to develop new ideas and work on personal projects. One of their employees, Dave Myers, came up with the application of an ultra-thin fluoropolymer to make guitar strings that were longer lasting and easier to use. W.L. Gore launched them under the brand name ELIXIR® strings; they are now the No. 1-selling acoustic guitar string. Coating strings to protect them is not new but, until this breakthrough, coatings affected sound quality. Myers was able to rely on the company's unique culture and formed a cross-functional team to advance the idea across a two-year period. Google also used the strategy and this produced Gmail, which was the first e-mail system to have a search facility. Google have recently revised their attitude to the 15% principle, moving to a more focused pipeline approach reflecting the growth of the company. We shall see how it fares.

3M sets a lot of store on structure. When a division gets too large, it is split up. It accepts failure and estimates that only two in every 100 ideas actually reaches the customer. It was one of the first companies to involve customers in shaping product ideas. In practice, some 3M employees use much more than their 15% bootlegging time, whilst others use none at all. What matters is that the rule exists as a visible permission/encouragement. This sets the context for experimentation.

Crossing chasms

One option for leading an organisation that wants to preserve the advantages of efficiency within functions with the opportunities for effectiveness afforded by horizontal collaboration is to leave these functions in place and use what Rosabeth Moss Kanter called 'boundary crossers' to 'cross pollinate' between functions. Such people have to speak multiple professional languages (research, marketing, IT and so on) in order to be effective in the different functional areas. Steve Plumridge, MD of Cantium Scientific, is an archetypal boundary crosser.

Nokia concentrate their efforts on boundary crossing to make horizontal structure work better by embracing social media to achieve new ways to connect and engage with employees. As an example, within a Nokia change programme they used a community site that connected 600 change leaders with 6,000 employees 24/7 to answer, or find answers, to any questions employees might have. Nokia also embraces online chats to connect people with ideas to leaders who have the budgets to make things happen. Being present and available is more effective than steering groups, gates, boards and endless presentations.

Reflections

Structure is an enabler to convert creativity into innovation. BBE structures must be designed to fit the strategy and the people in an age of complex and perpetual change.

We should look to biological models to find better ways to organise ourselves. If you want to do complex things quickly, this demands that you keep structures simple. Bees, termites, migrant birds and migrating jazz musicians understand that complexity requires a few simple rules to secure co-ordinated action.

Structure should facilitate the horizontal operation of your enterprise, since it is generally a weaker spot than the vertical dimension of structure through authority. Flattening the organisation structure is a utopian ideal, yet it cannot be realised, unless career routes are found that allow for 360-degree career mobility.

Since all structures have the weaknesses of their strengths, other 'devices' must be employed to minimise weaknesses arising from organisational structures, such as Hackman and Oldham's job design factors, bootlegging, boundary crossing etc. We must 'think outside the innovation pipeline' to find better ways to overcome the weakness of organisational structure.

Chapter 9

Developing innovation capacity and capability

The ancient Greek philosopher Democritus (c 460–c 370 BC) was thought to have observed that Man is deemed capable or otherwise not by his actions but by his intentions. He thus linked thoughts to actions long before business academics spotted their importance. To increase the effectiveness and efficiency of creative activity and its conversion to innovation in a BBE we need what I call ICCA: Intent, Capacity, Capability and Action. Here we focus on the capacity and capability to generate and maintain a climate that allows people to bring their heads, hearts and souls to work. We begin with the vexed question of whether to 'make' or 'buy' creative people.

To make or buy?

Many companies subscribe to the notion that the only way to build an enterprise where innovation and creativity thrive is by ensuring that the 'raw materials' are of the highest quality. This is confirmed by fundamental research conducted by Professor Adrian Furnham at University College London (UCL). His research confirms that we are essentially the product of our genes and development plays a relatively small part in developing our capability as human beings. The caveat to this impoverished view of human development is that we are more than able to develop creative capabilities if we have the willpower to do so. Armed with this wisdom, the smart money is on hiring people who come 'oven ready' with all the capabilities you need, or at least to select people based on their willingness to learn. Further research on the success of developmental coaching at UCL shows some surprising findings. Coaching is an effective development strategy when:

• There is excellent rapport and chemistry between the coach and the client – estimated to be nearly 50% of the contribution to success.

- The client has an important client goal to pursue for which there is no obvious and easy solution – approximately 25% contribution.
- The client believes that the coach can help – approximately 15%.
- The coach has a wide repertoire of skills and experience to draw upon to fit the client's preferred style – approximately 10%.

Assuming that you have decided to buy the right people or at least select people who are predisposed to learn, the next question is how do you best select the right people? A classic mistake is the assumption that the most intelligent people are likely to be the most ingenious. We have already noted that there is a huge difference between IQ and EQ or emotional intelligence. Enterprises which think that IQ is all that matters it will typically search universities for such people, with a focus only on qualifications as the measure of potential for innovation and creativity. We have already explored the difficulties of collaboration amongst experts when we discussed dyads earlier on. As well as attracting creative people, there is a case for creating attractive people (i.e. bringing their talent to its maximum capacity and utilisation). This can be achieved by mixing people who possess different 'natural intelligences', so that they address areas that are less developed in each other, or by providing the necessary support in terms of EQ. However, without any basic competence in emotional intelligence, the road may be hard and you may be better off by installing someone to manage the gap or not to hire them in the first place.

Innocent Drinks, in common with FujiFilm, Dyson and Prêt à Manger, place great emphasis on the hiring process rather than trying to develop creative talent. Given that Innocent has 'fans' amidst its customer base, it is even more important that they use a rigorous process to ensure that staff have the skills and values that they need rather than just being product enthusiasts. 3M also places emphasis on a balance between EQ and IQ: curiosity, problem-solving, collaboration and team skills. In honing job specifications and so on to target the people we want, it is vitally important that we encourage misfits. Unfortunately, the so-called 'professionalisation' of HR all too often encourages a regression to the mean in terms of selection. I suspect that neither Steve Jobs, Anita Roddick nor Richard Branson would get through the HR selection process in some companies these days, possibly just based on their appearance or social media profiles. Pre-judging people's capabilities based on an incredibly narrow and irrelevant set of data is a dangerous and stupid development in some companies' HR departments.

We have also seen that creative people are only half the requirement. To turn creativity into innovation also requires people who are good idea developers and obsessive finishers. It is rare to get all these qualities in one human being and getting them to mix together is another story altogether. This requires genuine diversity which we examine next.

Rich mixtures

Diversity is not just a nice idea. Men and women bring different things to the party. Some recent research indicates that there may be a genetic component to the popular notion that women are more intuitive than men. However, in discussing diversity here I wish to widen the word to include all forms of difference. Tom Peters suggested that business would be better if we surrounded ourselves with disagreeing (and even possibly disagreeable) people. I would add a further slant on this concept. There is enormous value in selecting people who import tension, unusual ideas and questions, even greater value if they are able to provoke others in ways that engage them in further levels of enquiry rather than the type of provocation that simply irritates. I sometimes provocatively refer to such people as 'idiots', since they will not be locked into accepted ideas about the nature of problems within an enterprise. The TV detective 'Columbo' is a good example of a 'genial idiot' who is very effective at using naïve questioning backed up by data to nail his suspects.

Alfred P. Sloan of General Motors illustrates the importance of creative tension in making better decisions. He is reputed to have said to his board of directors, 'Gentlemen, I take it that we have complete agreement on the decision here'. When everyone round the table nodded in assent he continued . . . 'then I propose we postpone further discussion of this matter until our next meeting to give ourselves time to develop disagreement and perhaps gain some understanding of what the discussion is all about'. In the context of businesses, 'idiots' include:

Naïve contributors – A naïve contributor is not hampered by the pre-existing norms, rituals and mindsets that exist within the main group.

This could be the new hire who is initially untainted by the culture, or someone well outside your business sector. The quickest way to invite naïve contributions is to invite children to comment on your enterprise. Uncontaminated by the daily grind and the need to cloak any feedback in acceptable clothes, kids see your enterprise for what it is.

Worker directors – Another example is the use of worker directors who bring important questions to the boardroom. This approach has been very popular in certain European countries for a number of years.

Consultants and outsiders – Outsider commentary can be systematic or accidental. An example of the systematic use of outsiders is when companies make use of outside consultants or customers to import difference to the enterprise, especially where attitudes need to be shifted. Another way to achieve this is by inviting stakeholder groups to important meetings, specifically to give an outsider view. Any good non-executive director can also add value by operating in this mode.

Sometimes diversity can be induced by using a catalyst and we examine this next.

Attracting creative people and creating attractive people at Virgin

I asked Sir Richard Branson for his views on whether talent selection matters more than talent development. Quite characteristically he answered with the 'not only but also' approach, coined by my namesake, the comic genius Peter Cook. Using the best strategies available rather than slavish adherence to one approach is the hallmark of a true master.

> We often talk about "Virgin people" as if our staff have a different genetic make-up to other people. You can see it in our branding teams, who come up with wonderfully inventive and quick-witted advertising campaigns or projects, right through to our cabin crew who are able to have a laugh and a joke with our customers – not something you often get on other airlines.

A lot of this does need to come naturally, but everyone should be able to change and improve through spending time at Virgin. In fact, one of the great benefits of working at Virgin is how exposed you are to different creative and innovative environments. Our companies will often collaborate with one another, which is great to see. Staff get to meet new people from different industries, experience a fresh way of thinking and be challenged to step outside of their comfort zone. Whilst our most creative people do have something about them that makes them inherently 'Virgin', it's a fair assessment to say they will have improved their abilities by working in the Virgin Group. Equally, they will bring something new to the table, and what it means to be a Virgin person will continue to evolve.

Catalysing innovation and creativity?

One choice for leaders is to develop creative capacity by using external resources wisely. A good innovation and creativity catalyst will improve the effectiveness and efficiency of creativity and innovation, whichever is being looked for in a given situation. They do this much like a catalyst works in science by reducing the 'activation energy' to get to the world of great ideas and to convert those ideas into sustainable innovations. In science, a catalyst's effectiveness is reduced by 'inhibitors' or 'poisons', but in business a good catalyst will covert 'poisonous people' into advocates, or at least neutralise their effect on a team or the organisation, through a range of non-directive or directive facilitation strategies. The catalyst is used in small doses to promote the innovation chain reaction, much as in science. It is an ideal solution for those enterprises who wish to have innovative thinking on tap as and when they need it but who do not wish to have that capability embedded into business permanently.

Developing internal talent

Another way is to develop creative capacity internally. This can be done on an individual level, at the level of teams or across the enterprise as a whole. Individual creativity can often be developed through K. Anders Ericsson's (1993) concept of 'deliberate practice'. This requires the systematic desire to extend one's repertoire beyond one's comfort zone. This could mean theoretical practice to acquire essential knowledge (e.g. by reading books on creativity and innovation or just reading outside your professional expertise). Since much of creativity is about skill and attitudes, experiential practice is also necessary, perhaps offering to facilitate groups requiring an injection of creativity and learning by trial and error and trial and success. If the risks in your business are too great to allow massive failure, it makes sense to pick lower-risk situations for deliberate practice, perhaps where the urgency is less pressing or in situations where it is certain that an incremental approach to innovation is almost bound to be needed and where mistakes can illuminate the path to success. Here is my best advice on developing talent, individually, in teams and in organisations as a whole:

Individuals – The individual is perhaps the easiest level to work with as you can adjust your approach to meet their own goals, learning style and pace. Coaching is a powerful method for developing internal talent when the protégé wants to learn and the chemistry between the coach and protégé works.

Teams – A team has to agree that it wishes to learn and one way to do that is to find something that the majority want to do better or differently. This is the realm of Organisation Development (OD).

Organisations – Some of the methods we have discussed under the headings of large group interventions, hackathons, strategy retreats, LVT, OST are relevant to help whole organisations embrace innovation and creativity.

Can you teach innovation and creativity?

Aristotle may not have been a management consultant or a primary school teacher but he wisely observed that educating the mind without educating the heart is no education at all. I was fortunate in my formative years to gain access to both types of education. A great epiphany across this time was being asked to teach innovation and creativity over many years at MBA level to groups. Indeed teaching is one of the best ways to learn, although I would expect few modern schoolteachers would be able or willing to admit this. I initially worked as a naïve practitioner, eventually developing a very wide and flexible repertoire of approaches to suit people of all persuasions, be they pure theorists, experimenters, reflective practitioners or pure pragmatists. What I have learned from 18 years of doing this is difficult to boil down into the confines of a book on the subject, but the essentials are contained here and you will find more on the accompanying website. What follows are essentially the practical manifestations of the 12 principles for creativity, which we explored in Chapter 3.

Lesson 1 – Manage the people – The first point of entry is to understand the people you are working with and make sure they all understand each other. It is always time well spent doing this. People need to feel a great sense of comfort if they are to reveal half-baked ideas or even liquid knowledge to each other. You need to at least know what they are great at in a professional context and what inspires them professionally. I usually want to know about their passions and hobbies outside of work, since these give a clue to the roots of their inspiration and offer a strong anchor for releasing their creativity.

Lesson 2 – Manage the climate – The four climate dimensions we discussed in Chapter 3 are extremely informative here and I use them as a flexible template for experiential and reflective energisers to move individuals and groups towards 'activation energy'. Amongst the more unusual things I have done in practice include taking groups out to forests to collect flora and fauna for no explicit purpose, levitated people in chairs, conducted guided imagery and hypnosis and built things from junk. The trick is to do something that fits the people and, ideally, an activity that foreshadows the topic to be scrutinised, which is why an extremely wide repertoire of experiences is needed. Whilst the essential need is to develop trust, there is also room to do all of the above using traditional means.

Lesson 3 – Manage the problem – As discussed in Chapter 4 it is nearly always a mistake to jump into problem–solution thinking in all but the simplest of problems and opportunities. In practice, this means managing the time required to dig backwards to understand the real issues that lie behind the presenting topic.

Lesson 4 – Manage the process – In teaching people innovation and creativity, often the journey is just as important as the destination; this requires excellent coaching and rather less manic obsession with the idea that outcomes are everything. Goal focus matters but goal obsession is unhelpful. This is a subtle but important point.

Climate change

Whereas culture is often persistent in the amount of effort that it requires to change it through the interaction of elements of Johnson's paradigm, the climate of an enterprise is something that can be changed quite quickly with dramatic results. Climate differs from culture in the sense that climate is about how the enterprise feels at a particular time, whereas culture is about the way things are habitually done. A metaphor for climate is that of the weather conditions of an enterprise. We think of geographical areas (and businesses) as having a characteristic type of climatic environment, which allows us to develop certain expectations of what the scenery will look like, what clothes its inhabitants might wear, how comfortable we will feel there, how predictable the weather might be, how strange it might feel for someone who is used to another sort of climate, etc. The climate of the United Kingdom is temperate, however, we can create different microclimates within this temperate climate. For example, in Kew Gardens a forced environment can be created to allow different plants to grow. Within the umbrella of an 'industry climate', businesses and parts of them can also create microclimates in order to suit specific purposes. A creative climate can help significantly, in both good and bad times, making people feel better about simply being at work, easing communication between those who are there and allowing fire fighting to happen more effectively. We visited the values that lay behind a climate where innovation and creativity flourish in Chapter 3. The next question is that of how leaders develop such a climate. Göran Ekvall's original work (1983) identified ten dimensions of climate, which Mark Brown expanded to thirteen through the Dolpin Index in Chapter 2.

Ekvall's climate dimensions		
Commitment	Playfulness	Shared view
Freedom	Idea proliferation	Work recognition
Idea support	Stress	Pay recognition
Positive relationships	Risk taking	
Dynamism	Idea-time	

Leaders can enable more creative climates. Here are some practical strategies:

- Designing and administering flexible reward and recognition schemes where the elements are based on individual passion rather than wants and needs. This is a kind of 'mass personalisation' of reward and recognition.
- Unwinding complex policies and procedures to give leaders and managers more latitude in decision-making. For example, reducing the rulebook to 50% of its previous size (without using a photocopier set to 'reduce').
- Training employees not to accept the first and most obvious solution to a problem/opportunity. Insist that no idea is put into action until at least twenty alternatives have been developed and evaluated.
- Coaching individuals to work with **V**olatile, **U**ncertain, **C**omplex and **A**mbiguous environments (VUCA) rather than fight with it, so that they will relish new challenges.
- Encouraging people to use informal networking to get ideas (e.g. encourage meetings in cafés and bars and organise 'daydreaming' workshops and think tanks). Tim Smit's example at the Eden Project is a good illustration of climate development.
- Learning from the examples of Google and Innocent about the importance of the physical environment. A good place to start on this is by reading Cris Beswick's book *The Road to Innovation*.

Developing innovation and creativity at Dyson

Do you concentrate more on 'attracting creative people' to work at Dyson or 'creating attractive people' through training and so on?

Inventive, quick-witted and bold are characteristics I always seek. We have engineers from all walks of life but they all share the same philosophy. They see the problem, and don't stop until they find the solution. I always wanted to attract graduates with little or no work experience. They make excellent first time recruits and it's easy to attract good people if you give them responsibility and freedom at an early stage. They are encouraged to make mistakes, to get things wrong and strive to correct them. That philosophy hasn't changed at Dyson since we started.

Is creativity something that can be learned through study, practice or technique, or are you in the camp that suggests you either have it or you don't?

You can learn almost any skill in life. What I always want from my team is for them to share my drive but also have the confidence to disagree with me. That was the case when I started with just 5 people and it is still the case for the 5,000 people we have at Dyson now. No successful business is built on yes men. I always look for young people who are full of fresh, unsullied ideas for our expanding robotics, electronics, sound and motor departments. They all have to be fearless and unafraid to explore new possibilities. I believe in inexperience and a hunger to learn by doing.

Do Dyson do any formal training in tools and techniques for divergent and convergent thinking? If so, can you say more on this?

What we teach our engineers at Dyson is highly secret but what I will say is that there is no substitute for the practical application of ideas. Our process is very much based on solving problems in small teams but not forgetting the big picture.

At Dyson we actively encourage "wrong thinking" – to think outside the box as much as possible and not to be afraid to explore new possibilities to create disruptive technology. It is the mindset I have always taken. No one believed in my idea of a bagless vacuum cleaner – especially one with a clear bin! But after 5,127 attempts it worked better than any other vacuum cleaner. This philosophy has not changed since 1993, when the first Dyson DC01 was made. Take our latest Dyson Big Ball Cinetic for example. Its compact cyclone pack with flexible rubber tips means that it can clean for ten years – that's up to two tons of dust – with no need to wash filters. This kind of technology is only possible by exploring new possibilities and not being afraid to challenge convention.

Innocence and creativity at Innocent Drinks

Innocent Drinks (see www.innocentdrinks.co.uk) has revolutionised the healthy drinks and food business in the UK and Europe. I spoke with Dan

Barrett, Head of Innovation, about their approach to innovation and creativity. From the moment you walk through the door the built environment is a living, breathing exhibit of the 12 principles for innovation and creativity we discussed in Chapter 4. Innocent's mission is 'make natural delicious food and drink that helps people live well and die old' – compellingly simple and worthwhile.

Innovation in branding

Above all else, Innocent is a great example of innovation in branding and the 'packaging' of ideas. An example of Innocent's use of an involvement strategy for branding includes the 'big knit', where people knit miniature hats for Innocent smoothies. It is a strategy that is both fun and which has also raised millions of pounds for charities. Dan commented on brand-based innovation:

> Before 2011 we sold orange juice in cartons. So did all our competitors. The customer could not tell the difference. So we redesigned the pack to show the product and its distinctive features. At the same time we launch a distinctive apple juice made from a unique blend of apples. This care in product design comes down to the names we use for products such as "skip to the beet" for our fresh beetroot juice blended with apple juice, carrot juice, lemon juice and a touch of ginger.

Ideas model

The company is constantly engaging with and listening to its drinkers. However, come from multiple sources at Innocent, working beyond 'level 5' in Rothwell's Innocent sticks to tried and tested methods of product development through testing new products on customers and involving their customers in new product development. This is particularly important when introducing new concepts such as their 'Innocent bubbles' range. This is a blend of fruit juice and spring water which has been carefully differentiated from 'flavoured water' products.

Innocent HR factors

Innocent relies on careful selection of its staff against a clearly designed set of values: be natural; be entrepreneurial; be responsible; be commercial; be generous. They say of these:

When we're all old and grey and sitting in our rocking chairs, we want to be able to look back and be really proud of the business we all helped to create. We think the best way of achieving this is by living the values that are closest to our hearts. Our five values reflect what we are, how we do things, and where we increasingly want to be. And they hang above every loo in the building so we get to remember them everyday.

Innocent Drinks: www.innocentdrinks.co.uk

Management are not so much a controlling force, rather mentors who give clear direction and objectives. Explicit real-time feedback is used as a means of performance improvement rather than saving it up for the annual appraisal. It is rare to find such good uses of such simple but vital tools.

Innocent operate two headline Reward and Recognition schemes. The 'Lord and Lady of the Sash' are monthly awards for which appreciation is given along with a financial award that can be used for things like a family and friends dinner, thus emphasising Innocent's family values. Once a year the company has its own version of the Oscars, the 'Golden Bottle' awards, for outstanding work through the year.

People are radically co-located to encourage mixing between disciplines. This encourages diversity of thinking and physical movement, which we have noted is good for creativity and mindfulness. A sense of team and mixing between disciplines is also modelled through quarterly retreats. Innocent Drinks is a textbook example of a climate and culture that supports innovation, creativity and enterprise down to the last detail.

Supporting innovation and creativity

It is claimed that the philosopher Neitsche said: 'for the creator to create suffering is needed' . . . Well, perhaps Mr Neitsche would not have got a job in HR at a corporate company with his rather impoverished views of human capital development! Nevertheless, he points out that some staff are simply not motivated by happy clappy HR strategies to make them enthuse and effuse positivity. As we have seen, creative endeavour is sometimes enhanced by a sense of being 'up against something'. The removal of such challenge by sanitising the corporate workplace is often a mistake for those people that feel the need to be involved in some kind of unarmed struggle with ideas, resources and people. So, one way to support innovation and creativity is to create challenge in the enterprise. Here are some other examples of how leaders can support innovation and creativity through good HR, financial and information resources.

Ten years after – Semco and Trust

In a grand utopian experiment, Ricardo Semler introduced a radical set of HR policies in his industrial conglomerate Semco in the 1990s. These included things like:

- Phasing out administrative jobs and having a war on bureaucracy.
- Divide and prosper – Using small cells as the basic building block of the enterprise, as we discussed earlier under 'mathematics'.
- Upside-down management – Staff appraise their bosses and are responsible for hiring and firing. At the time of writing General Electric and Accenture are removing annual appraisals, although they are not turning management on its head.

- Self-set salaries, goals and bonuses. The organising principle is management by peers rather than hierarchy.
- Worker directors and a socialist approach to unity between bosses and workers. This is what HR people call 'unitarism': workers and bosses work for the same goals.

Frederic Laloux has resurrected *The Semler Way* recently in his book *Reinventing Organisations* (2014). Laloux espouses similar ideals using exceptional organisations as his case studies. The beauty of Semler's case study is that it gives us an opportunity to look over the medium term at whether it has been a sustainable success. The company has indeed lasted and this offers some validation of what some consider unusual business practices. Which ones would fit with your enterprise?

Holiday like a Virgin

Richard Branson first heard about Netflix's HR policies when his daughter e-mailed him saying, 'Dad, check this out . . . I believe it would be a very Virgin thing to do to not track people's holidays'. She explained that a friend's company did the same thing and they experienced a marked upward spike in morale, creativity and productivity. As a result Virgin introduced a policy to allow people to take as much holiday as they liked – a true innovation vacation.

Netflix's approach permits all salaried staff to take holiday whenever they want for as long as they want. No prior approval is needed and there is no tracking of their days away from work. The assumption is that of responsible behaviour and that staff absence will not damage the business – or careers! Clearly such approaches work best in high commitment companies; this perhaps explains why the Virgin way is not copied more often in companies where people work to live rather than the other way round. Netflix's HR policy states 'Just as we don't have a nine-to-five policy, we don't need a vacation policy' (see www.virgin.com).

From rewards to recognition

Pay is a Herzberg dissatisfier. This means that dissatisfaction occurs if it is felt that pay is insufficient, but increasing pay beyond what is expected will not always produce long-term motivation. Other elements of the motivational mix are far more relevant to the higher order needs on Maslow's triangle such as self-actualisation and ego. Recognition is a Herzberg satisfier and can offer a stronger long-term incentive to greater feelings of well-being and engagement. A number of organisations have sprung up to support employee recognition, such as O C Tanner, yet in my view these are not really necessary if the enterprise can devise simple structures for recognition such as that used by Innocent and Metro Bank. At the simplest level, the best form of recognition is the two words 'thank you', said with heart and meaning. Most attempts to systematise recognition run the risk of losing hold of the personalisation that makes recognition such a powerful weapon of mass motivation. Simple basic acts of kindness, such as those practised at the Eden Project (see Food, Glorious Food) are often more effective than formulaic approaches.

Diagon Alley – working across divisions

One of the challenges of working horizontally or diagonally in organisations is the ability to make networks work and to share knowledge and skills across functional and geographical distance. Ingentis develops HR software, which facilitates horizontal collaborations and therefore enables innovation within and across disciplines, geography and time. Ingentis software is compatible with SAP, Oracle, PeopleSoft as well as other leading HR systems and visualises the whole organisational structure of a company. It shows organisational units, positions and employees, creating transparency within the company and facilitating collaboration based on knowledge, skills and other criteria.

Deutsche Telekom AG used Ingentis to visualise its 220,000 employees in 50 companies from 29 countries via intranet in an organisational chart. Executives use the software to discuss organisational changes in meetings and presentations. By properly managing big data, enormous amounts of information can be insightfully processed at lightning speed. Furthermore, the simulation tool allows different structural scenarios to be modelled directly (e.g. how will the structure change if positions are created or regrouped in a certain organisational unit?).

Another example is the Danish business conglomerate Maersk. With Ingentis, the company shows the information of over 60,000 employees in 130 countries in their intranet, enabling them to better connect and collaborate with like-minded and dissimilar people. This functionality is also extended beyond the company via links with external profiles on social platforms like LinkedIn.

Michael Grimm, Managing Director Ingentis, www.ingentis.com

Food, glorious food

Tim Smit, CEO of the Eden Project asks his people to prepare a meal for 20 of their co-workers on a yearly basis, for the joy of joining in and widening their work experience. It's something I also used to do many years ago whilst leading scientific Research and Development teams. I would cook a ten-course Chinese meal, we would play games and music into the evening, learning much more about each other than would be possible in a meeting at work.

Financing innovation

Does more investment equate to more innovation and creativity? In surveys of spending on Research and Development, the UK has consistently shown low ratios of spending compared to other large industrialised countries, yet it continues to score highly on surveys of innovation, ranking second in the world in the 2014 Global Innovation Index. Is success in innovation more to do with what you do with your R&D investment rather than the actual size of that investment?

Funding innovation at Dyson

James Dyson has some views on what the UK should do to encourage entrepreneurs and retain share ownership and intellectual property within the individuals and companies that create the initial value:

At Dyson we spend £3 million a week on research and development. Dyson is a family business, and remains privately owned. This means we can reinvest profits into new research and technology. When it comes to intellectual property I have always been clear. Patents are essential in protecting your ideas. Without a patent, there is no point in developing the technology; especially if you have global ambitions.

If the UK is truly going to be a world leading developer of high-end technology, it needs to strengthen its intellectual property laws further.

Whereas ideas cost very little, successful innovation often costs a lot. The entrepreneur needs to be capable of securing the relevant financial resources at the right time. The onus is partly on the individual to understand the networks within the enterprise and to be able to package ideas in ways that are appealing to those who have access to financial resources. It is also incumbent on those who control financial resources to have a better understanding of the creative process such that they can make better decisions in this area. The example of Space Synapse in Chapter 5 is instructive here in terms of working with monolith-funding bodies. Here are some things that governments can do to support innovation:

If you want to breed whales, encourage minnows – As I write, there have been a number of scandals about how the UK Government allows large corporations to pay virtually no tax. At the other end of the scale, there is precious little encouragement for entrepreneurs to start businesses. This needs to be rebalanced to encourage smaller enterprises. However, more focus needs to be placed on supporting winners.

Let a thousand flowers bloom, but water high-growth enterprises – Some radical innovation comes from start-ups. So, if we want more innovation we need more start-ups. That said, the ratio of start-ups to successful businesses is reckoned to be around just 10% with only 35% of start-ups surviving after five years in the USA. The success rates of first-time entrepreneurs are just around 20% and only rise to around 30% with seasoned entrepreneurs. Small businesses are overburdened by administration from governments. Reducing taxation for the first few years when growth is critical may help reduce failure rates. In the UK, there is also a trend of intellectual property loss from companies selling out to larger concerns. It is an unusual situation supported by company law on ownership and contributes to a net loss of ownership of such companies. Companies such as Dyson and Virgin are the exception due to their private ownership. It is something that needs to be reviewed.

Get the balance right – There is a balance to be struck between the private and public sector if prosperity is to be maintained. The public sector in the UK has continued to grow through the recession, from 5.4 to 6.4 million people in the last 20 years or so. The public sector has also increased its level of debt by approximately four times in this period. We need a vibrant public sector but one that is as small as possible and no smaller, if enterprise is to flourish and not be stifled by the weight of non-value-adding red tape. We simply cannot afford to run an economy based on tanning rooms, coffee shops, fast food joints and ever-growing levels of public services without an equivalent economy that provides the income to afford such things.

Encourage procurement from smaller companies – The recycling system from large corporations to smaller enterprise is an engine of innovation. If larger enterprises enabled procurement from smaller companies then that would channel some much-needed business to this sector and help it to grow.

Information, big data and innovation

Creating, disseminating and embodying information, both tacit and explicit, is a key strategic resource to be leveraged in the information age. The conversion of data to information, knowledge and wisdom offers a key to organisational learning and sustainable competitive advantage for BBEs. As I write, it seems that Tesco did not manage to convert the petabytes of big data that they have on customer behaviour into enough information, knowledge and wisdom to head off their recent decline in fortunes. Clearly the possession of data is one thing; using it is quite another.

James March and Herbert Simon (1958) predicted the dilemmas associated with information management in their seminal book *Organisations* some 50 years ago. They could not have possibly foreseen the exponential growth in information that we have experienced in the last 20 years. In the book they proposed that people in business would make rational choices if all the relevant information was available to them, but:

> If the rational man lacked information, he might have chosen differently if he had only known. At best, he is "subjectively"

rational, not "objectively" rational. But the notion of objective rationality assumes there is some objective reality in which the "real" alternatives, the "real" consequences, and the "real"utilities exist.

March and Simon, 1958

March and Simon proposed the concept of 'bounded rationality', where, consciously or otherwise, people make decisions based on the information available at the time. This leads to the idea that optimising is replaced by satisficing, where a good enough decision is preferred over the optimum decision. When there is more information than most people can reasonably use, a key role of managing information is the conversion of key data and information into knowledge and wisdom that will guide and inform decision making. Advances in our ability to handle data will, of course, help us to process larger amounts of it, yet it is better to 'swim with information' than to 'drown in data'. In Tesco's case, it was argued that their failure to spot warning signs of the need for change arose from the fact that their data set does not include insights on consumer decisions outside their Tesco shopping experience. Simply stated, incomplete data fits March and Simon's concept of bounded rationality rather well, using the old adage 'garbage in, garbage out'.

Roberto Ascione, CEO of Healthware International, has a passion to deliver faster, better information to help us live fitter, happier and more fulfilled lives. I asked Roberto for his thoughts on swimming with information rather than drowning in data within healthcare:

> We live in an 'I want it all, I want it now' society. But the amount of data has grown exponentially and we would collapse under petabytes of data if we actually tried to consume it all. Instead people need good quality information to make informed decisions about health and that's what we specialise in: a sort of individual data-driven health story which, by boosting true understanding, will promote better health outcomes for everyone.

Roberto alludes to the power of storytelling to convey complex information in a connected world of information overload. In this case, accurate and transparent stories, built on detailed data, knowledge and information rather than fairy tales.

Other important issues surrounding information are about who has it, how accurate it is and how current it is. Information depreciates in ways that other resources do not. The half-life of certain types of information can be incredibly short. If leaders keep information to themselves, as if stored in a battery, the value of that information may be zero by the time it reaches the people who are in a position to use it. In a Brain Based Enterprise, information must be distributed to those that need it in a timely fashion, as if via a 'National Information Grid'. People must then find strategies to handle information overload. This is a subject we will explore along with other practical leadership and management strategies on the associated book website.

Deliberate practice – encouraging innovation

Set up a dialogue with your HR or business directors on some of the following topics: How can you design reward and recognition strategies for individuals that are appropriate to their motivational strategies? What opportunities are there for allowing individuals to develop outside their specialism? How much time is set aside for speculative projects with no obvious immediate payback?

Reflections

Sometimes the best strategy is to buy the talent you need from the marketplace rather than attempting to develop it within the enterprise.

Developing people for innovation and creativity may not always involve training in innovative thinking and creative problem-solving techniques, but confidence to stand out from the crowd is required. Importing requisite diversity is one strategy; using catalysts is another and development the third.

It is possible to teach innovation and creativity but it mostly requires experiential learning (learning by doing) rather than just acquiring essential knowledge and the 'sheet music' of innovation and creativity.

The climate for innovation and creativity is more important than most businesses realise. A crucial role for leaders is the setting up of a climate where innovation and creativity are business as usual aspects of corporate life. Unlike culture, climate may be readily changed and the curation of a climate for innovation and creativity is a function of leadership.

If collaboration and learning across functions is to take place then trust is the underlying software of collaboration.

Information and knowledge management systems have been mostly designed for a 'vertical information age'. They need to be redesigned for an age in which innovation comes from combining ideas from different disciplines. This shift from 90-degree data management to 360-degree knowledge management will, in some cases, require a fundamental system redesign.

Chapter 10

Becoming a true learning enterprise

Changing change management

As long ago as 500 BC, the Greek philosopher Heraclitus was thought to have said: there is nothing permanent except change. Now, of course, we believe that change is a new phenomenon. There is also a tendency to believe that change in a VUCA environment does not require planning and that the best we can have is some kind of 'free improvisational approach to change'. This comes out of a fundamental misunderstanding of what improvisation is in my long experience as a facilitator of complex changes and as an improvising musician. The vast majority of people who are skilled improvisers are, in fact, able to do so due to extensive practice. What is perceived as improvisation is mostly 'prepared spontaneity' based on a lot of deliberate practice. Talking to Sheila E confirms the importance of preparation in improvisation. Sheila was Prince's drummer and musical director, and has worked with Stevie Wonder, Lionel Ritchie, Beyoncé and many world-class musicians. Skills of anticipation, being decisive in uncertain situations and staying effective when faced with complexity and ambiguity are the key skills of such people. Paradoxically, complexity and uncertainty in business also requires good preparation and skills in managing the unknown and the unknowable. Improvisation is a core skill for change mastery and this includes what we have described as emotional intelligence to sense and respond.

Experience is a double-edged sword in change management. It can ossify, which is why some people say 'You can't teach an old dog new tricks'. In the hands of masters, experience gives people a wider repertoire to improvise from, such as the example of Sir Richard Branson, who looks at business opportunities with a fresh pair of eyes every time. This is the hallmark of a master craftsman in the business of change.

There is no need whatsoever for older entrepreneurs not to try new things. In fact, those of us who have a fair few years behind us are often in an even better position, as we have made more mistakes to learn from!

Sir Richard Branson

There is also a movement of people trying to convince us that there has been some kind of genetic change with so-called 'Millennials', who crave change and who reject organisation and stability. Our biology has not changed over 20 years. What has changed is the amount of 'thin slicing' of our lives, as our days are interrupted by phones, e-mails, social media and so on. This might reduce the amount of time we actually have to spend on everything, but it does not come down to genetics per se. Many people now operate within portfolio careers that require them to constantly update their knowledge and skills. However, it seems that Millennials would like to have many of the same outcomes from the thing we call work as Generation X and Baby Boomers. Crucially, they look towards authenticity, competence and excellent communication skills in their leaders. Like all of us, they expect to be informed and consulted about change, perhaps even more so than their parents, so that they can align their contributions towards changing goals.

To become changemasters, we must learn what Peter Senge (1990) calls personal mastery. This is learning to expand our personal capacity to create the results we most desire, and creating an organisational environment which encourages all its members to develop themselves towards the goals and purposes they choose. Mastery is often connected with an unconscious competence in a given field. Excellent performers in the field of music and the arts are often 'magical' in their approach. In some cases, they are unconsciously competent and thus make poor teachers of their subject. The concept of 'flow' is a relevant parallel here. What then can we learn about change in a complex and changing world?

Virgins and a VUCA world – Planning for uncertainty

I asked Sir Richard Branson about strategy for a VUCA world. When entering an unfamiliar business area, how does he set about grappling with the unknowns and unknowables? How did Richard apply himself to this when entering mobile telecoms and space travel?

Entering an industry as an outsider can come with both pros and cons, this was immediately apparent when we founded Virgin Atlantic. On the one hand it was a great bonus; coming from the music industry the one thing we were pretty confident about was that we knew how to entertain people. We'd give musicians or magicians free tickets on our flights if they would entertain passengers; we pioneered in-flight entertainment options and created lounges for our customers to use before boarding their flight. We had a fresh perspective and didn't approach tasks with pre-conceived ideas about what an airline should and shouldn't be doing.

This outsider's perspective would only take us so far, however. To pass the tests, gain our licence and earn the trust of new flyers we needed some strong industry knowledge. This started by hiring the right people with proven track records. The mentorship of someone who had been there and done it before, Sir Freddie Laker, was a great positive influence over the airline's early days. Having founded his own airline, he gave us a lot of vital advice and ensured we didn't make unnecessary mistakes. When stepping into a new industry there will always be a degree of risk involved, try and reduce that by seeking out the right advice.

The mathematics of change

Preparation is the mother of success

Over many years I have found great utility and value in this simple 'formula' devised by David Gleicher whilst he was working at Arthur D. Little in the 1960s. This was subsequently written up by Richard Beckhard in his book *Organisation Transitions*. This identifies the pre-requisites for successful change, given that most success in change is all down to thorough preparation. Gleicher originally stated that, for change to occur, the drive for change must be more potent than the 'costs' of change. I have placed my own emphasis on Gleicher's original construct based on our experiences in helping companies address change.

$$CT \times V \times F > C^3$$

CT = the level of creative tension (*dissatisfaction*) with the present situation.

V = a *shared*, potent and *desirable vision* of the future situation.

F = the awareness of some *actionable first steps*.

C = the '*cost*' of change, *emotionally* as well as *practically*.

If you ascribe mathematical values to each element it becomes apparent that change will not occur if any of the elements in the left hand side of the equation has a value of zero. I do not advocate getting overly hung up on the 'maths' of the formula. What matters most are the deductions you can make from a cursory glance at the change dynamics:

If the level of creative tension (CT) is low, the challenge becomes how to increase the level of leverage associated with the present situation. The creation of a sense of urgency is a function of creative leadership; this is most difficult to do when the enterprise is not in crisis. Beware the danger of 'manufacturing a burning platform' to achieve change when there is none. Trying to manufacture a crisis to lever change can be fraught with difficulty as it challenges the authenticity of a leader which kills any sense of trust required to make change happen. Yet, one of the paradoxes of change is how to get change to occur when there is no crisis.

My adaptation of Gleicher's formula indicates the need for a *shared, potent* and *desirable* vision (V). This is a function of great participation and engagement with the strategic thinking process. Many of the creative techniques we have discussed in this book can be used to develop powerful visions, which then overcome the need and dangers of manufacturing a crisis.

If the awareness of actionable first steps (F) is low, this points towards the need to increase the awareness of actionable first steps in change. This requires the use of a range of participation and engagement strategies to move people beyond compliance to commitment. If the cost of change (C) is high then the need is to lower the threshold 'cost' of changing. This is creative transition and typically involves coaching, facilitation and other approaches that allow people to make sense of change so that they may let go without critical losses.

Importantly, if any of the elements is missing, change will be difficult or can even fail. It is always worth passing your change through the formula to give you some foresight on where most attention is needed. Many change strategies use 'pain' as the primary lever or what is often called 'the burning platform'. What is genuinely difficult in change management is to gain momentum for change when there is no burning platform, using 'gain' as a lever for change and what Peter Senge (1990) calls 'creative tension'.

Deliberate practice – scanning the future

1. Apply Gleicher's formula to a change you are intending to undertake. You may care to ascribe scores from 1-10 for each element of the formula to give you a semi-quantitative index for the likelihood of successful change:

$$CT \times V \times F > C^3$$

2. What do you learn from your application? What will you do about it?

The biology of change

Just as a biological immune system will destroy a life saving skin graft with the same vigor with which it fights pneumonia, so will a cultural immune system fight off a beneficial new kind of understanding with the same vigor it uses to destroy crime.

Robert M. Pirsig, author of *Zen and The Art of Motorcycle Maintenance*, 1999

Change management strategies fit along a continuum from 'hard' to 'soft' approaches, although hard does not mean difficult and soft is not a soft option. At the 'hard' end, we have approaches such as Business Process Re-engineering (BPR) and Project Management. These methods work well when we are dealing with change that is purely mechanical in nature and where clear goals can be established in advance. These methods do not fare as well when there are many complicated 'wicked' people issues involved and where change requires some experimentation in order to even discover the goal. This accounts for some of the grand failures of BPR in the 1990s where it was inappropriately used in an attempt to tame truly wicked organisational problems.

At the other end of the continuum, we have approaches such as Systems Thinking and Organisational Development (OD). It is OD that offers the greatest possibility of success for VUCA-shaped organisational issues, offering a more biological approach to the topic than hard approaches. We examine the art and discipline of OD here for those leadership issues that do not lend themselves to a spreadsheet or other linear approaches to change.

Organisation development

The Greek writer Sophocles (497–406 BC) wisely pointed out that a mature thought will have a different outcome from a thought which is hasty. So it is true with the business of change that wisdom outlasts a surface approach. The Organisation Development (OD) approach assumes that a deep engagement with the head, heart and soul of the company is required over an extended time period if change is to occur. OD has its underlying roots in the fields of psychology, sociology, political science and anthropology. In a world that demands rapid change, OD may seem like a rather unpopular approach to change, due to its emphasis on diagnosis, full involvement of people in the proposed change and some uncertainty of outcomes at the outset. It may be slower and more emergent in nature but it is more effective and less costly than much of what passes for change management in the long run. OD typically uses external change agents – these do not necessarily have to be outside the company, but are people who can act independently, especially when group or whole organisation norms must be challenged. We can visualise OD as an interactive and iterative cycle:

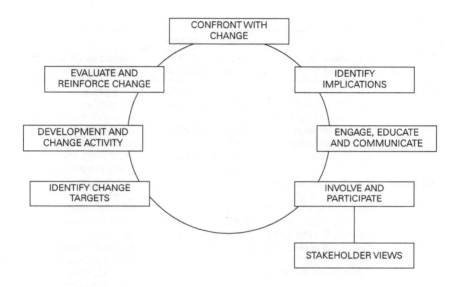

This cycle translates into a number of alternative OD strategies, depending on the level of need and the depth of change required:

Level of change	Depth of change		
	Behaviour (what is happening?)	Structure (what system is needed?)	Context (what is the setting?)
Enterprise	Poor morale, corrosive rather than creative tension, conspiracy theories, poor market focus. **Options: Survey feedback, benchmarking.**	Wrong goals; Wrong or misunderstood strategy; Wrong structure for purpose; Lack of external measurement systems. **Options: Change structure.**	Wrong place; Wrong market; Wrong people; Wrong technology; Wrong time. **Options: Change strategy, location, layout; change culture, liquidate the business.**
Inter-group	Poor co-operation, unhealthy conflict, unresolved feelings. **Options: Inter-group confrontation, role clarification and negotiation.**	Silo-based approaches to projects, interactions difficult. **Options: Redefine responsibilities, change reporting relationships, boundary crossers.**	Different sub-unit values, lifestyle, physical distance. **Options: Reduce mental and physical distance, job swaps, improve social interaction.**

(*Continued*)

Continued

Level of change	Depth of change		
	Behaviour (what is happening?)	Structure (what system is needed?)	Context (what is the setting?)
Group	Poor relationships, climate, commitment, poor leadership style. **Options: Process consultation, team development.**	Poor task and role definitions, leader's role overloaded. **Options: Redesign work or jobs, autonomous team working.**	Poor group composition, environment, resources, personality clashes. **Options: Change technology, layout, group composition.**
Individual	Poor fit of individual with goals, poor response to change, no learning opportunities. **Options: Coaching and career counselling, job design, career development strategies.**	Poor job definition, tasks too easy or too difficult. **Options: Job redesign, management by objectives.**	Poor selection, promotion and training, mismatch between rewards and objectives. **Options: Change 'raw materials', improve training, align incentives with performance.**

Assumptions

- OD is a humanistic approach to change. It assumes that people will become self-directed given the chance and a suitable structure in which they can respond.
- OD assumes that companies tend to suppress individual beliefs and values through their need to act as a single unit.
- OD assumes that win–lose conflict is unhelpful to the longer-term aims of the company and needs to be seen in terms of poor organisational design.

Strengths

- OD is perhaps the most inclusive approach to change as it attempts to involve all stakeholders, leading to long-term alignment.
- OD is a 'homeopathic' approach to change. It focuses more on the 'whole system' and may use low-level change to leverage larger effects in the company.
- OD takes account of political realities, which means that change, once agreed upon, is implemented more completely and rapidly.

Potential pitfalls

- That participation will lead to productive change. This is valid if the change is perceived as beneficial both rationally and emotionally, but is more unlikely to occur if the proposed changes are akin to 'Turkeys@Christmas'.
- It can take time to reach the required consensus to profit from speed and commitment in implementation.
- That more participation leads to improved decision making. In some cases it does lead to fudged decisions and low-level compromises. I've seen this happen a lot in public sector enterprises, although this is often due to political factors within such organisations and through external interference.

Minimising pitfalls

- Be clear that involvement and leadership are not always synonymous.
- Recognise that OD is a long haul rather than a quick fix and resource it appropriately, such as our examples of Nokia and FujiFilm Systems coming up.

OD not Oh Dear – The Wisdom of Change

I advocate a three-stage approach that seeks to understand and prepare for change before going into a design phase and only then implementing change. It is not such a clean process as the idea of three discrete stages would suggest, with many iterations and the need for improvisation and creativity to address unknown or un-knowable elements. Nonetheless, it helps to have a guide when fog walking.

Diagnosis

Fog walking – Whilst VUCA changes are essentially unknowable in advance, there is still a need to identify a destination for your change if people are to engage with it. If that is too difficult then at least identify intermediate destinations. Major change is often an untidy process and it is not possible to know at the start how it will turn out. Yet it is nearly always a mistake to think that you can make it up as you go along. It is not how serious improvisers in the arts generally operate and it is therefore a bad model to adopt in business. In such circumstances it is essential to establish means by which the top team can learn, adapt and respond continuously.

Meaningful measurement – Even if hard metrics are difficult to come by, it still matters that you set down some markers for where the business is currently and some ideas of how things will be different when changes have occurred, if only so that people can track progress. We have already discussed the need to choose measures that are meaningful rather than those which are convenient or easy.

Create positive not negative tension – Plan to create the conditions where change is possible. This may mean building an understanding of a desirable future before trying to dismantle what is currently in place. Change also requires people to feel that old ways are out of synch with future needs. Leaders must create positive tension with the status quo if there is no crisis to manage.

Develop change champions – If your change is to affect larger numbers of people, you will need to identify and later on mobilise and support a cadre of change champions. These people typically have wide networks, are regarded as opinion formers and therefore can engage the early majority, late majority and laggards in terms of the adoption curve from Chapter 6. They may not necessarily be from the 'innovator' group for the reasons we explored earlier.

Understand resistance – Diagnose resistance to change using the range of strategies identified by Kotter and Schlesinger, ranging from consultation to coercion, dependent on the circumstances and the stakes involved. Coercion sounds like a 'hot' word, yet in a turnaround situation, it may be one of the most effective ways to secure the enterprise's future. Participation may breed commitment but it takes longer than some of the methods on the right hand side of the grid. The key point is to use no more directive leadership than the stakes and context demand, as we explored in Chapter 3 under the issue of power.

Paradoxically, this often means getting those who are actively blocking change on board as well as the 'supporters club'. Anyone who has an

Strategy for handling resistance	Education and communication	Participation and involvement	Facilitation and support	Negotiation and agreement	Manipulation and co-option	Explicit and implicit coercion
Strengths	Offer the greatest chance of gaining active commitment and follow through			Can be fast and secure compliant behaviour in terms of change		
Weaknesses	May take longer than you have in critical turnaround situations			My leave people feeling disengaged and therefore store up problems for future change projects		

opinion is worth mobilising, whether it is positive or negative. By far the hardest group of people to activate are the 'indifferent majority'. Often these people make their decision when they see how the other groups react. Importantly, if they see that dissent is crushed, they may remain on the sidelines of change.

Design

Time and timing – Be clear on the timescale. It is inappropriate to have a full employee involvement programme in a business that is rapidly going to the wall. Conversely, it is often inappropriate to introduce change faster than it needs to be done in a 'steady state' operation.

Be a systemic thinker – Consider the impact of the change on the total system. Changes in one unit will usually affect other parts of the business.

Choose entry points – Decide whether you will adopt a Top-down, Bottom-up or Sideways-in strategy. Many changes use elements of all three designs, e.g. the strategic vision of change may be created at the apex of the enterprise (Quadrant 3 of our uncertainty grid), with some involvement from key players, with a bottom-up approach to deciding exactly how the strategy will be implemented (Quadrant 2).

Implementation

Preparation, preparation, preparation – Loosen up the business for change. Kurt Lewin described the process of change as a three-stage metaphor of unfreezing, changing and refreezing, as if you are changing

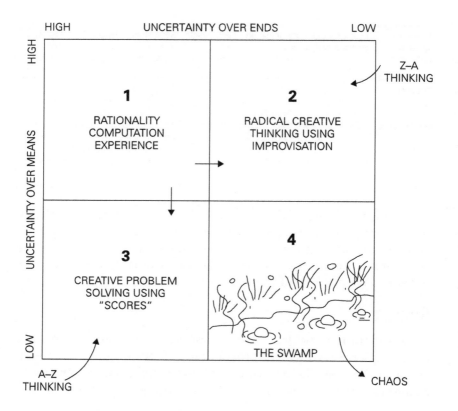

the shape of some ice from your freezer. Arguably refreezing rarely goes to full completion in an age of continuous change and leaders may try to hold enterprises in a state of fluidity and flux. Nonetheless, employees need to have some stability in order to give their best. Too much 'unfinished business' in an enterprise leaves a residue in terms of the energy that can be directed towards the future.

Apply energy – General Motors former CEO Jack Welch says the number one thing that leaders need is energy. Energy when things are good and especially when they are bad. Work hard at it! The people who have carefully designed the change process may not always be the best individuals to generate the energy required to implement the change. Mobilise your change champions and provide forums for keeping their motivation and commitment.

Communication, communication, communication – Spot early signifiers of change that are consistent with longer-term goals and reward and recognise them. Set up systems to assist with the management of ambiguity. These may include forums to enable people to make sense of chaos and paradoxes as 'the new' clashes with 'the old'.

Iterate – Solve new problems as they occur. New issues will probably arise as the change comes to the implementation stage and it is unlikely you will have captured it all on a project plan or spreadsheet. It is important to build in the capability of reacting to these issues into any plans. A process for listening to people's concerns and responding positively to them should be explicitly established. Nokia is a good example of a company that is working on change in a VUCA business environment. We visit Finland next.

Perpetual change at Nokia

Nokia's story is one of perpetual change from timber to telecoms, starting in 1865 when mining engineer Fredrik Idestam set up his first wood pulp mill in Finland. In its history Nokia has made rubber boots, tires, telephone and power cables . . . and indestructible phones.

Nokia did not see the arrival of the iPhone to its ultimate decline and sale to Microsoft, which just goes to show how strategic reconnaissance is necessary even in the world's greatest companies. Nokia has now started a journey to transform its business once again. Joel Casse, Global Head of Leadership Development takes up the story.

Nokia sets about developing leaders that learn and thrive under conditions of uncertainty. Nokia leaders see their role more as people who support and challenge their teams. This is different from command and control. We expect leaders to strike a balance between shaping the content and shaping the context. Their role, with input from the team, is to make sense of their business context.

Nokia leaders are expected to engage, listen to and take on ideas and perspectives from their teams. This is in keeping with the nature of the workforce who value being connected through a variety of internal and external social media; who want to be engaged and involved; who are informed and have access to data; and who are educated and want to grow. In short this is very much in keeping with the idea of a Brain Based Enterprise.

To enhance our leaders' tolerance of a **V**olatile, **U**ncertain, **C**omplex and **A**mbiguous (VUCA) business environment we invite lecturers to our corporate programmes that engage our leaders' thinking about how technologies disrupt; how we conduct business; and how we lead. We bring in speakers who challenge our leaders' thinking to go beyond expert intuition – characterised by quick, snap judgments based on familiarity of situations – to strategic intuition characterised by leaders who are open to diversity and different perspectives and who can connect the dots from disparate parts.

Developing leaders

Our communication about change with leaders uses the 5W's and H approach, especially:

- **Why** leadership needs to change. We need to ground change with scientific observations on Nokia's business environment.
- **What** the new leadership looks like, i.e. Nokia's new leadership model.

For example, in recruitment all leaders and HR consultants are expected to use the leadership framework in behavioural-based interviews. The leadership model is also used to make decisions on promotions, successions and development planning. We also review management systems like span of controls to identify what might hinder a leader from effectively taking the time to develop people.

- **How** to role-model the new leadership. This outlines how we exemplify Nokia's new way to lead in some simple and practical behaviours. For example we hold regular 1 in 90 discussions, which are quarterly performance and development dialogues with team members. Another example is the Rule of 3, where leaders strive to keep topics, decisions, inputs to a maximum of three things to focus everyone's attention to lead with more clarity.

Nick Obolensky, designer of the change programme and author of *Complex Adaptive Leadership* (2014) observes:

> The programme focused on middle managers who have a crucial role in working across the enterprise, which is where much value

creation occurs. Co-coaching was used to multiply the effect and impact of 1:1 coaching on performance across Nokia. Reflective practice is now a core element of individual and organisational learning. Leaders spend five minutes reflection every day and ten minutes every week on how to apply what has been learned into the next two weeks. This micro routine aligns well with Dr Daniel Levitin's work on neuroscience and pays enormous dividends.

Nick Obolensky, personal interview

Early impact

It is early days in terms of a full evaluation of the impact of the programme. Yet there are some early signs of change:

- We start to see leaders who are proud about being a leader at Nokia. For instance, we have held talk-show-like meetings where about 1,000 leaders have joined to hear leaders talk about how they apply the new way to lead.
- Our most senior teams have completed the new 360-degree leadership assessment. These leaders have become loyal advocates of the new way to lead and are now promoting the benefits of the 360-degree method and ensuing development plans.
- Leaders make time to conduct 1:1 discussions with team members to discuss objectives, development, and well-being.
- The senior executive team has dedicated time to discuss as a team what commitments they will make to showcase the new leadership mindset.

Breaking barriers

We identified some barriers to developing leadership that responds to VUCA environments. Nokia seeks to achieve a balance between developing leaders that drive value creation and that are talented in leading change:

1. Leaders struggle to let go control as they still see their role to be in the operational side and to get results. This is no surprise. Historically businesses have always rewarded and indeed recruited people for their IQ and for their ability to drive results NOT for engaging with people nor their ability to suggest, push and lead change. This is why at Nokia we expect leaders to empower people, to let go of the doing and take on a coach or sponsor role rather than a show and tell role.

This way we also make sure that learning about how to deal with change takes place across the organisation.

2. Leaders tend to become experts in their fields – they know the answers, draw on their past experience and try to repeat and apply what has worked for them in the past. Clearly with technology propelling change, leaders need to learn to try new things and learn from others. Recognising this, we have specifically included in our leadership framework such competencies as creativity, dealing with ambiguity, and innovation management. Another concrete example how we help leaders step out of their comfort zone and make them painfully aware of the change taking place around us is through our recent #Maketechhuman dialogue.

3. The systems and processes (like levels of approvals, gates, steering groups, etc.) which have served well the authoritative leadership styles will get in the way of supportive and challenging leadership which aims for innovation and value creation. Nokia has identified that too many levels of approvals are going counter to our aim to increase empowerment. We have also revamped our performance and talent management system by eliminating labels (e.g. improvement required or valued) and distribution curve, so that leaders can own the results and be more engaged in the development of their employees.

If change is continuous, then the organisation must learn continuously. What then does a true learning organisation think, look and feel like?

Anatomy of learning organisations

Learning organisations are organisations where people continually expand their capacity to create the results they truly desire, where new and expansive patterns of thinking are nurtured, where collective aspirations are set free and where people are continually learning how to learn together.

Peter Senge, 1990

Learning organisations are good at change. They are resilient and antifragile – that is they get stronger when shocked by disorder and environmental change. More importantly they are good at change when there is no burning platform, thus they stay ahead of the pack. I recall having a conversation with one of Pfizer's senior directors some years back, who was preening after they were rated the number one pharmaceutical company. I warned that the danger with being number one is that complacency can set in and there is only one way down, a prophecy that unfortunately came true. True learning organisations manage to adapt and learn even when there is no obvious need to do so. My model uses the well-known 4W's and H creativity checklist to define the essentials:

What – This concerns the level of learning. Single loop or **adaptive** learning is concerned with avoiding mistakes and is the realm of continuous improvement in most enterprises. Double loop learning is called **generative** learning and is concerned with challenging assumptions and attitudes in order to change underlying behaviours. Triple loop learning or **transformative** learning is concerned with the 'why' of learning (i.e. a fundamental change in mind-set or paradigm to create new meanings). Continuous improvement is essential as a rite of passage for any good organisation, but it is insufficient to achieve greatness. Fundamental organisational change is mostly concerned with generative and transformative learning. Increasingly the role of the change catalyst is to help enterprises become more aware of the unconscious assumptions that support everyday behaviour such that people can create new business models. It is an essential role for most organisations these days as 'the last thing a fish notices is the water it swims in'.

Who – A learning organisation means exactly what it says. It is not a lot of individuals attending training courses as some people think, but individual learning may play a part. Learning organisations learn at the group, inter-group, enterprise and extra-enterprise level of the OD matrix. Enterprise-wide learning is more difficult than the individual level and some observers argue that enterprises cannot learn. I do not agree. It really depends on leadership to set the conditions in place for collective learning, in other words the culture, structure, skills and resources we have discussed earlier. The degree to which individuals and the whole enterprise learn is a function of careful selection and great leadership.

Where – Learning organisations undertake what I call '360-degree learning'. Inside the enterprise, from the market, from customers, even competitors. It is what Peter Senge and Robert Fritz call 'systems thinking' and requires the ability to think across and beyond the boundary of the enterprise as a system of interconnected components. Learning organisations are not frightened to learn from the light or the darkness. In other words when things go wrong, this is one of the most important places where learning can occur. Metro Bank is a prime example as they make a habit of learning from customer complaints when others prefer to ignore them.

When – Learning organisations learn when they least expect or need to learn. This means that enterprises must make space for accidental learning as well as deliberate learning. W.L. Gore's approach to bootlegging time is one such approach to making space for accidental learning. A learning diet for a learning organisation should include learning about today, tomorrow and the longer now. Somewhat strangely, it must also include learning from history, since that is where most of the avoidable mistakes are buried. I have spent a lot of my life helping enterprises unearth priceless gems from failed projects that have been buried, in order to save face or protect the egos of a few people who would rather erase the project from the enterprise's memory.

How – Far too many conversations turn towards training as soon as the word learning is mentioned, yet a training course is just one of the huge multiplicity of ways to learn. Depending on whether our need is to learn knowledge, skills or attitudes, a veritable feast of learning methods exist:

- **Knowledge** – Books, the Internet, online learning programs – more or less any electronic media. We have left the age where knowledge needs to be taught by teachers and entered the age where we need to learn how to assimilate vast quantities of data and information and convert it to knowledge and wisdom. This is an invaluable skill for the twenty-first century.
- **Skills** – Skills tend to need to be practised rather than just internalised; for this reason, there remains a need to actively experience skill development. Imagine trying to learn to type without a keyboard or learning to ride a bike by only reading a book. Some skills may be learned online now and there is a place for learning skills by seeing how others approach them (e.g. using video case studies). However,

for certain soft skills, there is no substitute for direct experience, sometimes in safe conditions, sometimes in live situations, to learn.

- **Attitudes and values** – Whilst education can affect your attitudes and values, this is mostly an experiential art form. Coaching and mentoring can help when the subject is receptive and willing to learn. We have also explored this topic in Chapters 3 and 9.

Learning from colleagues, customers and competitors

Companies and markets inevitably copy one another's strategies and practices through competitive intelligence, employee churn and so on. 'Theft' is a valid strategy for benchmarking or 'keeping up with the Joneses'. However, keeping up is rarely a sustainable source of advantage. It is the business strategy equivalent of 'copy and paste'. Talking with John Etheridge from Soft Machine, a virtuoso guitar player who has worked with Stephane Grappelli, John Williams and Nigel Kennedy, brings this into sharp focus. Etheridge points out that many of the great guitar players did not have formal lessons and this meant that they introduced elements into their playing that were formally 'wrong'. Examples include Jeff Beck, who developed a unique way of using his right hand that owes nothing to guitar teaching manuals, Jimi Hendrix and jazz virtuoso Joe Pass. This 'wrongness' gives these players a unique 'signature' that has given them longevity and sustainability compared with people that fit into a 'copy and paste template model'.

So, theft in all walks of life does not always lead to greatness. In business, idea theft is particularly problematic, due to the requirement for ideas to fit into the 'host' organisation. Most organisations are complex adaptive systems. This is rather like the need to consider the host when conducting an organ transplant if rejection is to be avoided. Tom Peters' notion of 'creative swiping' in business is a much better strategy than theft. Creative swiping often means learning from multiple sources and, more importantly adapting the ideas to best-fit your own situation. This minimises the risk of rejection and gives ideas your own unique treatment for longer-term value.

For many years the Rover Group outperformed all of its competitors in the automotive sector, eventually falling into decline due to macro-economic factors in the British economy. Yet the story of what gave them a source of competitive advantage over an extended period is worth repeating. Part of their success was due to taking creative swiping across business units very seriously. Rover pioneered horizontal collaboration across geographical and functional boundaries. They linked this to a scheme, which rewarded innovation from creative swiping. Unusually, both the originator of an idea and the 'thief' were rewarded for demonstrating the adaptation and application of ideas in different settings, which was a key to the success of the scheme. All the above was pursued within the business as a whole rather than as a fad in a single unit. Rover also attributed their success to the fact that they did not switch business fads week to week and stuck to a few principles over an extended period. This is a valuable and durable piece of learning in itself and is just as relevant now as it was then. Fad surfing rarely succeeds in business although there is a lot of it about.

Another well-trodden approach to learning is the use of employee suggestion schemes to encourage learning from colleagues, customers and competitors. BASF implemented more than 23,000 suggestions in 2014 which generated £38 million. BASF has embedded a culture of suggesting ideas over many decades such that it has become part of the culture. The economics are heavily in favour of employee suggestion schemes, although they must be installed properly as they can just as easily damage engagement. This approach extends beyond the boundary of the enterprise through 'open innovation'. Both BASF and GSK post lists of wants and needs to encourage potential collaborators to connect with them. Essentially this is beyond 'level 5' of Rothwell's model which we explored in Chapter 6.

Unlearning hurts

The standard railway gauge is four feet eight and a half inches and approximately 60% of the world's railways are built to this gauge. Legend has it that this was itself influenced by the tools used to make wagons that used the same wheel spacing, which was influenced by the existing ruts in the road. Allegedly, the initial ruts were made by Roman war chariots. The Romans built their wagons to accommodate two horses, which equated to approximately five feet. If legend can be trusted, it could be said that the modern railway gauge was determined by the Roman Empire. The moral of this story is that old habits die hard. Nassim Nicholas Taleb points out in *Antifragile* that it has also taken us a similar amount of time to realise that suitcases could have wheels put on them.

Unlearning is the process of letting go, adapting or forgetting past beliefs and behaviours that have somehow become inconsistent with current and future needs. Anyone who has tried to give up a habit such as smoking will have an idea of what unlearning is all about. An incredible amount of energy is invested in persuading us that we need to learn and change. Just think of the number of seminars, events and programmes that feature learning in the main title. Rather less time is spent requiring us to forget or adapt out of date habits. For example it is very difficult to book up to attend an 'Unlearning' seminar, where success is measured on the quantity of knowledge, skills and attitudes that attendees are prepared to remove from their curriculum vitae. Furthermore many performance appraisal systems tend still to focus on 'industrial archaeology', reviewing past performance rather than future challenges. As I write, Accenture is getting rid of its annual performance appraisal process for 330,000 employees in favour of project-based learning. General Motors has also announced the elimination of annual appraisals in favour of a continuous feedback culture. At the very least, the balance of appraisals should be 20:80 in favour of looking back:looking forward. Clearly Accenture and GM's approach was based on archaeology. Very few businesses have rituals and systems that ask employees questions such as 'What did you forget today?' or 'What norm did you successfully challenge today?' and so on.

Successful twenty-first century change management has more to do with unlearning rather than learning. Unlearning is considerably harder to achieve in practice, since much of the learning has been internalised as a collective mind-set or paradigm. We visited Johnson and Schole's model of the paradigm in Chapter 7. This illustrates the self-reinforcing nature of these systems and the need for considerable work in changing cultures. We next examine FujiFilm – an enterprise that had to unlearn rapidly whilst doing one of the most difficult things –transforming itself by competing with – and eventually devouring – its existing business.

Business cannibalism

Innovation is hard enough when you are battling with the market, but what happens when you must cannibalise your existing business with no certainty that your new enterprise will succeed? FujiFilm Speciality Ink Systems (see www.FujiFilmsis.co.uk) has roots set firmly in the traditional process of screen printing, a technology that may be linked back as far as the Egyptians. Their products are typically used to generate both small, highly decorated objects (labels, CD containers) and large images, such as posters, vehicle livery etc. FujiFilm took the bold decision to move into the digital print business as an early adopter when all their investment was in screen-printing. Peter Kenehan, MD takes up the story.

It had become apparent that ink jet printing presented a threat to traditional screen-printing. Digital technology obeys Moore's Law rather well and pretty much every 18 months produces a doubling of the output available from the technology. Because of this fast pace of change we think of time in digital R&D in terms of 'dog years' (i.e. one analogue year = seven digital years). In 1999 we set up a small unit inside the existing factory as a 'Skunkworks', to grow a digital business. We mostly took key technical staff from inside the company who were willing and able to make the journey and added commercial expertise and someone who was already working in the ink jet business. Our preferred business model was the 'razor/razor blade' approach, to develop a long-term consumable revenue stream from ink (the blades) but we didn't have access to the delivery system (the razor). We developed a partnership with Inca, who had a breakthrough printer technology without a route to market, whereas we had access to a market with an incipient need for new technology, making this partnership a perfect match. Our business strategy was emergent, learning rapidly from what we did and improving along the way. We explored three business models initially but have ended up concentrating on the first two:

1. Selling printer systems plus ink.
2. Selling ink to companies that made ink jet machines or cartridges.
3. Waiting for a mature market and then supplying replacement ink products.

Within four years the unit was brought back into the mainstream of the business and digital now represents around 95% of our activity.

FujiFilm Speciality Ink Systems – Precision engineering and chemistry

Growing pains

The initial vision was to find a way to market without damaging the existing screen-printing business. It quickly became apparent that we would need to cannibalise the existing business rapidly which generated internal resistance. To add to the difficulty, whilst the new unit was physically separate from the rest of the factory, it was physically co-located within the target for its cannibalism. A lot of people were initially sceptical and expected the unit to fail. This changed when it became apparent that ink jet offered the company a much bigger market place.

X factors

HR director Malcolm Frier points out that it was essential to recruit people into the business who would be resilient and who wanted to go on this uncertain journey. This is essentially a 'buy' rather than 'make' HR strategy. The choice of a leader who was credible, had a reputation, had good networks, was commercial and had a technical background was also critical to success. The development of regional champions was pivotal to moving the business from cottage to industrial scale. Pete points out that the epiphany in the USA was when we installed a demonstration machine in Kansas. Once the US MD saw it he moved instantly from a 'passenger' to a digital champion. This serves to demonstrate that ideas often need to be visualised in order for them to be adopted, especially when the concepts are hard to grasp at a distance.

Failure as a spur to success

Significant technical problems dogged the early days and for 6–9 months a constant problem with one product threatened to put us out of business. We were saved by the mentoring of an experienced senior Japanese FujiFilm manager who insisted on a rigorous approach to root cause analysis rather than constantly repeating the mistake. From this came a mind shift from quality control to quality assurance and a focus on process control that enabled us to successfully make thousands of products from hundreds of raw materials on a 'right first time' basis, making us the envy of the chemical industry.

HR as an enabler

Culturally, it became apparent that some people were unable to make the transition from analogue to digital. Malcolm observes 'We did not succeed at converting some sales people to the new business when the prevailing assumption was that sales people could sell anything'. One of Malcolm's key contributions was to make the decision to keep the focus on people who could embrace digital technology rather than trying to develop multifunctional (analogue and digital) people.

In terms of the standard HR levers, the new unit was treated exactly the same in performance management terms. Constant communication with the main business was key to prevent attack on the fledgling enterprise.

In terms of performance management, the company has worked hard on the development of adaptability using a closer form of 1:1 development which sits alongside people's academic progress. To be in digital requires continuous learning, both academically and pragmatically. To be an effective player in the new FujiFilm, people must be 't-shaped'. We were helped enormously by having corporate owners such as BP and Saratoga Private Equity since they gave the company large amounts of autonomy over an extended period to prove the technology and diffuse it into the market.

Peter Kenehan and Malcolm Frier, FujiFilm Speciality Ink Systems.

Reflections

The enterprise with the most flexibility stands to move fastest and remain resilient and robust in the face of a volatile, uncertain, complex and ambiguous marketplace. The discipline of purposeful improvisation is the core leadership skill to face a VUCA world.

Rapid change requires that people are rapid and creative learners. This is subtly different from people who flit from fad to fad. To do this the skills of emotional intelligence are essential to maintain resilience.

Preparation is everything in change. Our adaptation of the Gleicher formula gives you some foresight on the future before it has happened.

To gain meaningful participation in change, you will need to adopt an Organisation Development (OD) approach to change rather than a piecemeal approach to the subject. Surface approaches to change only affect the surface.

Adaptive learning is necessary but insufficient to keep ahead. Learning companies need to learn at the generative and transformational levels to maintain excellence. Nokia are a good example of a company who are experimenting with complex adaptive leadership.

'Cut and paste' approaches to learning rarely lead to greatness. Change rarely works like a memory stick where you can 'plug and play'. Creative swiping is a more reliable strategy for transferring practices within and across enterprises.

Learning companies must unlearn. Unlearning is harder than learning, but unlearn we must if we are to face new challenges and live more harmoniously with planet earth.

It is much harder to compete with yourself in terms of changing direction internally than facing an external threat. The example of FujiFilm teaches us valuable lessons about business cannibalism.

Bibliography

Adams, Scott, (1996). *The Dilbert Principle*, London: Boxtree.

Adams, Scott, (1999). *The Joy of Work*, New York: Harper Collins.

Argyris, C. and Schön, D., (1974). *Organisational Learning: A Theory of Action Perspective*, Reading, MA: Addison-Wesley.

Ball, Philip, (2009). *Branches*, Oxford: Oxford University Press.

Ball, Philip, (2009). *Flow*, Oxford: Oxford University Press.

Ball, Philip, (2009). *Shapes*, Oxford: Oxford University Press.

Barrett, F.J., (1998). 'Creativity and Improvisation in Jazz and Organizations: Implications for Organizational Learning', *Organization Science*, Vol. 9, No. 5, 605–622.

Bateson, Gregory and Bateson, Mary Catherine, (2004). *Angels Fear: Towards an Epistemology of the Sacred (Advances in Systems Theory, Complexity & the Human Sciences)*, London: Hampton Press.

Beckhard, Richard, (1987). *Organization Transitions*, Boston MA: Addison-Wesley.

Berns, Gregory, (2010). *Iconoclast*, Boston MA: Harvard Business School Press.

Berliner, P.F., (1994). *Thinking in Jazz: The Infinite Art of Improvisation*, Chicago: University of Chicago Press.

Beswick, Cris and Gallagher, David, (2010). *The Road to Innovation*, London: Let's Think Beyond Publishing.

Branson, Richard, (2014). *The Virgin Way*, London: Virgin.

Branson, Richard, (2006). *Screw It, Let's Do It*, London: Virgin.

Brown, Mark, (1988). *The Dinosaur Strain*, London: Element.

Burnard, P., (2012). *Musical Creativities in Practice*, Oxford: Oxford University Press.

Burns, T. and Stalker, G.M., (1994). *The Management of Innovation*, Oxford: Oxford University Press.

Campbell, A., (1991). 'Brief Case: Strategy and Intuition: A Conversation with Henry Mintzberg', *Long Range Planning*, Vol. 24, No. 2, 108–110.

Chandler, Alfred, (1962). *Strategy and Structure: Chapters in the History of the American Industrial Enterprise*, San Francisco: Beard Books.

Chandler McDonald, Kim, (2013). *Innovation: How Innovators Think, Act and Change our World*, London: Kogan Page.

Christiansen, Clayton, (2013). *The Innovator's Dilemma: When New Technologies Cause Great Firms to Fail*, Cambridge MA: Harvard Business Press.

Collins, Jim, (2001). *Good to Great*, London: Random House.

Cook, Peter, (2006). *Sex, Leadership and Rock'n'Roll: Leadership Lessons from the Academy of Rock*, Carmarthen: Crown House.

Cook, Peter, (2015). *The Music of Business*, Faversham: Cultured Llama.

Csikszentmihalyi, M., (1990). *Flow: The Psychology of Optimal Experience*, New York: Harper and Row.

Csikszentmihalyi, M., (2013). *Creativity: The Psychology of Discovery and Invention*, New York: Harper Perennial.

de Bono, Edward, (1984). *Lateral Thinking for Management*, London: Penguin.

Deng, Ming-Dao, (1992). *365 Tao: Daily Meditations*, San Francisco CA: HarperOne.

Drucker, Peter, (2006). *Innovation and Entrepreneurship*, New York: Harper Business.

Dunbar, Robin, (2010). *How Many Friends Does One Person Need?: Dunbar's Number and Other Evolutionary Quirks*, London: Faber & Faber.

Ericsson, K. Anders, (2009). *Development of Professional Expertise: Toward Measurement of Expert Performance and Design of Optimal Learning Environments*. New York: Cambridge University Press.

Ericcson, K.A., Krampe, R.Th. and Tesch-Rómer, C., (1993). 'The Role of Deliberate Practice in the Acquisition of Expert Performance', *Psychological Review*, Vol. 100, 363–406.

Ekvall, Göran, Arvonen, Jouko and Lindblad, Ingrid Waldenström, (1983). *Creative Organizational Climate: Construction and Validation of a Measuring Instrument*, Stockholm: The Swedish Council for Management and Organizational Behaviour.

Ericsson, K. Anders, (1993). *Protocol Analysis: Verbal Reports as Data*, Cambridge MA: Bradford Books.

Festinger, Leon, (1957). *A Theory of Cognitive Dissonance*. London: Pinter and Martin.

Furnham, Adrian, (2008). *Personality and Intelligence at Work: Exploring and Explaining Individual Differences at Work*, London: Routledge.

Furnham, Adrian, (2010). *The Elephant in the Boardroom: The Causes of Leadership Derailment*, London: Palgrave Macmillan.

Furnham, Adrian and MacRae, Ian, (2014). *High Potential: How to Spot, Manage and Develop Talented People at Work*, London: Bloomsbury.

Ghiselin, Brewster, (1985). *The Creative Process*, Berkeley: University of California Press.

Gardner, Howard, (1999). *Intelligence Reframed*, New York: Basic Books.

Gladwell, M., (2006). *Blink: The Power of Thinking Without Thinking*, London: Penguin.

Gladwell, M., (2008). *Outliers: The Story of Success*, New York: Little, Brown and Co.

Gleick, James, (1987). *Chaos*, London: Abacus.

Godin, Seth, (2008). *Tribes: We Need You to Lead Us*, London: Penguin.

Goleman, D., (1995). *Emotional Intelligence: Why It Can Matter More Than IQ*, New York: Random House.

Griffin, M., Humphreys, M. and Learmonth, M., (2015). 'Doing Free Jazz and Free Organizations, A Certain Experience of the Impossible?' Ornette

Coleman Encounters Jacques Derrida, *Journal of Management Inquiry* Vol. 24(1) 25–35.

Gundling, E., and Porras, J.I., (2000). 'The 3m Way to Innovation: Balancing People and Profit', Kodansha International, Tokyo, Japan.

Greenfield, Susan, (2004). *Tomorrow's People*, London: Penguin.

Halley, Julianne and Winkler, David, (2008). 'Classification of Emergence and its Relation to Self-organization', *Journal of Complexity*, Vol. 13(5), 10–15.

Handy, Charles, (1989). *The Age of Unreason*, London: Arrow Books.

Handy, Charles, (1993). *Understanding Organisations*, London: Penguin.

Handy, Charles, (1994). *The Empty Raincoat*, London: Random House.

Handy, Charles, (1998). *The Hungry Spirit*, London: Random House.

Henry, Jane, (1991). *Creative Management*, London: Sage.

Henry, Jane and Walker, David, (1991). *Managing Innovation*, London: Sage.

Heron, John, (1989). *The Facilitator's Handbook*, London: Kogan Page.

Hirshberg, Jerry, (1998). *The Creative Priority: Driving Innovative Business in the Real World*, New York: Harper Business.

Isenberg, S.G. and Treffinger, D.J., (1985). *Creative Problem Solving, The Basic Course*, Buffalo: Bearly.

Johnson, G., (1987). *Strategic Change and the Management Process*, Oxford: Blackwell.

Johnson, G. and Scholes, K., (1993). *Exploring Corporate Strategy*. London: Prentice Hall.

Johnson, G., Scholes, K. and Whittington, R., (2007). *Exploring Corporate Strategy*, London: Financial Times/Prentice Hall.

Johnstone, Nick, (2005). *Lou Reed Talking*, London: Music Sales.

Kao, John, (1996). *Jamming: The Art and Discipline of Business Creativity*, New York: Harper Business.

Kanhneman, Daniel, (2011). *Thinking Fast and Slow*, London: Penguin.

Kanter, R.M., (2002). 'Strategy as Improvisational Theatre', *MIT Sloan Management Review*, Winter, 76–81.

Kirton, Michael, (1989). *Adaptors and Innovators*, London: Routledge.

Kline, Nancy, (2002). *Time to Think*, London: Cassells.

Koestler, Arthur, (1964). *The Act of Creation*, London: Hutchinson.

Kotler, Phillip, (2010). *Principles of Marketing*, London: Pearson.

Kotter, John, (1996). *Leading Change*, Boston MA: Harvard Business School Press.

Lee, Rupert, (2002). *The Eureka Moment*, London: The British Library.

Laloux, Frederic, (2014). *Reinventing Organisations*, Brussels: Nelson Parker.

Leybourne, S.A. and Kennedy, M., (2015). 'Learning to Improvise, or Improvising to Learn: Knowledge Generation and 'Innovative Practice' Project Environments' Knowledge & Process Management. Available at: www.researchgate.net/. . ./235252930. (Last accessed 8 October 2015).

Leybourne, S.A., (2009). 'Improvisation and Agile: A Merging of Two Ideals?', *International Journal of Managing Projects in Business*, Vol. 2 No. 4, 519–535.

Levitin, Daniel, (2007). *This is Your Brain on Music*, London: Atlantic Books.

Levitin, Daniel, (2015). *The Organized Mind: Thinking Straight in the Age of Information Overload*, London: Penguin.

Lewin, K., (2008). *Principles of Topological Psychology* (trans. Fritz Heider, Grace M. Heider) Read Books.

March, J.G. and Simon, HA., (1958). *Organizations*, New York: Wiley.

McGrath, R. and MacMillan, I., (2009). 'How to Rethink your Business during Uncertainty', *MIT Sloan Management Review*, Vol. 50 No. 3, 25–30.

Michalko, Michael, (2006). *Thinkertoys: Handbook of Business Creativity*, Berkeley CA: Ten Speed Press.

Michalko, Michael, (2011). *Creative Thinkering: Putting Your Imagination to Work*, Novarto CA: New World Library.

Miller, Arthur I., (2000). *Insights of Genius*, Cambridge MA: The MIT Press.

Mintzberg, H. and Waters, J.A., (1985). 'Of Strategies, Deliberate and Emergent', *Strategic Management Journal*, Vol. 6 No. 3, 257–272.

Morgan, Gareth, (1986). *Images of Organization*, London: Sage.

Morgan, Gareth, (1993). *Imagination: The Art of Creative Management*, London: Sage.

Obolensky, Nick, (2014). *Complex Adaptive Leadership: Embracing Paradox and Uncertainty*, Aldershot: Gower.

Odle, Chris, (1990). *Practical Visualisation*, Wellingborough: Thorsons.

O'Connor, Joseph and Seymour, John, (2002). *Introducing NLP*, San Francisco CA: Harper Element.

O'Reilly, III, C.A. and Tushman, M.L.,(2004). 'The Ambidextrous Organization', *Harvard Business Review*, Vol. 82 No. 4, 74–81.

Osborn, Alex, (1993). *Applied Imagination: Principles and Procedures of Creative Problem-Solving*, London: Creative Education Foundation.

Peters, Tom, (2010). *The Little Big Things: 163 Ways to Pursue Excellence at Work.* New York: Harper Business.

Peters, Tom, (1989). *Thriving on Chaos: Handbook for a Management Revolution*, New York: Harper Business.

Peters, Tom, (2004). *In Search of Excellence: Lessons from America's Best-Run Companies*, London: Profile Books.

Pink, Daniel, (2008). *A Whole New Mind: Why Right-Brainers Will Rule the Future*, New York: Marshall Cavendish.

Pirsig, Robert, (2014). *Zen and the Art of Motorcyle Maintenance*, New York: Vintage Books.

Porter, Michael, (1993). *Competitive Advantage*, New York: Free Press.

Purkiss, John and Royston-Lee, David, (2012). *Brand You*, Harlow: Pearson Education.

Radjou, N., Prabhu, J. and Ahuja, S., (2012). *Jugaad Innovation: Think Frugal, Be Flexible, Generate Breakthrough Growth*, San Fransisco CA: Jossey-Bass/Wiley.

Redfield, James, (1994). *The Celestine Prophecy: An Adventure*, London: Bantam.

Redfield, James and Adrienne, Carol, (1995). *The Celestine Prophecy: An Experiential Guide*, New York: Warner Books.

Reed, Lou, (2005). *Lou Reed Talking*, London: Music Sales.

Robinson, Sir Ken, (1998). *All Our Futures: Creativity, Culture, and Education*, London: Department of Education.

Robinson, Sir Ken, (2011). *Out of Our Minds: Learning to be Creative*, London: Capstone.

Rogers, Everett M., (1962). *Diffusion of Innovations*, Glencoe: Free Press.

Rowling, J.K., (1997). *Harry Potter and the Philosopher's Stone*, London: Bloomsbury.

Rowling, J.K., (1998). *Harry Potter and the Chamber of Secrets*, London: Bloomsbury.

Sawyer, Keith, (2007). *Group Genius: The Creative Power of Collaboration*, New York: Basic Books.

Sawyer, Keith, (2013). *Zig Zag: The Surprising Path to Greater Creativity*, San Fransisco CA: Jossey-Bass/Wiley.

Schein, E.H., (1985). *Organizational Culture and Leadership*, San Francisco CA: Jossey-Bass.

Semler, Ricardo, (2001). *Maverick!: The Success Story Behind the World's Most Unusual Workplace*, London: Random House Business.

Senge, Peter, (1990). *The Fifth Discipline*, London: Random Century.

Senge, Peter, Kleiner, Art, Roberts, Charlotte, Boss, Richard and Smith, Bryan, (1994). *The Fifth Discipline Fieldbook*, London: Nicholas Brealey Publishing.

Smit, Tim, (2011), *Eden*, London: Corgi Books.

Szent-Györgyi, Albert, in: IEEE (1985). Bridging the present and the future: IEEE Professional Communication Society conference record, Williamsburg, Virginia, October 16–18, 1985, p. 14.

Taleb, Nassim Nicholas, (2012). *Antifragile*, London: Penguin.

Taleb, Nassim Nicholas, (2008). *The Black Swan: The Impact of the Highly Improbable*, London: Penguin.

Tushman, M.L., and O'Reilly, III, C.A., (1996). 'Ambidextrous Organizations: Managing Evolutionary and Revolutionary Change', *California Management Review*, Vol. 38 No. 4, 8–30.

Trompenaars, Fons and Hampden-Turner, Charles, (2001). *21 Leaders for the 21st Century – How Innovative Leaders Manage in the Digital Age*, London: Capstone.

VanGundy, Arthur B., (1988). *Techniques of Structured Problem Solving*, Springer: Netherlands.

Wallas, G., (1926). *The Art of Thought*, New York: Franklin Watts.

Weber, M., (1905). The Protestant Ethic and 'The Spirit of Capitalism', Translated by Stepen Kalberg (2002), Los Angeles CA: Roxbury Publishing.

Weick, K.E., (1979). *The Social Psychology of Organizing*, 2nd edn, Reading MA: Addison-Wesley Publishing Company.

Weick, K.E. and Sutcliffe, K.M., (2007) *Managing the Unexpected: Resilient Performance in an Age of Uncertainty*, San Francisco CA: Jossey-Bass.

Index